Template for p

Manchester University Press

Template for peace

Northern Ireland 1972–75

Shaun McDaid

MANCHESTER UNIVERSITY PRESS

Published by Manchester University Press
Altrincham Street, Manchester M1 7JA, UK
www.manchesteruniversitypress.co.uk

British Library Cataloguing-in-Publication Data is available

Library of Congress Cataloging-in-Publication Data is available

ISBN 978 0 7190 9976 2   paperback

First published by Manchester University Press in hardback 2013

This edition first published 2016

Printed by Lightning Source

For John and Mary

Contents

Acknowledgements

This book began life as a PhD dissertation. I am most grateful to my supervisor, Fearghal McGarry, for his sound advice and encouragement; and to Andrew R. Holmes, my co-supervisor, for the same reasons. Both have provided much-appreciated support. Thanks also to Sabine Wichert, who supervised my dissertation in first year, for her valuable input.

Thanks to staff from the Queen's University Belfast School of History and Anthropology for their encouragement including: David Hayton, Mary O'Dowd, Catherine Clinton, Paul Corthorn and Peter Gray. Thanks to Alvin Jackson, my thesis examiner, for his constructive criticisms, and ongoing support. I also thank Paul Bew, my internal examiner, for his valuable comments and suggestions. I also benefited from discussions with members of the Irish Politics Research Cluster at the Queen's University Belfast School of Politics, International Studies and Philosophy.

I am grateful to the following friends and colleagues who read draft chapters, making helpful comments and criticisms: Jessie Blackbourn, Josephine Doody, Stuart Aveyard and James Greer. Elaine Farrell read all of it, in various incarnations, and I am grateful for her support over the years. I am also grateful to Kacper Rekawek for many years of support, advice and ongoing collaboration. The usual disclaimer applies.

For lively discussions about history and politics while completing the book, my thanks also to Sean Farrell, Gareth Mulvenna, Conor Browne, Marisa McGlinchey, Iosif Kovras and Neophytos Loizides. I must also mention my former office mates Raoul McLaughlin, Chris McCoubrey, Chris Loughlin, Aidan Enright, Matthew Lewis and Erica Doherty.

My thanks to everyone at Manchester University Press for all their work, assistance, and for showing faith in the project.

Many thanks to the staff at all the archives and libraries (listed in the bibliography) where I have researched – in particular Ross Moore at the Linen Hall Library. Thanks to colleagues at the Queen's University Belfast Institute of Governance for welcoming me there: Gemma Ní Chaoimh, Siobhán McAllister, Marie Lynch and especially to Phil Scraton for his support and encouragement.

Potential breach of my word limit prevents my mentioning everyone whose company I enjoyed during the writing of this book. Friends and colleagues from the past and present cohort of the Queen's University Belfast School of History and Anthropology, School of Politics, International Studies and Philosophy, and staff and students from the School of History and Archives, University College Dublin, all played their part – not to mention those from the Sonic Arts Research Centre, Guthrie House and the 'B-Siders'. You know who you are.

I must also name Vasileios Chatziioannou, Orestis Karamanlis, James Williams, Jose Argudo, Tej Pochiraju and Matthias Euler, who have all helped in various ways.

Thanks to all my friends and family in Donegal and further afield. Special thanks must, of course, go to my parents, John McDaid and Mary McDaid for all they have done for me; especially to Mary who proof-read the manuscript. And to Ania, for all her love, support and good humour throughout the writing process.

Shaun McDaid,
Belfast, December 2011

Abbreviations

AG	Attorney General
ASU	Active Service Unit
CBI	Confederation of British Industry
CENT	Central Secretariat (files)
CESA	Catholic Ex-Servicemen's Association
CJ4	Northern Ireland Office files
CLF	Commander of Land Forces
DEFE	Ministry of Defence (files)
DFA	Department of Foreign Affairs
DHSS	Department of Health and Social Services, Northern Ireland
DM	Deutsche Mark
DT	Department of the Taoiseach
DUP	Democratic Unionist Party
ECHR	European Court of Human Rights
ECR	European Conservative and Reformist (Group)
EEC	European Economic Community
EPP	European People's Party
ESB	Electricity Supply Board
EXMEMO	Executive Memorandum
FCO	Foreign and Commonwealth Office
FIN	Department of Finance (files)
FPCU	Free Presbyterian Church of Ulster
FRG	Federal Republic of Germany
GFA	Good Friday Agreement
HC	House of Commons
HMG	Her Majesty's Government
HQNI	Headquarters, Northern Ireland (British Army)
IDU	Inter Departmental Unit (on Northern Ireland)
ILP	Irish Labour Party
INLA	Irish National Liberation Army
IRA	Irish Republican Army

JUS	Department of Justice, Republic of Ireland
LAW	Loyalist Association of Workers
LEC	Law Enforcement Commission
MEP	Member of the European Parliament
MOD	Ministry of Defence
MP	Member of Parliament
MW	megawatt(s)
NAI	National Archives of Ireland
NATO	North Atlantic Treaty Organisation
NIES	Northern Ireland Electricity Service
NIFC	Northern Ireland Finance Corporation
NILP	Northern Ireland Labour Party
NIO	Northern Ireland Office
NIPC	Northern Ireland Political Collection, Linen Hall Library
NUM	National Union of Mineworkers
OE	Office of the Executive
OIRA	Official Irish Republican Army
OSF	Official Sinn Féin
OPEC	Organisation of Petroleum Exporting Countries
PIRA	Provisional Irish Republican Army
PREM	Prime Minister's Office
PRONI	Public Record Office of Northern Ireland
PR–STV	Promotional representation, single transferable vote
PSF	Provisional Sinn Féin
PSNI	Police Service of Northern Ireland
PUP	Protestant Unionist Party
PUS	Permanent Under Secretary
RANI	Resettlement Agency Northern Ireland
RMP	Royal Military Police
RNAS	Royal Naval Air Service
RUC	Royal Ulster Constabulary
SAS	Special Air Service
SDLP	Social Democratic and Labour Party
SIS	Secret Intelligence Service
SOSEC	Secretary of State's Executive Committee
TD	Teachta Dála (Member of the Irish Parliament)
TNA	The National Archives
TUC	Trades Union Congress
UCDA	University College Dublin Archives
UDA	Ulster Defence Association
UDI	Unilateral Declaration of Independence
UDR	Ulster Defence Regiment

UFF	Ulster Freedom Fighters
UKREP	United Kingdom Representative
ULC	Ulster Loyalist Coalition
UN	United Nations
UPNI	Unionist Party of Northern Ireland
USC	Ulster Special Constabulary
UUC	Ulster Unionist Council
UUP	Ulster Unionist Party
UUUC	United Ulster Unionist Coalition
UVF	Ulster Volunteer Force
UWC	Ulster Workers' Council
VAT	value added tax
VPP	Volunteer Political Party
VUPP	Vanguard Unionist Progressive Party
WBLC	West Belfast Loyalist Coalition

Introduction

From its inception in 1921, Northern Ireland was governed solely by the Ulster Unionist Party (UUP).[1] However, in 1972, the Northern Ireland parliament (Stormont) was prorogued[2] by the British government amidst a deteriorating security situation, which the region's devolved government proved incapable of improving. Stormont, for over fifty years the totemic manifestation of unionist dominance in Northern Ireland, was replaced by direct rule from Westminster. Unionists were dejected at the collapse of their beloved parliament, which they regarded as a bulwark against a united Ireland. This dejection was matched by the euphoria of nationalists, who saw in the advent of direct rule the demise of unionist domination and the possible re-opening of the constitutional question. The political uncertainty generated by these events gave rise to increased inter-communal violence and suspicion between the two communities, which was already at a high level since the outbreak of widespread violence in 1968.[3]

The (Conservative) government at Westminster was unenthusiastic about assuming responsibility for the region, and sought to restore a measure of devolution to Northern Ireland as soon as was practicable. However, there was no question of a return to the old, unionist-controlled Stormont system. Instead, the government supported the establishment of a power-sharing administration, in which nationalists and unionists would participate together. This became official government policy in March 1973, when the White Paper, *The Northern Ireland Constitutional Proposals*, was published by the Secretary of State, William Whitelaw.[4] Consequently, a power-sharing executive was formed in November 1973. It consisted of a coalition comprising a pro-agreement faction of the UUP, the nationalist Social Democratic and Labour Party (SDLP) and the cross-community Alliance party. Power-sharing was not the only controversial matter contained in the White Paper. It also provided for the establishment of institutionalised co-operation between Northern Ireland and the Republic of Ireland, the 'Irish dimension'. This commitment to all-Ireland co-operation was formalised in December 1973, when the Sunningdale Agreement was signed by the British and Irish governments. Many issues were agreed at Sunningdale. However, the most controversial of these was the decision to establish a Council of Ireland with limited executive functions. The Council could, at its discretion, assume responsibility for administering certain public services on an all-island basis. Despite its limited remit, nationalists portrayed it as a staging-post on the road to Irish unification, and unionists were all too eager to believe them; the latter not being prepared to countenance any involvement by the Republic in Northern Ireland's affairs.

On 1 January 1974, the power-sharing administration assumed office. For many people in Northern Ireland, particularly hard-line loyalists, the pace of change was too great. Less than five months later, the executive collapsed in the face of a loyalist general strike organised by the Ulster Workers' Council (UWC), a motley assortment of Protestant trades unionists, paramilitaries and politicians. The UWC was strongly opposed to the Irish dimension, and this was the primary motive for its strike. But the UWC also had a more atavistic, sectarian character, and it was ill-disposed to seeing Catholic and nationalist politicians in positions of power. Thus, for the second time in two years, a devolved Northern Ireland administration collapsed in the face of a political crisis.

The UWC strike confirmed to the British government that a solution could not be imposed on the Northern Ireland majority by Westminster diktat. The following year, in May 1975, a Constitutional Convention was established to allow Northern Ireland's politicians the chance to devise an acceptable form of government for the region. Its proceedings were dominated by the unionist parties, and, as many commentators predicted, it called for a return to the old Stormont system. However, the Labour government, elected in 1974, continued to follow the policy of the previous Conservative administration: that devolved government would not return to Northern Ireland in the absence of power-sharing, and some form of Irish dimension. There were significant similarities between the Conservative and Labour governments, in relation to constitutional policy in Northern Ireland. They also pursued similar security policies, such as engaging in discussion with paramilitary groups, in an attempt to reduce the violence throughout the region. The analysis of this series of key events lies at the heart of this book.

Throughout this entire period, the people of Northern Ireland experienced other forms of crisis, both economic and social. This included economic contraction both within the UK and abroad, inspired by events such as the global Oil Crisis of 1973. Social problems, some peculiar to Northern Ireland, also presented formidable challenges, such as segregation, sectarianism, weak economic growth and poor housing. This book also explores how the various parties in Northern Ireland approached social and economic policy formation, and places this analysis in the wider context of developments in the British and world economies at the time.[5]

The recent availability of a vast tranche of official documents from archives in Belfast, Dublin and London has allowed for a more detailed study of the high politics and processes of policy formulation than has hitherto been possible.[6] By studying these documents, it was possible to address a number of key questions previously debated by scholars from a range of disciplinary backgrounds such as: were nationalist and unionist politicians able to work together effectively in government, or was the power-sharing executive plagued by divisions throughout its precarious tenure? Did the Dublin government seek to use the proposed Council of Ireland as a means to achieve Irish unity? In the aftermath of the UWC strike, did the British government seriously consider withdrawing from Northern Ireland? These, and other, issues are considered in light of this newly available evidence.

Official documents, like other historical sources, often display an inherent authorial bias. Information gleaned from these sources is supplemented by material from private political party archives, the political party literature produced during the period, memoir accounts of the major officials and politicians who were involved in these events, and information from a range of contemporary newspapers and periodicals.[7] It also engages with a vast corpus of extant secondary literature, confirming or challenging its findings where necessary.

To date a number of accounts which engage this period have been published by scholars from a range of disciplines. Often, the events of 1972–75 are covered as part of a broader historical survey. This body of work includes monographs by Alvin Jackson, Paul Bew, Peter Gibbon and Henry Patterson, Joe Lee and Michael Cunningham.[8] Most accounts of this nature draw from a wide range of sources, ranging from official publications to private papers. However, because these works were published within thirty years of the 1972–75 period, they have not enjoyed access to official documents relating to these years. Paul Bew's *Ireland: The Politics of Enmity, 1789–2006*, has utilised official documents to discuss the high politics of this period, particularly the possibility of British withdrawal from Northern Ireland during Harold Wilson's second premiership. Because of the broad scope of his book, however, the attention devoted to these matters is necessarily restricted.[9] Similarly, Bew, Frampton and Gurruchaga's study of Northern Ireland and the Basque country has used these sources, but their work is aimed at contributing to a wider debate on the politics of security policy, and spans a broader chronology, thus it does not provide an exhaustive account of the initiatives of this period.[10] Recent studies drawing on documentary evidence have also been published by P. J. McLoughlin and Cillian McGrattan. In his recent biography of John Hume, McLoughlin draws on archival material, but his primary focus is on explaining Hume's contribution to nationalist ideology. McGrattan's study covers the forty-year period from 1968–2008, and provides a critique of the work of a number of political scientists associated with advocating consociational theory.[11] The events of 1972 to 1975 are discussed in detail, but are approached through the prism of path-dependency theory in an attempt to explain why the conflict in Northern Ireland became 'entrenched'. However, the use of path-dependency theory, which claims that decisions taken at 'critical junctures' influenced or constrained the later policy options of the participants, often fails to appreciate the historical nuances of the period, and results in a teleological interpretation of why the conflict developed as it did.[12]

An equally important focus of the present study is an interrogation of the comparisons that have been drawn between the Sunningdale package and the Belfast (Good Friday) Agreement of 1998. The latter accord was wryly described as 'Sunningdale for slow learners' by Seamus Mallon, former SDLP Deputy-First Minister of Northern Ireland. Mallon's observation has been accepted at face value in Anthony Craig's book covering the 1966–74 period.[13] Similarly, Michael Kerr's recent work accepts the premise that the untimely demise of the Sunningdale settlement can be characterised as Northern Ireland's 'lost peace process'.[14] Some of the policies established during this period, as Alvin Jackson has noted, 'remained relevant to many of the planned initiatives [in Northern Ireland] since then'.[15] Undoubtedly, there are similarities between the political structures established during both periods. The Sunningdale package can thus be said to have provided a model from which the Good Friday settlement was eventually negotiated. However, Mallon's quip is misleading, since the difference in the political context in which the two accords were concluded could hardly be starker, not least the levels of violence during the 1970s and the fact that the IRA and loyalist paramilitaries were not included in political negotiations. A more historically informed comparison of these two periods will deepen our understanding of both.[16] Such an understanding is all the more important, given the tendency, among some authors, to attempt to extrapolate lessons from the Northern Ireland 'peace process', and 'export' these lessons to other zones of conflict.[17]

The evidence presented in this book demonstrates that a simple comparison of the two accords is insufficient to explain why the current peace settlement took so long to achieve. The naively optimistic view that the Sunningdale settlement represented a 'lost peace process', and that the IRA's intermittent ceasefire of 1975 was a 'missed opportunity' to achieve a peaceful settlement, is rejected.[18] Between 1972 and 1975, the British government's emphasis was on creating an executive consisting of moderate political parties. Those engaged in paramilitary violence were excluded. As a result their violent campaigns continued, and spoiled the executive's chances of success.

Following the UWC strike, the British government discussed a number of policy options. These discussions confirmed that direct rule would remain until such times as Northern Ireland's politicians could agree a settlement acceptable to the government. To secure the government's acceptance, such a settlement required power-sharing in government, some form of Irish dimension, and guarantees for unionists that Northern Ireland would remain in the UK for as long as a majority so wished. Successive British governments continued to demand that these conditions were met before restoring devolution to Northern Ireland. As the following chapters show, these stipulations provided a template for the future negotiations, eventually resulting in the Belfast Agreement of 1998, and Northern Ireland's ongoing peace process.

Notes

1 Ulster unionists ensured that, when Ireland was partitioned, the Northern Ireland state would have an in-built unionist majority. For the history of Northern Ireland, especially pre-1972, see for example P. Bew, *Ireland: The Politics of Enmity, 1789–2006* (Oxford: Oxford University Press, 2007); P. Buckland, *A History of Northern Ireland* (Dublin: Gill and Macmillan, 1981); D. Harkness, *Northern Ireland since 1920* (Dublin: Helicon, 1983); T. Hennessey, *A History of Northern Ireland, 1920–1996* (Dublin: Gill and Macmillan, 1997); H. Patterson, *Ireland since 1939: The Persistence of Conflict* (Oxford: Oxford University Press, 2002); S. Wichert, *Northern Ireland since 1945* (London: Longman, 2nd edn, 1999). For the history of the UUP, G. Walker, *A History of the Ulster Unionist Party: Protest, Pragmatism and Pessimism* (Manchester: Manchester University Press, 2004).
2 To prorogue: when an elected assembly is suspended without being dissolved.
3 For the outbreak of the conflict, see N. Ó Dochartaigh, *From Civil Rights to Armalites: Derry and the Birth of the Irish Troubles* (Basingstoke: Palgrave Macmillan, 2nd edn, 2004); S. Prince, *Northern Ireland's '68: Civil Rights, Global Revolt and the Origins of the Troubles* (Dublin: Irish Academic Press, 2007); B. Purdie, *Politics in the Streets: The Origins of the Civil Rights Movement in Northern Ireland* (Belfast: Blackstaff, 1990).
4 *The Northern Ireland Constitutional Proposals* (HMSO: 1973).
5 For the role of economic development and 'normalisation' in the current peace process, K. Bean, *The New Politics of Sinn Féin* (Liverpool: Liverpool University Press, 2007), pp. 16–50.
6 A number of studies exist which discuss matters such as paramilitary organisations, political parties, the working classes and local politics during this period. See for example, S. Bruce, *The Red Hand: Protestant Paramilitaries in Northern Ireland* (Oxford: Oxford University Press, 1992); R. English, *Armed Struggle: The History of the IRA* (London: Macmillan, 2003); G. Murray and J. Tonge, *Sinn Féin and the SDLP: From Alienation to Participation* (Dublin: O'Brien, 2005); J. Greer, 'Losing the province: a localised study of Ulster unionism, 1968–1974' (PhD thesis, Queen's University Belfast, 2011); S. G. Gillespie, 'Loyalist politics and the Ulster Workers' Council strike of 1974' (PhD thesis, Queen's University Belfast, 1994); G. Mulvenna, 'The protestant working class in Northern Ireland: political allegiance and social and cultural challenges since the 1960s' (PhD thesis, Queen's University Belfast, 2009); H. Patterson and Eric P. Kaufmann *Unionism and Orangeism in*

Northern Ireland since 1945: The Decline of the Loyal Family (Manchester: Manchester University Press, 2007); K. Rekawek, *Irish Republican Terrorism and Politics: A Comparative Study of the Official and the Provisional IRA* (London: Routledge, 2010).

7 For memoir accounts see for example B. Faulkner, *Memoirs of a Statesman* (London: Weidenfeld and Nicolson, 1978); A. Currie, *All Hell Will Break Loose* (Dublin: O'Brien, 2004); B. McIvor, *Hope Deferred: Experiences of an Irish Unionist* (Belfast: Blackstaff, 1998); R. Ramsay, *Ringside Seats: An Insider's View of the Crisis in Northern Ireland* (Dublin: Irish Academic Press, 2009); K. Bloomfield, *Stormont in Crisis: A Memoir* (Belfast: Blackstaff, 1994), and *A Tragedy of Errors: The Government and Misgovernment of Northern Ireland* (Liverpool: Liverpool University Press, 2007); P. Devlin, *Straight Left: An Autobiography* (Belfast: Blackstaff, 1993); G. FitzGerald, *All in a Life: An Autobiography* (Dublin: Gill and Macmillan, 1991); M. Hayes, *Minority Verdict: Experiences of a Catholic Public Servant* (Belfast: Blackstaff, 1995); E. Heath, *The Course of My Life: An Autobiography* (London: Coronet, 1999); R. Maudling, *Memoirs* (London: Sidgwick and Jackson, 1978); J. Peck, *Dublin from Downing Street* (Dublin: Gill and Macmillan, 1978); M. Rees, *Northern Ireland: A Personal Perspective* (London: Methuen, 1985); H. Wilson, *Final Term: Labour Government 1974–76* (London: Weidenfeld and Nicolson, 1979) and W. Whitelaw, *The Whitelaw Memoirs* (London: Aurum, 1989). For a broader account based on contemporary newspaper sources, G. Gillespie, *Years of Darkness: The Troubles Remembered* (Dublin: Gill and Macmillan, 2008).

8 See for example Jackson, *Home Rule: An Irish History, 1800–2000* (London: Weidenfeld and Nicolson, 2003), pp. 260–319; P. Bew, P. Gibbon and H. Patterson, *Northern Ireland 1921–2001: Political Forces and Social Classes* (London: Serif, 3rd edn, 2002); J. J. Lee, *Ireland 1912–1985: Politics and Society* (Cambridge: Cambridge University Press, 1989), pp. 435–51; M. Cunningham, *British Government Policy in Northern Ireland 1969–2000* (Manchester: Manchester University Press, 2001) primarily bases its findings on government publications and policy statements.

9 Bew, *Ireland*, pp. 509–23.

10 J. Bew, M. Frampton and Í. Gurruchaga, *Talking to Terrorists: Making Peace in Northern Ireland and the Basque Country* (London: Hurst, 2009).

11 For the classic introduction see Arend Lijphart, 'Consociational democracy', *World Politics*, xxi: 2 (1969), pp. 207–25. His ideas are further developed in such works as *Democracy in Plural Societies* (New Haven: Yale University Press, 1977) and 'Consociation: the model and its applications in divided societies' in Desmond Rea (ed.), *Political Co-operation in Divided Societies* (Dublin: Gill and Macmillan, 1982), pp. 166–86. In 1975, Lijphart argued that a number of conditions necessary for a consociational settlement were not present in Northern Ireland. See 'Review article: the Northern Ireland problem; cases, theories and solutions', *British Journal of Political Science*, v: 1 (1975), pp. 83–106.

12 P. J. McLoughlin, *John Hume and the Revision of Irish Nationalism* (Manchester: Manchester University Press, 2010); C. McGrattan, *Northern Ireland, 1968–2008: The Politics of Entrenchment* (Basingstoke: Palgrave Macmillan, 2010). For a cri-

tique of the path-dependent approach, F. Ross, 'An alternative institutional theory to path dependence: evaluating the Greener model', *British Politics*, ii: 1 (2007), pp. 91–9.

13 A. Craig, *Crisis of Confidence: Anglo-Irish Relations in the Early Troubles, 1966–1974* (Dublin: Irish Academic Press, 2010), p. 193.

14 M. Kerr, *The Destructors: Northern Ireland's Lost Peace Process* (Dublin: Irish Academic Press, 2011).

15 Jackson, *Home Rule*, p. 281. It remains to be seen how committed successive governments were to this policy, or whether they simply accepted it as the 'least worst' option.

16 Diachronic comparisons within the same political unit can be particularly fruitful. However, context is crucial, since the chosen political entity is never really the same at different chronological junctures. See A. Lijphart, 'Comparative politics and the comparative method', *American Political Science Review*, lxv: 3 (1971), p. 689. The differing contexts between the political accords in Northern Ireland during the 1970s and 1990s are explored in the conclusion.

17 For a critique, see R. Wilson, *The Northern Ireland Experience of Conflict and Agreement: A Model for Export?* (Manchester: Manchester University Press, 2010); E. O'Kane, 'Learning from Northern Ireland? Uses and abuses of the Irish "model"', *British Journal of Politics and International Relations*, xii: 2 (2010), pp. 239–56.

18 Kerr, *Destructors*; N. Ó Dochartaigh, '"Everyone trying", the IRA ceasefire, 1975: a missed opportunity for peace?', *Field Day Review*, vii (2011), pp. 51–78.

1

From direct rule to power-sharing, 1972–74

The formation of the power-sharing executive was the result of protracted political discussion and constitutional planning. The careful negotiation of the executive was the culmination of a series of political initiatives, designed by the British government, following the prorogation of the Stormont parliament. These initiatives were intended to foster an accommodation between nationalist and unionist parties. The ultimate aim was to restore to Northern Ireland a radically different form of devolved government, which involved power-sharing between the opposing factions.

The collapse of Stormont stimulated a wide-ranging political discussion, among both nationalist and unionist parties, about how Northern Ireland should be governed. All the main parties published policy documents setting out their own proposals for the region. To better understand both the significant political compromises made by the parties that formed the executive, and the entrenched opposition to reform of its opponents, these policy proposals are discussed in detail. The state of both nationalist and unionist politics from the collapse of Stormont onwards, are also discussed. This period witnessed the continued fragmentation of the unionist bloc and the SDLP's consolidation of its position as the voice of Northern Ireland's nationalist minority.

The British government had a decisive influence on the moderation of the policy positions of the Northern Ireland parties because it refused to countenance any settlement not based on the core principles of power-sharing and an Irish dimension, whilst maintaining Northern Ireland's right to remain part of the United Kingdom as long as a majority desired. Thus the analysis of its policy documents, particularly the 1972 Green Paper, *The Future of Northern Ireland: A Paper for Discussion*, the March 1973 White Paper, *The Northern Ireland Constitutional Proposals*, and the reactions of local parties to those documents, provide the context in which the executive was formed and the December 1973 Sunningdale Agreement was concluded.

The Sunningdale settlement was a significant development in the relationships between the British and Irish governments, and the elected representatives of Northern Ireland. For the first time since 1925, these three groups signed an agreement with significant political ramifications for all three signatories. The Sunningdale Agreement placed the relations between each group on a new footing. One relationship which has received much comment is that between the Irish government and the nationalist SDLP. It has been widely written that, during the period in question, the SDLP had a significant influence on the Dublin government.[1] Archival sources, however, reveal the extent of the divisions between these groups, and suggest that they were by no means united on policy.

Finally, despite the diverse ideological preferences of its members, the executive itself was by no means irrevocably divided and destined to collapse regardless of the political climate. Indeed, the evidence illustrates that relations between the nationalist and unionist politicians were often close and harmonious. Instead, it was opposition to any Irish involvement in Northern Ireland's affairs, and a lack of enthusiasm for power-sharing among the wider unionist community, which seriously undermined its chances of success. This unionist opposition was engendered by the collapse of the Stormont parliament in March 1972.

The fall of Stormont and unionist and nationalist politics

The principal reason for the introduction of direct rule was the deteriorating security problem in Northern Ireland. This was an embarrassment to the British government, which was blamed for this situation, despite not being in full control of the security apparatus in the region. On 22 March, the Prime Minister, Edward Heath, informed Northern Ireland premier, Brian Faulkner, that the UK government intended to assume responsibility for all security matters.[2] Faced with this derogation of its powers, the Northern Ireland government resigned.[3] Thenceforth, the region was governed directly from London. The office of the Secretary of State for Northern Ireland was created, with William Whitelaw as its first incumbent.[4] Under direct rule, Northern Ireland was primarily governed by Orders-in-Council: decisions of the Privy Council, approved by the Queen.[5] This was to reduce the pressure which Northern Ireland matters would have on Westminster's timetable following direct rule.

Most unionists reacted furiously to the introduction of direct rule.[6] Around 100,000 of their number staged a protest at Stormont, with a further 200,000 subsequently participating in an anti-direct rule strike, which halted industrial activity for two days.[7] This was a clear symbol of the 'alarm throughout the unionist community' resulting from Stormont's prorogation.[8] The collapse of Stormont prompted an outpouring of anti-British sentiment among Northern Ireland's unionist community, with the Union Jack at Belfast's City Hall replaced by an Ulster Banner, and 'crowds of girls waving flags' jeering at British troops.[9] Whilst traumatic for the general unionist community, direct rule had an even more serious effect on unionist politics, in particular the UUP, which went from being a party of government to 'a body of incoherent and ineffectual protest'.[10] However, some time before the introduction of direct rule, it had already begun to show signs of fragmentation, faction and division.

McGarry and O'Leary have argued that direct rule resulted in a 'considerable fragmentation' of the unionist bloc.[11] However, even before direct rule was considered necessary, there were signs that divisions both within the UUP, and the unionist bloc as a whole, threatened to undermine its long-term electoral dominance. Support for the party had already begun to decline following the reforms to the allocation of housing and the local government franchise introduced by the Northern Ireland government in 1969.[12] Many disenchanted UUP voters turned to the Protestant Unionist Party (PUP), led by Dr Ian Paisley. The PUP, formed in 1966, criticised the aforementioned reforms instigated by Prime Minister Terence O'Neill as 'appeasement' of nationalists.[13] 'Paisleyism' became synonymous with opposition to reform. The PUP won two key Stormont by-elections in 1970, narrowly defeating the UUP candidates in each.[14] In September 1971, Paisley went on to form the Democratic Unionist Party (DUP), a more secular version of the PUP.[15] Paisleyism was neither the sole, nor most serious, threat to the UUP. For some years, the party had been internally divided, a problem exacerbated by the events of March 1972.

Marc Mulholland has demonstrated that the most significant division within the UUP, which emerged in the 1960s, was between those who sought to bring Catholics into the 'Unionist alliance' (integrationists) and the traditionalists who opposed this tendency (segregationists).[16] A more serious split was still to come. This time the divisions were primarily between those who believed that political reforms were necessary to placate Catholic and British government opinion, and those who were completely opposed to any reform of the Stormont system.

In February 1972, a protest movement was formed within the UUP, known as the Vanguard movement. Vanguard was founded by William Craig, a former home affairs minister. Craig completely opposed reforming Northern Ireland's system of governance. Support for the Vanguard movement was widespread. A rally organised at Belfast's Ormeau Park in March 1972 attracted 50,000 people, the largest loyalist rally since Carson's Balmoral gathering in 1912.[17] Addressing the crowd, Craig spoke of 'liquidating the [republican] enemy', and claimed loyalists would 'do or die' to prevent direct rule.[18]

However, members within the movement were divided over what future form of government Northern Ireland should enjoy. Some supported an independent Northern Ireland. Vanguard's publication, *Dominion of Ulster*, written by Professor Kennedy Lindsay, attempted to garner support for this notion, arguing that an independent Ulster would be economically viable.[19] It is unlikely most Vanguard supporters favoured Ulster independence, but its strong anti-reformist rhetoric was extremely popular.[20] Vanguard's presence within the UUP was a clear signal to the party leaders that whatever reforms it undertook would be watched carefully, and potentially vetoed, should its supporters be able to mobilise enough opposition to any such proposals.

The political dynamics of northern nationalism were markedly different to unionism. The Social Democratic and Labour Party (SDLP), founded in 1970, attracted the overwhelming support of the nationalist electorate, as there was simply no credible alternative for nationalist voters. The old Nationalist Party had provided indifferent leadership, and it was soon eclipsed by the more active SDLP. More extreme republican parties attracted little support. For example, the Republican Clubs, the Northern Ireland branch of Official Sinn Féin (OSF), received a derisory 1.8 per cent of votes in the 1973 Assembly elections.[21] Provisional Sinn Féin (PSF), the political wing of the Provisional Irish Republican Army (PIRA), was then an illegal organisation, and could not contest elections. It was legalised in April 1974 by the then Secretary of State, Merlyn Rees, but it, too, lacked significant nationalist support.[22] Thus the SDLP was relatively free from electoral competition from within the nationalist bloc. The party itself, however, was not entirely free of divisions and faction.

The original SDLP leadership was a combination of civil rights activists, Labourites and constitutional nationalists.[23] There were significant tensions between those of more nationalist inclination (such as John Hume and Seamus Mallon) and those with a greater focus on socio-economic issues (particularly Belfast parliamentarians, Gerry Fitt and Paddy Devlin). These divisions within the party, regarding issues such as the Council of Ireland, will become more apparent in later chapters. The proposals of the various political parties on how Northern Ireland should be governed following the collapse of Stormont will now be examined.

The policy proposals of the Northern Ireland parties

The UUP policy proposals were published in September 1972 in a paper entitled *Towards the Future: A Unionist Blueprint*. The party favoured the return of a strong devolved parliament in Northern Ireland. It was not particularly concerned about the structure of such a parliament, but insisted it have significant powers.[24] The powers in question included the internal security of Northern Ireland, control of the prison and legal system, agriculture, education, regional development, health and social services and local government, the same powers devolved to Northern Ireland under the Government of Ireland Act (1920). However, the UUP also sought tax varying powers 'to apply financial measures to further the regional economy', such as the power to introduce special rates of value added tax (VAT).[25] To counter nationalist anxiety, a bill of rights was proposed as a 'safeguard for minorities'.[26] This proposed bill was to include the right to 'freedom from discrimination on religious grounds', and 'freedom of political association'. The *Blueprint* stated that Sections 5 and 8 of the Government of Ireland Act made provision for discriminatory practices to be challenged in the courts, although this had never happened in Northern Ireland's history.[27] It was claimed that those who complained 'were not anxious to have their claims legally examined or that they found it difficult to do so by reason of lack of means or evidence'. The provision of legal aid was proposed to 'ensure that public pressure is put on those complaining to seek recourse to the law'.[28]

The *Blueprint* also included a section on 'Relations with Southern Ireland', which called on the government of the Republic to recognise the right of the people of Northern Ireland to 'self-determination'. A 'solemn binding agreement between the three governments concerned as in 1925', recognising that right, was proposed. An amendment to Articles 2 and 3 of the Irish Constitution, which laid claim to Northern Ireland, was not sought, but the question of extradition of paramilitary suspects was raised. If a court in the Republic decided an offence was political, then it was non-extraditable. The UUP argued that either a new extradition treaty, which did not exclude political offences, or a common law enforcement area in the British Isles be introduced. The *Blueprint* then mooted the idea of a 'joint Irish inter-government council' to discuss matters of mutual interest in the economic and social field.[29]

The Vanguard movement took a less constructive approach to the opportunities for political discussion created by the introduction of direct rule. Its members continued to reject proposed reforms, calling for the restoration of the old Stormont system. They publicly challenged claims that the Catholic community had any grievance or 'suffered from any inequality before the law or any injustice at the hands of government or public authority which justified the violence or even passive protest against the state'.[30] In contrast to the UUP and Vanguard, Ian Paisley's DUP favoured the complete integration of Northern Ireland with the rest of the United Kingdom. In 1971, Paisley predicted the introduction of direct rule, and argued that total integration would be the best way to safeguard the union.[31] Nationalist politicians, however, harboured more radical ideas.

The SDLP's policy document, *Towards a New Ireland*, was also published in September 1972. It was a strongly nationalist document, emotive in tone. The tragic events of Bloody Sunday in January 1972, which provoked a furious reaction from nationalists, influenced its content.[32] The party argued that there could be no solution to the Irish question 'in a purely Six County context', and demanded a British declaration that Ireland would be best served being 'united on terms acceptable to all the people of Ireland'. It also called for an 'interim system of government' shared between the UK and Ireland, referred to as 'the Joint Sovereignty of Northern Ireland'. The structures proposed included two Commissioners (one British, one Irish) to give assent to legislation. Like the UUP, the SDLP also advocated devolved local government. For the SDLP, this was to consist of an 84-seat assembly elected by proportional representation, single transferable vote (PR-STV), and a 15-member executive. No parliamentary representation in Dublin or London was sought, emphasising the 'newness' of the SDLP's proposed system of governance.[33] The party also sought an all-Ireland body, the National Senate of Ireland, which would integrate government services and plan for the eventual unification of Ireland. It argued, rather naively, that the new Ireland would 'still Protestant fears', but, as the majority of Northern Ireland Protestants wished to remain in the UK, the mention of Irish unity actually accentuated these fears. The document was certainly a radical one: as Bew and Patterson noted, the policies contained in *Towards a New Ireland* took 'a more stridently anti-partitionist line' on Northern Ireland than even the Dublin government.[34] An analysis of the policy proposals of the Northern Ireland political parties is important because it illustrates how their policies evolved during the subsequent years, through the executive negotiations and Sunningdale. However, the Northern Ireland political parties did not, at that time, have the power to implement any of these proposals. The government of Northern Ireland was the sole responsibility of the British government. It duly published a Green Paper on 20 September 1972 entitled *The Future of Northern Ireland: A Paper for Discussion*.

The British proposals in context

In early March 1972, the Home Secretary, Reginald Maudling, brought his Northern Ireland policy proposals before the cabinet. Historians have not hitherto been particularly kind to Maudling. Roy Foster has argued that his only contribution to Northern Ireland policy was 'nothing more than the notorious concept of an acceptable level of violence'.[35] Joe Lee referred to him as 'an unfortunate choice' of Home Secretary 'from a Northern Ireland point of view'.[36] His policy proposals are examined in more detail below, but it is argued that Maudling's contribution to policy making was more extensive than previously thought.

There were also policy proposals emanating from the deputy principal secretary to the Stormont administration, Kenneth Bloomfield. Documents in Ministry of Defence files reveal that Bloomfield was furtively advocating the adoption of a form of power-sharing to a Home Office representative as early as December 1971. He was anxious that no one at Stormont should find out about his proposals. Bloomfield informed Home Office official, Philip Woodfield (later of the Northern Ireland Office) that he thought 'hard and long' before telling him 'of the conclusions towards which he had been reluctantly driven'. These conclusions represented 'a deep change in his assessment of the situation' and his view of what was needed. In his opinion, no settlement was possible, and violence would continue, unless policies were applied 'which not only met adequately the demands of the Catholics but were also acceptable to the South'. Further to the British government's reassurance that there could be no Irish unification without the consent of the majority in Northern Ireland, Bloomfield suggested that the government should also state 'there would be unification if the majority came to desire it'. He advocated a referendum on the question of unification as a means of testing public opinion on the subject, as soon as the political situation in Northern Ireland was sufficiently stable. He favoured 'periodic referenda' but ones which did not ask the same simple question: 'unification or not?' He felt the questions asked [in referenda] should follow a progression, depending on the way in which relations with the Republic developed.

> To begin with, committees or councils for co-operation in certain [fields] should be set up. If these proved useful, a referendum would be held after several years on a proposal to extend the field of co-operation and perhaps deepen its nature: and so on step by step. The progression [might] lead in the end to the final question of unification.

Bloomfield recognised that to 'reveal this intention fully' would provoke strong 'Protestant opposition'. He also argued for a progressive policy in relation to Catholic participation in government. This policy would have to be driven by London, since he 'saw no hope of Stormont evolving by its own efforts into a parliamentary and governmental system acceptable to the Catholics'. He was critical of Faulkner's belief, that if violence was eliminated, 'the Catholics would come round to co-operation'. He believed that 'civil disobedience and parliamentary abstention would continue', even if Faulkner's hoped-for improvement in security materialised. For Catholics, 'nothing less than a share in governmental power would do: that is to say community government'. Bloomfield's difficulty with this was that 'the unionists were quite unable to bring themselves to offer it: the Catholics would not accept it as a gift from the unionists'. Thus, a solution might only be found if the British government decided 'to intervene directly'. He thought the British government should impose a new constitution and reform the electoral system. PR-STV should be used to 'elect an enlarged house from which a community government would be appointed on a basis reflecting party strengths in the house, with blocking provisions in the government as well as the house to safeguard minority interests in selected fields'.

Bloomfield stressed that his proposals would be likely to meet with strong opposition should the Northern Ireland parties be consulted. However, he thought that the politicians would accept such a plan 'if it was imposed on them', as would the general public. If the politicians rejected the settlement, he believed that the British were faced with introducing direct rule. Woodfield enquired if Bloomfield had reason to believe his views were shared by his colleagues in the Northern Ireland civil service. The latter stressed that while he had not specifically discussed these views with anyone, he found that 'with the exception of one or two who were incurably addicted to the "bash them" approach, his senior colleagues had recently become seized of the importance of Southern opinion as well as Catholic opinion [in Northern Ireland] if lasting solutions were to be found'. The minute concluded with Woodfield's suggestion that Bloomfield's proposals 'be given a good deal of weight'.[37] These proposals were relayed to Prime Minister Edward Heath, who was reported to have read them 'with great interest' and sought to discuss them with Bloomfield in person.[38] However, Heath later recalled that the men never got around to a face-to-face meeting.[39] Nevertheless, it is clear his suggestions were taken seriously at the highest levels of government. Interestingly, Bloomfield makes no mention of these proposals in either of his memoirs.[40]

In March 1972, some of Bloomfield's proposals were advocated by the Home Secretary. Maudling argued that the desire of most unionists to remain in the United Kingdom should be supported by the government, but only if unionists accepted the overriding authority of the Westminster parliament. He also suggested periodically staging plebiscites to reassure Protestants that the constitutional position was secure. According to Maudling, law and order powers should be transferred to Westminster, and internment ended when it was considered safe to do so. He argued that Northern Ireland policy should encourage and support the 'participation of the minority community in the life and public affairs of the Province by adapting administration, legislature and Government'.[41] The latter phrase implied the consideration of an institutionalised role for Catholics in any future Northern Ireland government – in other words, power-sharing. Maudling's proposals were thus similar to those advocated by Bloomfield in December 1971. At cabinet level, however, there was, as yet, little enthusiasm for either 'community government' or direct rule. Heath is reported to have broadly favoured the long-term aim of finding a solution to the Northern Ireland problem in an all-Ireland context.[42]

Paul Bew has argued that in early 1972 'there appears to have been a growing consensus amongst the most senior officials at the Home Office and the Foreign Office that a period of direct rule was inevitable and that some new form of power-sharing was the way forward for Northern Ireland'.[43] The memorandum, which Maudling prepared for the cabinet, supports this view. Later that year, the British government tried to undertake a political initiative. This followed the military success of Operation Motorman, which re-established an Army presence in republican strongholds where no security forces had operated.[44] A political conference was organised at Darlington in September 1972. However, it was boycotted by the SDLP and the DUP, and thus did not prove particularly successful.[45] In Belfast, a Church of Ireland clergyman, the Rev Joseph Parker, whose fourteen-year-old son had been killed by a bomb two months previously, staged a five-day hunger strike to protest the boycott of the conference by these two parties. During the fast, he collected a petition of 7,000 signatures protesting against the 'political bankruptcy of the Irish nation'. SDLP leader Gerry Fitt visited Parker, but refused to attend the conference.[46]

There were several reasons why these parties refused to participate. Unionists were angered when Whitelaw met leading figures within the PIRA,[47] and his offer of an amnesty to those interned for participation in illegal marches. Alternatively, nationalists were angered by his decision not to phase out internment altogether.[48] This, coupled with the damage that the events of Bloody Sunday did to the British government's reputation, influenced the SDLP's refusal to attend the conference. The SDLP may also have realised that its more radical proposals in *Towards a New Ireland* would have been dismissed by both the UUP and the British government. Brian Faulkner invited William Craig to attend the Darlington conference as his advisor, but he declined. Craig's refusal signalled a widening of the gap between the policies of the UUP and those of Vanguard, as the latter's policy documents had already indicated.[49] Politically the conference was a failure. According to one newspaper, its only substantial achievement was that some of the factions 'sat down and talked'.[50] However, the month following its conclusion, the influential British Green Paper, *The Future of Northern Ireland: a paper for discussion*, was published.

This Green Paper stated that the British government's aim in Northern Ireland was 'to find a system of government which will enjoy the support and the respect of the overwhelming majority.' It also insisted 'the view of HM Government has always been that no change should be made to the status of Northern Ireland without Northern Ireland's free agreement'. The SDLP's proposals for joint sovereignty were rejected as incompatible with the 1949 Ireland Act, which stated that the consent of Northern Ireland's parliament was required for any change in the constitutional position. The four possible options outlined in the paper were: integration; a purely executive authority (council); a limited law-making body (convention); a return to meaningful devolution in the form of a powerful legislature and executive. Relations with the Republic were also mentioned.[51] Many of the ideas in the Green Paper became British government policy when Whitelaw published the *Northern Ireland Constitutional Proposals* in March 1973.

The White Paper provided for the re-establishment of a devolved local assembly in Northern Ireland, with significant executive powers. However, there were clear differences between the old Stormont system and the proposed new Assembly. PR-STV was to be used in elections, and the terms 'government' and 'parliament' would no longer be used. The head of the devolved administration was to be referred to simply as 'Chief Executive'. There would now be only one Prime Minister in the United Kingdom. Whitelaw's proposals explicitly rejected the principle that an executive could be formed by a single party if 'that party draws its support and elected representation virtually entirely from one section of a divided community'.[52] A return to exclusively unionist government was out of the question. The only realistic option, left open to the Northern Ireland parties wishing to form a local executive, was power-sharing between nationalists and unionists. The White Paper (like its predecessor, The Government of Ireland Act 1920), contained the provision that 'the United Kingdom Parliament will continue to have the power to legislate in respect of any matter whatever in Northern Ireland', regardless of the existence of the devolved administration. The passing of 'discriminatory legislation' by the proposed assembly was also outlawed. This reinforced the fact that Northern Ireland was part of the United Kingdom and that the writ of the Westminster parliament took primacy over any local administration. The British proposals also sought to remove the issue of the constitutional status of Northern Ireland from any future discussions: 'there will be no weakening whatever in Northern Ireland's links with the Crown. Where executive power is not devolved . . . it will be exercised either by The Queen in Council or by Her Majesty's Government'.[53]

Despite the unequivocal support for the constitutional *status quo*, problems remained for unionists. Whitelaw's proposals stated that the British government favoured, and were prepared to facilitate, the 'establishment of institutional arrangements for consultation and co-operation between Northern Ireland and the Republic of Ireland'. A future tripartite conference was suggested to discuss the implementation of the policies proposed in the White Paper. The conference would deal with three outstanding objectives: the acceptance by the Republic of the constitutional status of Northern Ireland; all-Ireland co-operation; and the 'provision of a firm basis for concerted governmental and community action against terrorist organisations'.[54] Nationalist politicians were, for the first time, presented with an opportunity to actually govern, and the proposed all-Ireland institutions could be presented by them as a positive step towards closer political links with the Republic. Few unionists could criticise the proposed all-Ireland action against terrorist organisations, but concerns remained over how much influence the Republic would have concerning the affairs of Northern Ireland.

Reaction to the White Paper and the Assembly elections in Northern Ireland

The British White Paper was keenly debated by the UUP at a special meeting of the party's governing body, the Ulster Unionist Council (UUC). A motion authorising Faulkner to have further talks with Whitelaw on aspects of the White Paper which were deemed unsatisfactory was passed by 381 votes to 44. A further motion, proposed by Vanguard, calling for the outright rejection of the White Paper was defeated by 381 to 231 votes. There were 100 abstentions, which illustrates the lack of consensus within the UUP regarding the White Paper.[55] The defeat of Vanguard's motion was the immediate cause of the formal split between the UUP and the Vanguard movement. The latter subsequently became a political party in its own right, the Vanguard Unionist Progressive Party (VUPP).[56] The VUPP stated that one of its primary aims was to make the Assembly proposed in the White Paper 'a nonsense'.[57] The party labelled William Whitelaw a 'usurper in our land' and advocated a campaign of civil disobedience against the British government: 'the spirit that refused ship money to Charles I and tea-money to George III will pay neither rates nor tribute to their modern imitator'. The same Vanguard publication criticised Whitelaw for not cracking down on a civil disobedience campaign led by 'the law-breaker, Mr John Hume, MP'.[58]

Following the above-mentioned UUC vote, the UUP published a policy statement entitled *The Northern Ireland Constitutional Proposals: A Constructive Approach*. This document argued that there was nothing in the White Paper for unionists to fear. The union with Great Britain was 'firmer under the new proposals than ever before'. It downplayed differences in the names of the new institutions and claimed that the proposed Council of Ireland was 'basically the same as that proposed by the Unionist Party'. Regarding power-sharing the UUP argued that it had never been its policy 'to insist on one-party government', but contended that there could be no place in any Executive 'for those who are not prepared to accept the right of the people of Northern Ireland to decide their future by a free vote . . . and to work for the benefit of the community inside the framework thereby decided'. In a clear-reference to the VUPP, the document criticised hard-line loyalists 'proposing to make the Assembly unworkable', and claimed that 'the fewer wrecking elements' elected to the Assembly, the more likely it was that security powers would be devolved to Northern Ireland.[59] The reactions of the other political parties to the British White Paper emerged during the course of both the local government and Northern Ireland Assembly elections which took place in May and June 1973 respectively.

The SDLP's reaction was generally positive, since the White Paper contained 'enough SDLP policy for the party to support the British government's legislation'.[60] The SDLP *District Council Election Manifesto* presented the British White Paper proposals as a series of SDLP 'demands' which had been conceded. The party 'demanded proportional representation (STV) ... We have got proportional representation ... We demanded the removal of contentious issues from local politics ... this has now happened ... We demanded local government structures that would be free from the dead hand of permanent unionist domination ... This too has now happened'.[61] Such posturing did little to convince unionists of the SDLP's *bona fides*. By contrast, the UUP manifesto made more reference to actual local government issues than the SDLP document, and spent little time on constitutional issues.[62] The lesser emphasis on constitutional matters in UUP local government literature, coupled with the SDLP's presentation of the White Paper as a series of 'gains' for nationalists, further estranged many unionists.

The cross-community Alliance party welcomed the White Paper proposals. They contained much of what it had been arguing for since 1972, including proposals for an institutionalised Irish dimension.[63] In the subsequent local elections, the UUP emerged as the victor with 41.4 per cent of the vote. The Alliance party came in second with 13.7 per cent, 0.3 per cent ahead of the SDLP.[64] The UUP still commanded a great deal of support in the community and secured a good result. Internally, however, further splits were forthcoming. These divisions were manifested publicly before the Northern Ireland Assembly elections in June 1973.

The UUP Assembly election manifesto contained a carefully worded statement about the party's view on power-sharing. The party stated it would not sit in government with those whose 'primary objective' was to break the union with Great Britain. This left open the possibility for a coalition with the SDLP. Faulkner argued that if the SDLP was prepared to work within a Northern Ireland framework, then breaking the union could no longer be its 'primary objective',[65] but Faulkner's creative use of words did not satisfy everyone in his party. In an effort to present a united front at the elections, Faulkner asked UUP candidates to sign a pledge supporting party policy. Ten of the thirty-nine UUP candidates refused, and contested the election as 'unpledged' unionists. This group was led by Harry West, a former Stormont agriculture minister.[66]

The pledged UUP manifesto, *Peace, Order and Good Government*, stated that a devolved government must be 'such as to inspire trust and confidence in all but an irredeemable hard-core of militants'. Devolution of policing powers was called for, with sufficient freedom for the Assembly to 'decide priorities of expenditure'. It was also suggested that a potential role be developed for minor parties, independent politicians, and opponents of the White Paper in principle by proposing a committee system where those 'who could not or would not join in actual government could find meaningful participation'.[67] This committee system was similar to that proposed by Faulkner in 1971 as a means to include nationalists in the process of government. However, those 1971 proposals were rejected by the SDLP as not going far enough to meet the necessary reforms.[68]

By 1973, the SDLP's rhetoric focused on promoting the concept of a united Ireland. Its Assembly election manifesto stated that the two Irelands should 'ultimately come together . . . not in any false or forced manner . . . but by planned and agreed steps'. Unionist voters were not likely to have viewed this as the manifesto of a party whose primary aim was not to break the union with Great Britain. Further to this, the party proposed the abolition of the 1954 Flags and Emblems (Northern Ireland) Act, which prohibited the flying of the Irish tricolour. It also argued for the promotion of the Irish language, and stated that the proposed all-Ireland institutions would 'remove barriers' to all-island integration. While also mentioning employment and education, the manifesto was largely concerned with the constitutional question; membership of the European Economic Community (EEC) was also mentioned as a possible stimulus for Irish unity.[69]

The Alliance party also referred to the EEC in its manifesto, arguing that Northern Ireland could benefit from the provision of money 'in quantities previously undreamt of' from that organisation, and from Westminster. The British proposals were, in its view, 'a reasonable basis to achieve peace, justice and self-respect', and did not constitute 'a sell out'.[70] Despite being initially opposed to the Irish government 'being represented as a participating body in any talks on the future of Northern Ireland', the party now conceded that the former's participation was necessary.[71] Notwithstanding the party's cross-community image, its manifesto concluded by urging both unionist and nationalist voters to give their second and subsequent preferences to Alliance candidates in order to 'keep out [their] worst enemy'.[72]

Ian Paisley's DUP manifesto contrasted sharply with that of Alliance. It contained little detailed discussion of the White Paper, but argued that the proposals were a capitulation to republican violence, and that the Council of Ireland provision was a 'half-way house to a united Ireland'. The party repeated its demand for the complete integration of Northern Ireland with the rest of the United Kingdom.[73]

The most militant opposition to the White Paper emanated from the VUPP. Its manifesto dismissed critics who described it as an extremist party, claiming that it was not extremist to 'work for the defeat of a minority that would dispossess the majority of their freedom and rights'. The VUPP argued that it would be better for Northern Ireland to be independent than accept the British proposals.[74]

The elections took place on 28 June 1973. The pledged UUP won twenty-four seats in the Assembly. However, the unpledged UUP took a quarter of all UUP votes, winning eight seats. The SDLP won nineteen Assembly seats, making it the second largest political party in Northern Ireland. Other anti-White Paper unionists had reasonably good results at the polls. The VUPP took seven Assembly seats, while the DUP won eight. The Alliance party received 9.2 per cent of the vote, less than the DUP and VUPP, but won eight Assembly seats. In total, 60.4 per cent of the electorate voted for pro-White Paper candidates. However, a majority of unionists voted for opponents of Whitelaw's reforms: 29.3 per cent of unionists voted for the Faulknerite faction, while 35.4 per cent voted for anti-reform candidates, illustrating that the British proposals were not supported by a majority of unionists. Despite this, there was still a possibility to form an executive, consisting of the pledged UUP, SDLP and Alliance parties. A meeting of the Assembly was arranged for 31 July 1973.

The events of that day did not augur well for its future.[75] The first meeting of the Assembly was plagued by disruption from loyalist members. It took two-and-a-half hours to elect the Presiding Officer (speaker). The disruption was caused by Ian Paisley (North Antrim), Kennedy Lindsay (South Antrim), Johnny McQuade (North Belfast) and Glenn Barr (Londonderry). Lindsay's erratic opening speech referred not just to the unsuitability of Faulkner's choice of Presiding Officer, Nat Minford, but also to aspirins, gundogs and swivel chairs.[76] Minford was eventually elected, and adjourned the Assembly after receiving a tirade of abuse from Barr, Paisley and McQuade. The loyalists refused to leave the chamber, installed their own chairman and carried on a 'mock' Assembly. Public reaction to this performance was unfavourable, and Paisley later agreed to sit on the committee that agreed the Assembly standing orders.[77] That committee began its work in August 1973. Paisley took a very active part in its work, tabling five amendments on the first day. Many of the committee proceedings were tedious, with issues such as seating arrangements given much attention. So important was this issue that the committee decided to visit London, The Hague and Brussels to examine 'alternative seating arrangements in legislative chambers'. The SDLP members of the committee proposed that the Assembly should meet in Armagh city. It was eventually decided the Assembly would meet at the former House of Commons at Stormont. A proposal to introduce electronic voting machines in the chamber was ruled out due to the prohibitive costs involved.[78] The disorder of the first meeting of the Assembly was discussed by the standing orders committee. The speaker was given powers of censure relating to members who 'persistently and wilfully obstructed' the Assembly business, and those who used 'objectionable words' which they refused to withdraw upon receiving a reprimand.[79] An indication of the type of verbiage involved during parliamentary questions can be seen from the standing order relating to these. Questions were prohibited from containing 'statements of fact . . . arguments, inferences or imputations . . . adjectives . . . ironical expressions [or] hypothetical matter'. Debates were to be 'confined to the matter of such motion'.[80] However, an examination of the reports of the Assembly debates show that these rules were rarely followed.

Political discussions and executive negotiations

Following the first few sittings of the Assembly, a series of political meetings took place, with the purpose of forming an executive in accordance with the Northern Ireland Constitution Act. This was a difficult aim, since at that time the SDLP and UUP were not prepared to have face-to-face discussions. At a meeting in August 1973, the Alliance leader, Oliver Napier, informed Edward Heath that his party would seek to 'effect a compromise' between the Faulknerite UUP and the SDLP. Heath argued that the main obstacles to progress were: '(i) the police, and (ii) the Council of Ireland'. Napier agreed. He spoke of the need for clarity in relation to the functions of the Council, as 'it would be disastrous if the Executive broke down after, say, three months, because of dissension on this issue.' His party believed the issue of policing was potentially the greatest threat to progress, particularly because of opposition to the Royal Ulster Constabulary (RUC) from John Hume, 'the leader of the SDLP in all but name.'[81]

The issue of policing was raised by the UUP during its meeting with Heath. The position of the RUC was 'not negotiable' for the UUP. It also required clarity regarding the maintenance of the union and the proposed Irish dimension before it would enter into discussions about forming an executive. Failure to do so would lead the UUP to lose its 'support in the country'. Roy Bradford, East Belfast UUP member, highlighted the dangers of an executive forming and breaking up shortly afterwards over 'police, security or the Irish dimension'. Faulkner was critical of the manoeuvrings of Paisley, arguing that 'many of the present troubles besetting Northern Ireland could be laid at his door'.[82] Heath stated that 'it was clear that any Executive would have to be based on the Unionist Party, Alliance and SDLP'. This line of policy had been agreed by the British and Irish governments in the month preceding the Prime Minister's visit to Northern Ireland. Records of the British–Irish discussions show that Heath and Taoiseach Liam Cosgrave agreed that 'the outcome to be desired was that the official Unionists . . . should come together with the Alliance Party and the SDLP to form a coalition . . . which would meet the

requirements in the British government's White Paper'.[83] This illustrates that
the two governments rejected the SDLP's view that 'meetings on the formation of an Executive should be between delegates from the SDLP and the
Unionist Party', excluding the Alliance Party which it 'regarded as self-righ-
teous and inconsequential'. At this meeting, Heath asked Cosgrave if he felt
there was any chance of a deal between the SDLP and the anti-White Paper
loyalists regarding power-sharing. Cosgrave thought that such a deal would
be a 'disquieting possibility'. Heath then asked if Cosgrave could use 'any influence to bear on the SDLP to ensure against this outcome'.[84] The supposed
SDLP–loyalist discussions, to which Heath referred, turned out to be a rumour
started by Paddy Devlin to pressurise Faulkner to form an executive, but this
was unknown to the two premiers.[85] Both governments hoped that hard-line
loyalists would be disinclined to participate in any political settlement, and
sought to discourage the SDLP from negotiating with them.

In July of that year, the DUP showed little sign that it would play a positive
role in discussions about the future of Northern Ireland based on the British
White Paper. South Belfast Assembly member, T. E. Burns, told the Prime
Minister that 'it was impossible to get on with Roman Catholics whose attitude was feckless and irresponsible'. Paisley argued that 'the vast majority of
loyalist people in the Province could only be reassured if the Roman Catholic
community were to become fully integrated in the political life of the Province
and if the Dublin government were to renounce their territorial claims'.[86]
Paisley's argument about the Republic's territorial claim was a valid one. It
was an issue that was to be addressed by the Irish government at Sunningdale.
His attitude regarding the Catholic community was more questionable. How,
for example, could Catholics become totally integrated in the political life of
Northern Ireland without eventually having some say in its governance?
Without such a say, Catholics would have had to become unionists in order
to reassure the DUP that power could be shared with the minority
community.

Prior to negotiations regarding the formation of an executive, British officials met with members of the SDLP.[87] Issues such as internment, policing
and the Council of Ireland were discussed. On 10 September the SDLP
requested that the name of the RUC be changed to the 'Northern Ireland
Police Service'. However, it was clear that, for the SDLP, the major issue was
the proposed Council of Ireland. SDLP members informed the British officials
that they saw it as being an 'evolutionary' body, which, from an Irish nationalist point of view, can only have meant that it might eventually act as a mechanism for some sort of Irish unity.[88]

A meeting between Gerry Fitt, Paddy Devlin and Frank Cooper, Permanent
Under Secretary (PUS) of the Northern Ireland Office (NIO), confirmed that
the Council of Ireland was of primary importance for the SDLP. Fitt and

Devlin pointed out that they felt their views regarding the Council's importance were being misrepresented to the Dublin government by British officials, and that Dublin had therefore not kept up the momentum on proposals for a Council.[89] Fitt had previously hinted to British officials that the SDLP might be more open to negotiation than might be assumed from the attitude of John Hume, whose approach, Fitt stated, 'was based too much on Jesuit logic'.[90] The British were also in close contact with Hume, who along with Armagh Assembly member, Paddy O'Hanlon, informed British officials that they were involved in secret negotiations with members of the PIRA. They were more representative of the average SDLP supporter than Fitt and Devlin, who appeared to have been flexible regarding the Council of Ireland. Hume and O'Hanlon stated that members of the PIRA leadership had informed them that if good progress was made *a propos* the Council of Ireland, then it 'would be prepared to envisage a unilateral cessation of violence'. The claim about the PIRA's positive reaction to progress, concerning a Council of Ireland, is interesting given that it later opposed the Sunningdale Agreement. Of course, the PIRA could have changed its mind, or the contacts Hume and O'Hanlon had might not have been privy to the actual views of the PIRA's Army Council. But it is also possible that as two of the most vocal advocates of a powerful Council of Ireland, Hume and O'Hanlon were using the IRA as a bargaining tool to influence British officials into support for a strong Council.[91]

On 5 October 1973, discussions chaired by William Whitelaw concerning the formation of an executive got under way at Stormont.[92] Five days previously, 2,000 people from both sides of the community held a prayer meeting for peace at the interface of the loyalist Shankill and republican Falls areas of Belfast.[93] The main point of contention, during the negotiations, was the number of ministers each party would have on the proposed executive. The SDLP had nineteen Assembly seats, while the Faulknerite UUP had twenty-four. However, two of Faulkner's group voted against him in the Assembly. This meant that he could only rely on twenty-one members (excluding the Presiding Officer), just two more than the SDLP, which felt entitled to an equal number of ministries in the Executive.[94] The SDLP did not think any allowance should be made for the fact that the unionists outnumbered nationalists in Northern Ireland. It argued for an Executive comprising five unionists, five SDLP and two Alliance members.[95] Faulkner had originally been prepared to countenance 'seven unionists or nothing'.[96] After protracted discussions lasting over a month, William Whitelaw was able to devise a compromise acceptable to all parties. The executive designate would consist of six pledged UUP members, four from the SDLP and one from Alliance. The SDLP would be allocated two non-executive posts within the administration, the Alliance and pledged unionists, one each. The agreement to form an executive was a source of great personal pride to Whitelaw, who retrospectively argued that those involved had 'broken the mould of Northern Ireland politics based on sectarian division'.[97] In forming the executive, Faulkner was aware that many unionists, even those from the liberal middle classes, remained sceptical about power-sharing with the SDLP.[98] The new executive became known to the public on 21 November 1973.[99] The details on matters such as the proposed Council of Ireland and co-operation between Northern Ireland and the Republic on security matters would be worked out at a tripartite conference at Sunningdale, Berkshire from 6–9 December 1973.

The Sunningdale Agreement, the Dublin government and the SDLP

What was eventually agreed at Sunningdale did not reflect the wishes of most unionists. Loyalist parties who were invited to air their views, refused to attend, since they were excluded from any substantive discussions. The details of the Sunningdale conference have been well covered elsewhere.[100] However, all the parties involved, including the Irish and British governments, were able to reach agreement on a number of issues affecting the future governance of Northern Ireland. The three most important aspects of the agreement, published as 'The Sunningdale Communiqué', were, firstly, a declaration by both governments on the constitutional status of Northern Ireland; secondly, an agreement was reached between the Irish and British governments to co-operate against cross-border paramilitary activity; thirdly, and crucially, plans were made for an all-Ireland institution similar to that envisaged in 1920.

The Irish government 'solemnly declared that there could be no change in the status of Northern Ireland until a majority of the people of Northern Ireland desired a change in that status'. In turn, the British government declared that it would be prepared to facilitate a united Ireland, should the majority of the people of Northern Ireland wish to join such a polity. The Republic's declaration was important to unionists, since Article 2 of the Irish Constitution claimed Northern Ireland as part of the Irish state. In practice, this was no threat to Northern Ireland, since the writ of the Irish government only applied in the Republic. At Sunningdale, the Irish government recognised the importance of reassuring unionists that it had no irredentist intentions towards Northern Ireland. This was the first time an Irish government had explicitly recognised Northern Ireland, although previous governments had given it *de facto* recognition for many years. However, much of the value of the status declaration was lost when Irish republican politician Kevin Boland took the Irish government to court on the grounds that it was unconstitutional. The government's (successful) defence was that this was only a statement of policy, which damaged the declaration in the eyes of many unionists, who regarded it as an example of Dublin's insincerity.

Addressing the question of cross-border security co-operation, both governments agreed to establish a Law Enforcement Commission (LEC) to ascertain the 'most effective means' of dealing with cross-border violence. This was linked to the contentious issues of human rights and policing, which created great difficulties for the nationalist community in Northern Ireland.

The proposed Council of Ireland was the most controversial aspect of the Sunningdale Agreement. Plans were made for a Council 'with executive and harmonising functions . . . and a Consultative Assembly with advisory and review functions'.[101] This issue proved to be the most difficult for the executive designate.

The *Irish Times* 'Backbencher' column stressed the significance of the Sunningdale Agreement. Its author claimed that the logic of Sunningdale dictated that Fianna Fáil leader Jack Lynch should 'put his arms round Liam Cosgrave' and say that Sunningdale 'makes it possible to reunite the National Movement', and adopt its original title, Sinn Féin. This, the column claimed would be 'no more ludicrous than Gerry Fitt and Brian Faulkner with their arms around one another'.[102] Most commentators, then and subsequently, agree that the SDLP was the main 'winner' at Sunningdale. That consensus certainly reflects the view that Faulkner was 'pushed farther than he should have been and beyond his power to deliver'.[103] The idea that Faulkner, dubbed by one commentator as 'as cunning as a wagonload of monkeys', was overwhelmed during the negotiations does not seem credible.[104] Faulkner later claimed that the agreement of the Irish government to co-operate with Northern Ireland security forces, and the recognition of the status of Northern Ireland by Dublin, were major gains for unionism.[105] It is also worth noting that the Council of Ireland had a unionist veto on all issues relating to co-operation with the Republic and Dublin had, in any case, no intention of using the Council to unite Ireland.[106]

Some commentators have argued that the Dublin government and the SDLP were working in concert throughout the latter part of 1973. The reality, however, was rather different. Serious divisions existed between Dublin and the SDLP at the time, and contemporary documents challenge John Hume's retrospective claim that the SDLP's influence on the Dublin government 'in those days was total'.[107] Bew and Patterson have argued that meetings between the Irish government and the SDLP were 'remarkably successful' for the latter, and that by September 1973 their discussions had eliminated 'any significant differences of approach', in particular with regard to the Council of Ireland.[108] This argument is supported by Cillian McGrattan, who stated that 'a large degree of unanimity' existed between the Irish government and the SDLP during this period.[109] Similarly, P. J. McLoughlin has argued that after press leaks about a rift between the Irish government and the SDLP in July 1973, the Dublin coalition 'was seen to swing fully behind the SDLP's line on the Council of Ireland and policing'.[110] But what exactly did the Irish government do to 'swing fully' behind the SDLP's policies? As mentioned, the Irish government did not intend to use the Council as a staging post to a united Ireland. Dublin initially supported a Council with the potential to evolve into a strong all-Ireland body, but enthusiasm waned over time, and no policies were pursued which attempted to implement Irish unity – a stated goal of the SDLP. If indeed the Irish government and the SDLP were united in their approach to Northern Ireland, the SDLP would probably not have seen fit to chastise the Irish government for being 'generally partitionist' and accuse it of 'not being sincere in its approach to Irish unity'.[111] Policing was another area where divisions between the SDLP and the Dublin government were apparent. The SDLP pressurised the Irish government to support its calls for substantial police reform. McLoughlin has surmised that it is likely that members of the SDLP implied that they would seek the support of Fianna Fáil on the policing question if the coalition was not supportive.[112] Archival material from Dublin supports this supposition.

The SDLP informed the Attorney-General of Ireland, Declan Costello, '[it] might have to turn quickly to Fianna Fáil in the hope of getting their support on the policing question'.[113] The Fine Gael–Irish Labour Party (ILP) government, elected in February 1973, had a slender majority in Dáil Éireann, and the Fianna Fáil opposition could have used the government's Northern Ireland policy as a means to destabilise the coalition.[114] However, while accepting that the achievement of a 'common form of policing for the whole of Ireland under the Council of Ireland' was 'desirable', the most the Irish government advocated was that the police forces North and South of the border should 'account regularly' to the proposed Council of Ireland.[115] This reflected the coalition's recognition that there would be no Irish unity in the short to medium term. The Irish government had long tacitly accepted the principle of consent regarding Irish unity. The Taoiseach argued that the inflexibility and crudeness of the SDLP's tactics was a result of being 'new to power'. He claimed that the SDLP should be reassured that there would be a good chance that its views would be listened to, but that the Irish government had 'no wish to create difficulties for Faulkner and his followers'.[116] This suggests that the Irish government sought the participation of the SDLP in the power-sharing government, within a Northern Ireland framework. The vaguely defined Council of Ireland might perhaps satisfy the SDLP that its Irish aspirations could find practical expression, while at the same time the Irish government could avoid any real responsibility for Northern Ireland affairs. Given the high levels of violence and instability in the region, this was an entirely realistic position for the Irish government to take. The Dublin coalition and the SDLP therefore had some broad similarities in terms of policy, but the means by which each side sought to have those policies implemented was different, and their relationship at times uneasy. Crucially, they differed in one key respect: the SDLP sought to involve Dublin in Northern Ireland's affairs, while Dublin wished to keep a healthy distance from Northern Ireland. The character of the Dublin government's attitude to the SDLP is perhaps best summed up by a memorandum by the then Minister for Posts and Telegraphs, Conor Cruise O'Brien, who argued that the government 'should make it plain to the SDLP that while we wish to continue a close liaison with them, and while we are in agreement on broad policy aims, that the *tactics* suited to a political party are not necessarily those available to a government'.[117] Archival evidence, therefore, suggests the existing literature fails to fully appreciate the complexity of the relationship between the Irish government and the SDLP during this time.

The executive in office

The new executive took office on 1 January 1974.[118] It did not have an auspicious start. Three days after its first meeting, Faulkner faced a UUC vote on the Sunningdale Council of Ireland. Membership of the UUC was not confined to the UUP, which was divided into pro-and-anti Faulkner groups; it also included delegates from the Orange institutions and Vanguard members, to whom the Orange Order lent its support.[119] The composition of the UUC made it difficult for Faulkner to win its approval for the proposed Council of Ireland. However, because of the diverse background of its members, a UUC vote was a good test of unionist opinion in Northern Ireland. The UUC rejected the Council of Ireland proposals by 427 votes to 374.[120] Thus the anti-Council of Ireland faction had an advantage of almost 7 per cent against the Faulknerite unionists. Faulkner treated the result as a vote of 'no confidence' and duly resigned as party leader, whilst remaining head of the executive. His resignation as UUP leader further damaged his standing among many unionists, and also left him without the support of a political party machine.

Despite this setback, the possibility of getting power-sharing to work within the executive seemed promising. At its first meeting, it was agreed that, in taking decisions on any matter, 'any form of vote [was] to be avoided if at all possible', to ensure that such decisions reflected the views of all concerned. This would enable the administration to 'stand collectively' behind these decisions.[121] The executive minutes demonstrate that the executive, composed of politically opposed ministers, could work together and was not permanently divided along sectarian lines. After the UUC defeat, Faulkner told the executive that 'views were divided as to whether the result . . . accurately expressed Unionist opinion in the country'. This was despite the fact that the UUC represented many shades of unionist opinion. He wanted to 'ensure the country [supported] Sunningdale'. This was a major challenge, given the support for anti-Council of Ireland loyalists in the Assembly. The records show that Faulkner unionists believed that all-Ireland action against republican paramilitaries would broaden support for Sunningdale. The environment minister, Roy Bradford, noted that 'unless the Republic delivered on improving security then 'the prospect of selling Sunningdale [would] be immensely more difficult'. The executive agreed that Faulkner would write to the Taoiseach expressing its views on the 'law and order' situation and the 'dependence of the Sunningdale agreement on action by the Republic'.[122] Faulkner was soon presented with an opportunity to test support for Sunningdale. A strike by the National Union of Mineworkers (NUM) in England prompted Edward Heath to call a general election. In Northern Ireland, the sole issue of the election was Sunningdale – more specifically the Council of Ireland.

The pro-executive parties could not put forward agreed candidates in the election. This would have risked alienating their supporters. Faulkner noted that seven weeks of working together was not enough to change the mutual antipathies built up over fifty years. Anti-Sunningdale loyalists had no such difficulty. The unpledged UUP, VUPP and DUP formed the United Ulster Unionist Coalition (UUUC) and put forward agreed candidates. Their slogan, 'Dublin is just a Sunningdale Away', captured the imagination of many unionists.[123] The pro-Assembly election manifesto tried to reassure unionists that the party would 'not permit a council of Ireland to become a staging post for Irish unity', and that there would be no such Council until the Republic of Ireland acted 'effectively against cross-border terrorism'.[124] The SDLP manifesto called on the two traditions in Northern Ireland to stop pursuing 'total victory', whilst at the same time ignoring the sensitivities of many unionists by calling for the reform of the RUC which was, it argued, 'seen as the arm of a one party state'.[125] The majority of the unionist electorate was obviously unconvinced. The UUUC won eleven of the twelve Northern Ireland seats. Gerry Fitt (West Belfast) won the only pro-Sunningdale seat. This was a setback for the executive. A majority of unionists had sent a clear signal that they would not be forced into acceptance of a Council of Ireland. It may be regarded as optimistic to assume, as the author of a contemporary article in *Fortnight* magazine did, that unionists might have (reluctantly) accepted power-sharing without the proposed Council of Ireland, if an attractive social and economic platform could have been agreed by the executive.[126] Indeed, even during the Ulster Workers' Council (UWC) strike, the *Newsletter* stated that power-sharing had been broadly accepted in the community, but as a 'final concession'.[127] Despite the general election results, the executive still held office. The Assembly still conducted business, and there was, *at the time*, no sign that the executive was on the brink of imminent collapse.[128]

The executive parties, nationalist and unionist, did not regard the general election result as either ruinous to the Sunningdale settlement or its prospects for governing, but there were some concerns about the speed at which Sunningdale could be implemented. At a post-election meeting of the executive, Faulkner returned to the point, raised in his election manifesto, that progress on the formation of a Council of Ireland would have to be stalled if action by the Republic against the PIRA was not forthcoming. Within the executive, opinion was divided as to what *exactly* should be done in the aftermath of the election. Unsurprisingly, and pragmatically, unionists urged caution. The SDLP, however, favoured 'fast-tracking' the implementation of Sunningdale. This was clearly out of step with unionist feeling. Austin Currie thought that 'everything possible' should be done to implement Sunningdale. John Hume further argued that: 'If the Council of Ireland were to be removed, [the SDLP] would go, and [Northern Ireland] would be back in the hands of extremists.'

Regarding the Irish government's attempt to reassure unionists, Paddy Devlin said he was confident that Dublin 'would go for constitutional change after Sunningdale had been ratified'.[129] This contrasts with the recollection of Garret FitzGerald, whose memoirs clearly state that the government 'ruled out, with no serious discussion that I recall, the possibility of amending the Constitution' following the Sunningdale Agreement.[130] Unionist ministers argued that the election result was a form of mass protest. Agriculture minister, Leslie Morrell, 'agreed with Mr Hume that the vote [the eleven seats won by the UUUC] was a mass protest'. He warned that the SDLP had complained in the past that mass protest had been ignored: the executive should '*not* fall into the same trap' by ignoring the vote, as doing so risked a violent reaction from 'Protestant extremists'. Education minister, Basil McIvor, saw a 'class element' to the unionist opposition. Sunningdale, he argued, 'could be to the mutual advantage of North and South. But the message did not get through to the people in the high flats at Finaghy'. However, the size of the UUUC vote suggests that anti-Sunningdale sentiment was not confined to working-class communities. The executive decided to issue a politically ambiguous statement after its discussion, claiming it was 'united on policy' and calling on the British and Irish governments to fulfil the commitments made at Sunningdale.[131]

British–Northern Ireland contacts, March and April 1974

In February 1974, the outgoing British government was defeated in the general election. The Labour party returned to power with a minority government led by Harold Wilson. Wilson had previously provoked the ire of unionists when, in 1971, he had argued that a united Ireland might be possible within a fifteen-year timespan.[132] He appointed Merlyn Rees, MP for South Leeds, as the new Secretary of State for Northern Ireland. Rees has been caricatured as indecisive. Paddy Devlin is reported to have said that Rees was usually 'struggling with his conscience. The trouble is it always ends in a f***ing draw'.[133] His resilience was soon tested by the anti-Sunningdale UWC strike in May 1974.[134] That organisation, comprising Protestant trades-unionists, loyalist paramilitaries and VUPP members, such as William Craig and David Trimble, emerged from the rubble of the Loyalist Association of Workers (LAW).[135] The month prior to its official formation, 6,000 loyalists marched in Belfast to protest against the Sunningdale Agreement. Speakers addressing the crowd said loyalists would not put their necks 'under the jackboot of the priesthood', and would never countenance a united Ireland.[136]

Rees was a supporter of the previous government's Northern Ireland policy. One of his diary entries recorded the view that 'the realities are that a million Protestants ... cannot be bulldozed into the South. The other reality is that the government of the South does not want them ... [nevertheless, we have] got to make it possible for the minority in the North to feel that they belong in Northern Ireland and can work for a united Ireland'.[137] The Northern Ireland Constitution Act, with power-sharing and an Irish dimension, broadly satisfied those aims. Soon after his appointment, Rees met Brian Faulkner. The latter was pessimistic about his prospects if Assembly elections were called in response to UUUC demands. Rees refused to concede to these demands, to avoid further undermining the executive.[138] In late March and early April, opinion polls suggested that power-sharing still had a chance of success. In a survey conducted from 31 March to 7 April, 66 per cent of Protestants approved, or strongly approved, of power-sharing, while 59 per cent of Protestants and 90 per cent of Catholics surveyed thought that the executive 'should be given a chance'.[139] It could be argued that Rees was correct in not calling Assembly elections. This was consistent with the stated British policy of support for the executive.

The first meeting between the Secretary of State for Northern Ireland and the power-sharing executive took place on 26 March 1974. Rees stressed the importance of the meeting, arguing that 'only those resident in Northern Ireland could make a full assessment of the problems and even more important only they could solve the problems of the country'.[140] He later commented that the '"English disease" is to look for a "solution to the Irish problem"; our aim must be to find a Northern Irish solution.'[141] Rees admitted that the government was reconsidering its Northern Ireland policy. However, he confirmed that 'Sunningdale was still the basis for progress, and the House of Commons was firmly behind it.' He was critical of the Northern Ireland public for their 'apparent apathy' about politics and violence, arguing that it seemed to him that the Northern Ireland people were disinterested in politics as long as their own area was relatively safe.

In the discussion concerning the general election, Faulkner argued that the UUUC success had 'seriously slowed down the momentum of the Executive'. Roy Bradford highlighted the fact that many anti-Sunningdale votes came from areas which would 'in normal times be labelled "liberal" or "moderate"', proof that Basil McIvor had underestimated middle-class antipathy to Sunningdale. Bradford thus argued that the executive should 'put the brakes on political developments'. Austin Currie opined that while the Sunningdale Agreement had not fully satisfied any of the parties, it was the 'best possible compromise and the UK government must continue to underpin it' and pressure the Irish government to honour its obligations. He also claimed that 'some pro-Assembly unionists had lost confidence and that the Rev Paisley was manipulating and playing on these fears'. The executive must 'get the show back on the road'. There was much agreement between politicians of both persuasions at the meeting. Rees assured the executive of his full support, and confirmed that there was no intention on the part of HMG to depart from the terms of the Constitution Act. The records of this meeting clearly undermine the suggestion of Michael Kerr that the Labour government displayed antipathy towards power-sharing and the executive.[142] Rees also confirmed that he 'was giving thought to the weakening of certain groups by involving them in politics, and this could mean legalising the [Provisional] Sinn Féin organisation'.[143] This was part of a wider process of attempting to engage paramilitary groups in political discussion (a topic to which we will later return).

The Chief Executive met with the new UK Prime Minister the following week. The meeting was dominated by the issue of security (examined in the following chapter), but the Prime Minister also referred to political developments. He asked in particular about the disorderly scenes in the Assembly, enquiring 'if there had been many debates on bread and butter issues'. Faulkner replied that 'there had not been many such discussions although there had been a debate on pig farming recently which had been attended by the opposition'.[144] This could have done little to inspire Wilson's confidence in the Assembly. However, Wilson gave the executive his full support. He met with the entire executive on 18 April and informed its members of the 'government's determination to support the Executive'; if it 'were to fail, what confidence could there be of finding another [solution]'.[145] The executive, despite some minor disagreements, had established a cordial working relationship, and reached agreement on many sensitive matters. The meetings with Rees and Wilson confirm the new government's support for the power-sharing initiative. Despite the general election results, the executive appeared relatively stable and in no immediate danger of collapsing. The increasingly visible opposition of loyalist paramilitaries was, however, an ominous sign that difficult times lay ahead for the executive.

Conclusion

It is apparent that the UUP shifted its position significantly on devolved government. In the 1972 *Blueprint*, the party argued for a local administration with more power than the old Stormont system, but ended up accepting a devolved Assembly with substantially fewer powers than the old parliament. The all-Ireland body proposed by the UUP in 1972 made provision for a consultative body only. However, at Sunningdale, it accepted a Council with 'executive functions', albeit with a unionist veto on how these would be exercised. A significant section of the unionist electorate did not favour any involvement by the Republic in Northern Ireland, and this accounted for the loss of support experienced by the UUP. Power-sharing alone was not the primary reason why the UUP lost a chunk of its support, but undoubtedly some sections of unionism opposed this, based on the assumption that the SDLP was determined to have a united Ireland.

The SDLP also had to accept significant compromises, being forced to abandon many of the ideas in *Towards a New Ireland*. The UK government did not declare that the best solution would be eventual Irish unity, nor did it offer any hope of joint-sovereignty for Northern Ireland. However, some of the SDLP's demands were met, most notably the proposed establishment of a Council of Ireland with executive functions. The vague remit of the proposed Council, and Dublin's indifference to it, illustrate that this was not the major success for the party which many thought at the time. However, the fact that a majority of unionists perceived it as a success for the SDLP, and saw in it the potential for Irish unity, was an important factor in the UUUC success in the February general election.

Anti-Sunningdale loyalists were frustrated by their lack of success. The Assembly was in place; the executive was working. It appeared that this would continue to be the case. The general election in February 1974, however, was a boon to loyalists who sensed that public opinion was turning against the executive and thus inspired further loyalist resistance, which culminated in the UWC strike in May 1974. The Alliance party arguably gained most from Sunningdale. As a party with less than 10 per cent support, it now had two ministers, one within the executive.

The British and Irish governments were firmly committed to a power-sharing administration in Northern Ireland. The Irish government was in favour of a vague 'Irish dimension' to satisfy nationalists enough to work within a Northern Ireland framework, whilst also seeking to avoid too much involvement in that region's politics. There was little disagreement between the two governments in relation to the Constitution Act, and indeed much common cause between them. Contrary to some existing accounts, the Irish government and the SDLP were not working in tandem on all the issues. The relationship was complex, and at times fraught. Successive British governments assured the executive of all necessary support, and confirmed that the Sunningdale settlement was the only basis on which political progress could be made. One of the most contentious issues was the ongoing security problem, which will be discussed in the following chapter.

Notes

1 Jackson, *Home Rule*, p. 318; McGrattan, 'Dublin, the SDLP and the Sunningdale agreement: maximalist nationalism and path dependency', *Contemporary British History*, xxiii: 1 (2009), pp. 61–78; Kerr, *Imposing Power-sharing: Conflict and Coexistence in Northern Ireland and Lebanon* (Dublin: Irish Academic Press, 2005), p. 62.

2 Faulkner, *Memoirs*, pp. 151–2.

3 Patterson and Kaufmann, *Unionism*, p. 141.

4 Lee, *Ireland*, p. 441.

5 See Privy Council Office website. Available: www.pco.gov.uk/output/page534.asp.

6 Gillespie, *Years of Darkness*, p. 53.

7 *Irish Independent*, 28 March 1972.

8 Hennessey, *Northern Ireland*, p. 208.

9 *Irish Independent*, 28 March 1972.

10 Walker, *Unionist Party*, p. 212.

11 J. McGarry and B. O'Leary, *The Politics of Antagonism: Understanding Northern Ireland* (London: Athlone), p. 185.

12 Harkness, *Northern Ireland*, p. 166.

13 M. Mulholland, *Northern Ireland at the Crossroads: Ulster Unionism in the O'Neill Years, 1960–9* (Basingstoke: Palgrave Macmillan, 2000), p. 92. For biographical accounts of Paisley, compare S. Bruce *Paisley: Religion and Politics in Northern Ireland* (Oxford: Oxford University Press, 2007) and E. Moloney *Paisley: From Demagogue to Democrat* (Dublin: Poolbeg, 2008). See also E. and A. Pollak, *Paisley* (Dublin: Poolbeg, 1986) and C. Smyth *Ian Paisley: Voice of Protestant Ulster* (Edinburgh: Scottish Academic Press, 1987).

14 See G. Walker, 'The Ulster Unionist Party and the Bannside by-election 1970', Irish *Political Studies*, xix: 1 (2004), pp. 59–73.

15 Jackson, *Ireland 1798–1998*, p. 375.

16 Mulholland, 'Assimilation versus segregation: unionist strategy in the 1960s', *Twentieth Century British History*, xi: 3 (2000), pp. 284–307.

17 The Balmoral mass-meeting was attended by Conservative leader Andrew Bonar-Law, who pledged his support to the anti-Home Rule cause.

18 *Sunday Independent*, 19 March 1972.

19 *Dominion of Ulster* (Belfast, 1972). Lindsay was elected to the Northern Ireland Assembly in 1973 for the South Antrim constituency.

20 Patterson and Kaufmann, *Unionism*, p. 150. A June 1972 poll showed support for Vanguard at 31 per cent, just 12 percentage points behind the UUP. The Democratic Unionist Party (DUP), led by Ian Paisley, at that time only attracted the support of 11 per cent of those polled.

21 ARK website. Available: www.ark.ac.uk/elections/fa73.htm. For the Nationalist Party, B. Lynn, *Holding the Ground: The Nationalist Party of Northern Ireland* (Aldershot: Ashgate, 1997).

22 Faulkner, *Memoirs*, p. 255. The IRA and Sinn Féin split into two factions in December 1969 and January 1970. Official Sinn Féin (OSF) and the Official IRA (OIRA) wished to drop the party's abstention from parliamentary elections and pursue a radical leftist agenda. Provisional Sinn Féin (PSF) and the Provisional IRA (PIRA) supported more traditional republican tactics. See English, *Armed Struggle*, pp. 105–9.

23 John Hume, Ivan Cooper and Paddy O'Hanlon had been prominent civil rights independents, Austin Currie was in the Nationalist Party, Gerry Fitt was Republican Labour, and Paddy Devlin was in NILP. T. Hennessey, *The Evolution of the Troubles 1970–72* (Dublin: Irish Academic Press, 2007), p. 24.

24 UUP, *Towards the Future: A Unionist blueprint* (Belfast: Ulster Unionist Party, 1972), p. 13.

25 Ibid., p. 13.

26 The Alliance Party and NILP also supported a Bill of Rights for Northern Ireland. See *The Future of Northern Ireland*, Conflict Archive on the Internet (CAIN) website. Available: www.cain.ulst.ac.uk/hmso/nio1972.htm.

27 *Towards the Future*, pp. 13–17. The Government of Ireland Act prohibited religious discrimination, but it did not expressly forbid discrimination on political grounds.

28 *Towards the Future*, p. 17.

29 Ibid., p. 19.

30 Ulster Vanguard, *Spelling It Out: A Brief Statement of Basic Principles* (Belfast: Ulster Vanguard, 1972).

31 Walker, *Unionist Party*, p. 213.

32 For more on Bloody Sunday see chapter 2. For two recent interpretations of that day's events see, Hennessey, *Evolution* and N. Ó Dochartaigh, 'Bloody Sunday: error or design?', *Contemporary British History*, xxiv: 1 (2010), pp. 89–108.

33 SDLP *Towards a new Ireland* (Belfast: SDCD, 1972).

34 P. Bew and H. Patterson, *The British State and the Ulster Crisis: From Wilson to Thatcher* (London: Verso, 1985), p. 53.

35 R. F. Foster, *Modern Ireland 1600–1972* (London: Penguin, 1989), p. 591.

36 Lee, *Ireland*, p. 434.

37 The National Archives (TNA), Ministry of Defence files (DEFE), for Woodfield from Smith, 20 December 1971.

38 TNA, Cabinet Office (CAB) 164/1175, R. Armstrong to B. Trend, 7 January 1972.

39 *Bloody Sunday Inquiry Transcript*, Day 291, 29 January 2003. Available: http://report.bloody-sunday-inquiry.org/transcripts/Archive/Ts291.htm.

40 Robert Ramsay claims he confronted Bloomfield about these proposals when he found out about them years later, and the latter claimed he had 'almost forgotten about' them: *Ringside Seats*, pp. 107–8.

41 TNA, CAB 129/168, memorandum by the Secretary of State for the Home Department, 3 March 1972.

42 Hennessey, *Evolution*, pp. 326–9.
43 Bew, *Ireland*, p. 506.
44 R. Bourke, *Peace in Ireland: The War of Ideas* (London: Pimlico, 2003), p. 170.
45 Faulkner, *Memoirs*, p. 179.
46 *Irish Times*, 26 September 1972.
47 Harkness, *Northern Ireland*, p. 172. See chapter 2.
48 Lee, *Ireland*, p. 442.
49 Faulkner, *Memoirs*, pp. 177–8.
50 *Sunday Independent*, 1 October 1972.
51 *The Future of Northern Ireland* (HMSO, 1972).
52 *Northern Ireland Constitutional Proposals* (HMSO, 1973).
53 Ibid.
54 Ibid.
55 Patterson and Kaufmann, *Unionism*, p. 158.
56 Walker, *Unionist Party*, p. 216.
57 Whitelaw, *Memoirs*, p. 111.
58 Ulster Vanguard, *Government without Right* (Belfast: Ulster Vanguard, 1973).
59 *The Northern Ireland Constitutional Proposals.*
60 G. Murray and J. Tonge, *Sinn Féin and the SDLP: From Alienation to Participation* (Dublin: O'Brien Press, 2005), p. 48.
61 *SDLP District Council Election Manifesto* (May, 1973)
62 *Unionist Local Government Manifesto* (May 1973).
63 *Statement of Alliance Party's Position for Constitutional Conference* (September, 1972). The proposals were addressed to William Whitelaw and signed 'P. O'Neill'. The P. O'Neill in question was Phelim O'Neill, MP for North Antrim.
64 1973 local election results. CAIN website. Available: www.cain.ulst.ac.uk/issues/politics/election/rd1973.htm.
65 Faulkner, *Memoirs*, p. 194.
66 Ibid., p. 195.
67 *Peace, Order and Good Government* (Belfast: Ulster Unionist Party, 1973).
68 Faulkner, *Memoirs*, p. 103.
69 *SDLP Assembly Election Manifesto* (Belfast: SDLP, 1973).
70 *Alliance Assembly Election Manifesto* (Belfast: Alliance Party, 1973).
71 *Statement of Alliance Party's Position for Constitutional Conference* (September, 1972).
72 *Alliance Assembly Election Manifesto* (1973).
73 *Ulster Democratic Unionist Party 1973 Assembly Manifesto* (Belfast: Ulster-Democratic Unionist Party, 1973).
74 The minority were 'Irish republican and Marxist factions'. Ulster Vanguard, *A statement of Policy: Power for the People – Power for Our Land* (Belfast: Ulster Vanguard, 1973).
75 1973 Northern Ireland Assembly election results. CAIN website. Available: www.cain.ulst.ac.uk/issues/politics/election/ra1973.htm.
76 Faulkner, *Memoirs*, pp 200–1. For full text of the Lindsay's speech, see *Northern Ireland Assembly: Official Report*, vol. 1, 31 July 1973–19 December 1973, col. 35.

77 Faulkner, *Memoirs*, pp. 201–2.
78 *Northern Ireland Assembly Papers, 1–8, 1973–74* (Belfast: HMSO, 1974), pp. 11–33.
79 Ibid., p. 16.
80 Ibid., p. 52.
81 TNA, Foreign and Commonwealth Office (FCO) 87/283, meeting between the Prime Minister and the Alliance Assembly Members, 29 August 1973.
82 Ibid., meeting between the Prime Minister and leaders of the 'pledged' Unionists, 28 August 1973.
83 TNA, Northern Ireland Office files (CJ4)/391, note for the record, 2 July 1973.
84 TNA, CJ4/509, Secretary of State meeting with Brian Faulkner, 7 September 1973.
85 Currie, *All Hell*, p. 221.
86 TNA, FCO 87/283, note of a meeting between the Prime Minister and leaders of the Democratic Unionist Party, 29 August 1973.
87 Meetings took place on 10 September with the SDLP, on 25 September with Fitt and Devlin, and on 21 September with Hume and O'Hanlon. See TNA, FCO 87/228.
88 TNA, FCO 87/228, meeting between the PUS and the SDLP, 10 September 1973.
89 Ibid., meeting between the PUS and Mr Gerry Fitt and Mr Paddy Devlin, 25 September 1973.
90 Ibid., meeting between the PUS and the SDLP, 10 September 1973.
91 Ibid., meeting between the PUS and Mr John Hume and Mr Paddy O'Hanlon, 21 September 1973. One of O'Hanlon's contributions to the meeting was a warning that his PIRA contacts 'had mentioned some particularly beastly actions (he would not repeat them) which the Provisionals could well unleash if necessary'.
92 For memoir accounts of some prominent unionists see Faulkner, *Memoirs*, pp. 202–25 and McIvor, *Hope*, pp. 95–8.
93 *Newsletter*, 1 October 1973.
94 Currie *All Hell*, p. 218.
95 McIvor, *Hope*, p. 97.
96 Faulkner, *Memoirs*, p. 219.
97 Whitelaw, *Memoirs*, p. 120.
98 Patterson and Kaufmann, *Unionism*, p. 163.
99 Bourke, *Peace*, p. 212.
100 The memoirs of Faulkner, Austin Currie, Basil McIvor, Paddy Devlin, Maurice Hayes, Ken Bloomfield and Garret FitzGerald to name but a few.
101 All quotations from The Sunningdale Communiqué, CAIN website. Available: www.cain.ulst.ac.uk/events/sunningdale/agreement.htm.
102 *Irish Times*, 15 December 1973.
103 Hayes, *Minority Verdict*, p. 166.
104 *Sunday Independent*, 16 December 1973.
105 Faulkner, *Memoirs*, p. 237. Basil McIvor's memoirs are more pessimistic. He claims to have thought Sunningdale 'a pretty hopeless exercise'. McIvor, *Hope Deferred*, p. 100.

106 See chapter 3.

107 Kerr, *Imposing*, p. 62.

108 Bew and Patterson, *British State*, p. 58. The Council of Ireland will be dealt with in chapter 3.

109 C. McGrattan, 'Dublin, the SDLP', p. 69.

110 The leaks originated with Paddy Devlin. See McLoughlin '"Dublin is just a Sunningdale away?" The SDLP and the Failure of Northern Ireland's Sunningdale Experiment', *Twentieth Century British History*, xx: 1 (2009), p. 80.

111 National Archives of Ireland (NAI), Attorney General's Office files (AG) 2004/1/254, SDLP meeting with Sean Donlon in Belfast, 30 October 1973.

112 McLoughlin 'Dublin is just a Sunningdale away?', p. 82.

113 NAI, AG 2004/1/254, SDLP meeting with Sean Donlon, 30 October 1973.

114 M. Gallagher, *The Irish Labour Party in Transition, 1957–82* (Manchester: Manchester University Press, 1982), p. 196.

115 NAI, Department of the Taoiseach files (DT) 2004/21/3, Cabinet Minutes, 26 October 1973.

116 NAI, AG 2004/1/254, Department of the Taoiseach, Heath visit, 21 September 1973.

117 Ibid., O'Brien to Cosgrave, 5 November 1973.

118 Faulkner was Chief Executive. Gerry Fitt, Deputy Chief Executive. The other executive members were Herbie Kirk, finance; John Hume, commerce; Austin Currie, housing; Paddy Devlin, health and social services; Roy Bradford, environment; Basil McIvor, education, Leslie Morrell, agriculture; Oliver Napier, legal services; John Baxter, information services.

119 E. P. Kaufmann, *The Orange Order: A Contemporary Northern Irish History* (Oxford: Oxford University Press, 2007), pp. 82–3.

120 Patterson and Kaufmann, *Unionism*, p. 165.

121 Public Records Office of Northern Ireland (PRONI), Office of the Executive files (OE)/2/1, executive minutes, 1 January 1974.

122 PRONI, OE/1/2/1A, executive minutes, 8 January 1974.

123 Lee, *Ireland*, p. 444.

124 *Pro-Assembly Unionists: Imperial General Election Campaign* (February 1974).

125 *Another Step Forward with the SDLP: Manifesto 1974*.

126 I. S. Wood, *Crimes of Loyalty: A History of the UDA* (Edinburgh: Edinburgh University Press, 2006), 32.

127 *Newsletter*, 24 May 1974.

128 It remains unclear whether or not the executive could have survived had the UWC strike not occurred. G. Gillespie argues that it would have collapsed in any case due to an increasing loss of unionist support. 'The Sunningdale Agreement: Lost Opportunity or an Agreement Too Far?', *Irish Political Studies*, xiii: 1 (1998), 100–14.

129 PRONI, OE/10/10, executive minutes, 5 March 1974, note of a discussion on the political situation following the results of the general election 28 Feb. 1974.

130 Sunningdale in this sense means the conference in England, 6–9 December, 1973. FitzGerald, *All in a Life*, p. 223.

131 Finaghy is an area in South Belfast with sizeable working-class communities. PRONI, OE/10/10, executive minutes, 5 March 1974, note of a discussion on the political situation following the results of the general election 28 Feb. 1974. Emphasis as original. Even in affluent North Down, the UUUC candidate received 61 per cent of the vote. ARK election results. Available: www.ark.ac.uk/elections/cnd.htm.

132 Wilson, *Final Term*, p. 70.

133 Currie, *All Hell*, p. 268. The quote has also been attributed to a British civil servant.

134 The strike and its aftermath are dealt with in chapters 5 and 6.

135 See Wood, *Crimes*, pp. 33–6.

136 *Irish Independent*, 17 January 1974.

137 LSE, MERLYN-REES/1/1, Merlyn Rees diaries, transcripts of tapes, sides 1–2, 10.

138 TNA, FCO 87/334, note for the record by Frank Cooper, 4 March 1974.

139 Kerr, *Imposing*, p. 55.

140 PRONI, OE/1/24, executive meetings with Secretary of State, 26 March 1974.

141 TNA, CAB, 134/3921, ministerial committee on Northern Ireland (IRN (75)), 7 November 1975.

142 Kerr's account of this meeting, which omits some crucial aspects of Rees's remarks, contrasts sharply with that presented here. See *Destructors*, p. 172.

143 PRONI, OE 1/24, executive meetings with Secretary of State, 26 March 1974.

144 TNA, CJ4/788, meeting between the Prime Minister and Brian Faulkner, 1 April 1974.

145 PRONI, OE 1/24, meeting of the Northern Ireland administration with the Prime Minister, 18 April 1974.

2

The security problem

The two-year period, from the introduction of direct rule to the fall of the Northern Ireland Executive, accounted for the highest level of violence over the entire course of the conflict. Improving security on an all-Ireland basis was therefore a prominent political concern during these years. This was because cross-border attacks on Northern Ireland security forces were then commonplace. The Sunningdale Communiqué of 1973 made explicit reference to such attacks, and the British and Irish governments agreed to make the Northern Ireland frontier more secure. Cross-border security co-operation improved following the Irish general election of 1973, when a Fine Gael–ILP coalition replaced the outgoing Fianna Fáil administration.

The sensitive issues of internment, detention, reform of the police and extradition affected the prospects of the Sunningdale settlement. The unionist leader, Brian Faulkner, overestimated the importance which the SDLP placed on police reform and security policy. The SDLP was more concerned with the Council of Ireland, and was prepared to accept relatively cosmetic security reforms as a pre-condition to urging nationalists to whole-heartedly support the RUC.

The security problem, 1972–74: an overview

It has been argued, by academics and former politicians, that the security problem was the primary reason for the executive's untimely demise. Merlyn Rees claimed that violence jeopardised any 'prospect whatsoever of political progress'; while Joe Lee argued that the gunmen were 'able to sabotage concili-atory initiatives by provoking incidents guaranteed to rouse communal bitterness'.[1] The 1972–74 period witnessed intense loyalist and republican violence, resulting in 1,043 deaths. The majority of these were caused by the PIRA.[2] The OIRA posed a lesser threat to security, having declared an ambigu-ous ceasefire on 29 May 1972. This was in response to the hostile reaction to its assassination of Ranger William Best, an off-duty Catholic soldier from Derry. However, the terms of its ceasefire allowed its members 'to defend any area under attack by the British military or sectarian forces from either side'.[3] Both factions of the IRA opposed Sunningdale, but the PIRA's opposition was most significant.[4] Ed Moloney has argued that 'there was a widespread agreement within the republican movement that the [Provisional] IRA had better kill off Sunningdale, before Sunningdale killed it'.[5] This demonstrates the formidable challenge facing the proponents of the power-sharing settlement.

During the 1972–74 period the PIRA's *modus operandi* changed significantly. From 1970 until 1972, PIRA activity was characterised by urban bombing campaigns, particularly focused on economic targets. During this time, the group began using the car bomb to devastating effect.[6] One of its most notorious attacks occurred on 21 July 1972 in Belfast. Twenty-six bombs were detonated in the city centre, causing much carnage. The warnings given were inadequate; 11 civilians were killed, 130 seriously injured.[7] It remains unclear what the goal of the operation, subsequently known as 'Bloody Friday', was; but the wave of revulsion which it caused was used by British security forces as a pretext for re-establishing a presence in former 'no-go' areas.[8] Whilst its long-term political significance has been exaggerated, 'Operation Motorman' seriously curtailed the ability of the PIRA to operate in urban centres.[9] It also resulted in a change in the nature of the PIRA's operations. The decrease in urban bombings throughout 1973 and 1974 was matched with an increase in 'hit-and-run' style operations in border areas. These attacks were reminiscent of the IRA's 'Operation Harvest' (1956–62), which was characterised by raids on security installations in Northern Ireland by units based in the Republic, who swiftly retreated to the latter jurisdiction to avoid capture.[10] That campaign failed, largely due to the internment of IRA members on both sides of the border. The context of the attacks in the 1970s was different, however. PIRA attacks were more efficient, ruthless and carried out with superior weaponry. Furthermore, there was no internment of IRA suspects in the Republic in the 1970s; and many PIRA members lived on the southern side of the border. This situation angered many unionists, who considered the Irish government too lenient on the PIRA. Cross-border violence was thus an important political as well as security consideration throughout this period.

Loyalist violence was also rife in Northern Ireland, and primarily characterised by sectarian murders. However, British security forces were concerned about a possible loyalist 'backlash' against political reforms, and considered that loyalists might shift the focus of their attacks to the Republic.[11] The emergence of the Ulster Defence Association (UDA), as an amalgamation of various loyalist vigilante movements in 1970–71, augmented these concerns. Elements within the UDA adopted the *nom de guerre*, the Ulster Freedom Fighters (UFF) in 1973, to carry out an assassination campaign against Catholics.[12] The Ulster Volunteer Force (UVF) was also engaged in similar activities. Some loyalist attacks did take place in the Republic, the most serious being the Dublin and Monaghan bombings on 17 May 1974, during the UWC strike, which resulted in thirty-three deaths. Events, such as those mentioned above, influenced the British security forces' response.

British security policy in Northern Ireland, 1972 to February 1973

From the early 1970s, British security policy in Northern Ireland had two main aims: the reduction of paramilitary violence in Belfast and Derry and the improvement of security co-operation with the Republic of Ireland. There was also a realisation that local security forces would have to become more acceptable to the minority community to increase their effectiveness. To that end, the Ulster Defence Regiment (UDR) was created by the British Army in 1970. It was hoped the UDR would reduce the number of British troops in Northern Ireland and increase Catholic participation in the security forces. Initially Catholics made up over 18 per cent of the force. However, when it emerged that former members of the all-Protestant Ulster Special Constabulary, known as the B-Specials (disbanded in 1970), had been sent application forms for the new regiment, Catholic applications plummeted.[13] By 1973, only 3.9 per cent of UDR members were Catholics – hardly the kind of representative force that had been hoped for. It has been argued that 'cold-shouldering' of Catholics by Protestants within the force, and more significantly, threats against Catholic UDR members by the PIRA, further discouraged minority participation.[14] Protestant members of the force also faced significant personal risk, as Henry Patterson's analysis of the PIRA's campaign against Protestant security force members in Fermanagh and Tyrone during the 1970s and 1980s has shown.[15] Moreover, the UDR did not significantly reduce the levels of violence at this time.

The increase in cross-border PIRA attacks was discussed by Edward Heath and Jack Lynch at a meeting in September 1972. The meeting heard that there were twenty-eight such attacks in the same number of days in that month. The British expressed concern that the successes of 'Motorman' would be hampered due to lack of action by the Republic against the PIRA.[16] The following month, Lynch assured Heath that firm action was being taken by his government. He pointed to arms and explosives finds by the Gardaí at Lifford, County Donegal, and raids on PSF premises. While the attempt to arrest the then PIRA Chief-of-Staff Seán MacStíofáin was unsuccessful, the Gardaí had 'picked up his papers and learnt a great deal from them about the organisation and manning of the Provisional IRA. This had shown how out-of-date their information was'. Lynch expressed concern about the 'development of the Ulster Defence Association. He had always thought there would be no Protestant backlash', and 'was now concerned that a backlash was developing'.[17] Throughout the summer of 1972, armed and masked UDA patrols had erected barricades in loyalist areas, staged vehicle checkpoints on the main Belfast–Londonderry road and hijacked many vehicles in South and East Belfast.[18] In one of the summer's more bizarre events, an English Church of Ireland minister held an open-air religious service near Belfast for over 100 UDA men dressed in combat fatigues.[19] The UDA was involved in a number of attacks against British soldiers that month, following the death of a loyalist rioter, run over by an armoured car.[20] However, by 20 October, an uneasy 'truce' between the UDA and the British Army emerged. Roy Bradford, former Stormont development minister, and future member of the power-sharing executive, is reported to have telegrammed the UDA 'praising their efforts to restore harmony between "Loyalists" and troops'.[21]

The importance of security matters to the prospects of political stabilisation in Northern Ireland was again underlined at a further Lynch–Heath meeting in November 1972. According to Lynch, lack of resources and personnel on the Irish side of the border was one reason why security was not as tight as possible. The Irish forces were 'fully stretched' on the border, although they had succeeded in arresting Seán MacStíofáin. He was unexpectedly 'lifted' during a surveillance operation on former Belfast PIRA leader Joe Cahill. MacStíofáin subsequently went on hunger and thirst strike in protest at his arrest and sentencing to six months imprisonment.[22] Heath remarked that there existed 'the possibility of a significant favourable development in the situation in Northern Ireland', but that its success depended on a reduction in IRA violence. He added that British Security forces would 'co-operate with the Irish police and armed forces to whatever extent and in whatever way the Irish forces felt possible in order to reduce IRA activity'. Heath also assured Lynch that action was being taken against loyalist paramilitaries, including the 'second in command of the UVF'.[23] Urging the Irish government to improve security remained a central feature of British security policy throughout the following year. On 28 February 1973, Lynch's Fianna Fáil government was replaced by a Fine Gael–ILP coalition. This change of government had a significant impact on Irish security policy.

The security policy of the Fine Gael–ILP government

The security policy of the Fine Gael–ILP coalition was based on the principles of reducing violence on an island-wide basis and preventing Northern Ireland's instability crossing the border. The coalition used strong rhetoric to voice its opposition to republican violence during its tenure. There was significant historical precedent for this. Governments of all persuasions in the Republic, including those led by Fianna Fáil, took uncompromising action against republican subversion, particularly during the 1940s and the IRA's border campaign of 1956–62. The priority for successive Irish governments was the sovereignty and security of the southern state.[24] Irish parties became increasingly opposed to militant republicanism, since this posed a threat to that sovereignty. As far back as 1957, Fianna Fáil decided to rule out the use of force as a means of ending partition.[25] The outbreak of the conflict in Northern Ireland, however, led to a blurring of the lines of Fianna Fáil's Northern Ireland policy – as evidenced by the events of the arms crisis in 1970. This crisis involved a plot to import weapons for defensive use by nationalist groups in Northern Ireland. The money used for the purchase of these arms was obtained from a fund (IR£100,000) intended for 'relief of distress' in Northern Ireland.

Two government ministers, Neil Blaney (agriculture) and Charles J. Haughey (finance), were dismissed by Jack Lynch for their alleged involvement in this plot, which contravened official government policy. Blaney and Haughey were then charged with attempted illegal importation of arms. The charges against Blaney were dropped, but Haughey and three other defendants, Captain James Kelly (Irish Military Intelligence), Albert Luykx (Belgian-born businessman) and John Kelly (Belfast republican), were tried in court on the same charge. All were acquitted.[26] Full details of the 'arms crisis' have so far eluded historians, as has a completely satisfactory answer to the question of how much the Taoiseach Jack Lynch knew about the affair. Catherine O'Donnell has argued that Lynch was fully committed to Irish unity, and believed that unification would solve the Northern Ireland problem. This view tallies with that of one British observer writing in 1973: 'no-one in the Irish government other than Mr Lynch is deeply concerned with Northern Ireland; basically they consider it a nuisance which is interfering with their domestic and EEC problems'.[27] These observations challenge the view that Lynch was relatively free of republican ideology.[28] What is clear, however, is that cross-border security co-operation improved when Cosgrave replaced him as Taoiseach. It is also apparent that the northern conflict, and the threat it posed to the security of the state, seriously influenced southern Irish politics in the 1970s, with the 1973 Irish general election campaign dominated by security issues.

During the campaign, the transport minister, Michael O'Kennedy, attacked the security policies of Fine Gael and the ILP as 'rash, unsure and unreliable'. He claimed that Fianna Fáil, under Lynch, was the 'one party that could be trusted to contain the subversives and preserve peace'.[29] Two days before the poll, Fianna Fáil took out a full-page advertisement in the *Irish Times* headed 'An Alternative?' which again criticised Fine Gael and the ILP on security matters. It stated that 'it took a bomb in Dublin' to coax the majority of Fine Gael TDs to support Fianna Fail's Offences Against the State amendment, and that one wing of the ILP 'condones violence and the other says we shouldn't talk about the problem'.[30] Lynch himself stated that the election of a 'weak and divided' Fine Gael–ILP coalition would have 'tragic consequences' for the Republic. Both Fine Gael and the ILP strongly criticised Fianna Fáil's grandstanding during the campaign. ILP leader, Brendan Corish, claimed Lynch's comments could inflame opinion in Northern Ireland, thereby exposing the nationalist minority to sectarian violence.[31] Fine Gael used the issue of the arms crisis to raise doubts about Lynch's credibility in relation to the Northern Ireland question. Its foreign affairs spokesman, Richie Ryan, claimed that Lynch would not have acted against his cabinet colleagues in 1970, or moved to tackle the 'illegal armies in our midst', had it not been for the 'insistence of Fine Gael.'[32] Despite the strong anti-subversive rhetoric of the main Irish political parties, overt security co-operation with British forces in Northern Ireland remained a problematic and emotive issue. However, the Fine Gael–ILP coalition began to take more robust action against republican paramilitaries after the election.

At the time the coalition took office, British officials regarded the Republic's approach to cross-border violence as unsatisfactory. D. G. Allen of the Foreign and Commonwealth Office (FCO) noted that '[t]he security forces in the Republic appear to be reluctant to patrol vigorously near the border and have thereby *de facto* created a one mile no man's land'. This reluctance increased 'the difficulty of apprehending members of [PIRA] ASUs (Active Service Units)'. The Lifford area was particularly problematic.[33] Allen alleged that members of the Gardaí seemed 'unwilling to take prompt and decisive action against the IRA in the area' and that the Lifford ASU appeared 'to operate actively without fear of harassment'. In British security circles, there was a 'certain amount of suggestion, although no confirmation', that there had been some collusion between the Gardaí and the PIRA. Allen qualified his remarks by noting that the 'Gardai appear to be armed only with pistols', which partially explained any possible 'lack of enthusiasm to tackle gunmen armed with high velocity and automatic weapons'. The PIRA was regarded as the most serious threat to British security forces in border areas. There was only 'one "renegade" Official IRA unit operating in the border area . . . the Warrenpoint/Rosstrevor unit led by Paul Tinnelly, a group that has been disciplined by the Official Council staff in Dublin for carrying out explosives and other operations without permission . . . mainly bank robberies'.[34]

The British soon noted a marked improvement in security co-operation. In April 1973, William Whitelaw met Garret FitzGerald to discuss security matters. Whitelaw was 'grateful for all the efforts that were being made by the new Irish Government to increase co-operation against terrorism on both sides of the border'.[35] His observation is corroborated by the analyses of contemporary newspapers. One County Cavan based newspaper noted the increased number of Irish Army patrols in the border areas, with 'similar precautions' being taken on the northern side of the frontier.[36]

Around this time, security forces in the Republic increased pressure on the PIRA, and its political wing, Sinn Féin. Brendan Halligan, general secretary of the ILP, informed Sir Arthur Galsworthy, UK Ambassador to Ireland, that the government intended 'to close the Provisionals [sic] Kevin Street office again soon'. Halligan also said that 'the government were trying to decide what to do with Sean Stephenson [MacStíofáin] after his release' from prison. Some members of Garda Special Branch advised that releasing him 'would bring about major splits and increasing trouble in the Provisional leadership'.[37] Halligan asked for the British view of what should be done with MacStíofáin. Kelvin White (Republic of Ireland Department, FCO), warned that a republican split might threaten security, as 'breakaway groups tend to compete in violence'. White therefore urged that MacStíofáin be 'returned to gaol' as he was 'not martyr material'.[38]

The increased pressure on the PIRA by Irish security forces began to yield impressive results. At the end of March 1973, the Irish Navy apprehended the *Claudia* off the southern coast. The ship, manned by PIRA members, contained a substantial cache of arms, ammunition and explosives, including 250 7.62 mm Russian rifles, 100 anti-tank mines, and 500 high-explosive handgrenades. An Irish Army ballistics expert later confirmed that the weaponry on board was 'very serviceable' and would be very useful to any organisation involved in a guerrilla campaign.[39] An investigation by the British government found that it was 'virtually certain' that the *Claudia* weapons 'came from Libya', which had been under the *de facto* leadership of Colonel Muammar al-Gaddafi following a 1969 military *coup d'état*.[40] A 1974 press report alleged that Gaddafi provided funding and training for the PIRA, to the tune of £1 million, as well as aid to the Palestinian paramilitary groups, Black September and the Popular Front for the Liberation of Palestine.[41]

Following this seizure, there is further evidence of British-Irish security co-operation. On 14 April, the Irish Minister for Defence, Paddy Donegan, informed Galsworthy that he had been ordered by the Taoiseach to provide the British 'with the *Claudia* arms we wanted [to carry out tests on]. He stressed that Cosgrave wanted this to be done discreetly', and would deny any handover had taken place if the story leaked. Donegan assured Galsworthy that the 'Irish authorities would do everything they could to stop bad hats operating in the border areas. The problem was the length of the border and the nature of the terrain'. The Minister then referred to what D. G. Allen had classified as the *de facto* 'no man's land' at the frontier. Donegan claimed that the 'reason Irish troops kept one mile back was because of the dangers of British and Irish Army units firing at each other', which would 'delight the IRA'. He also informed Galsworthy that Irish troops listened to British Army radio traffic and were under orders to act when incidents occurred. Galsworthy was clearly impressed with Donegan, commenting that his 'enthusiasm for clobbering the IRA [was] to be encouraged'. However, he believed that a lack of communication between Irish government ministers was hampering the achievement of tighter border security. A meeting of Irish and British army experts was proposed to help secure more practical co-operation at local level.[42]

The Irish government re-assured the British authorities that all available assistance would be given by them to the Northern Ireland security forces. In May, justice minister Paddy Cooney said he had 'instructed the Garda to co-operate with [British forces] in the suppression of criminal activities across the border'. Galsworthy confirmed that the British had indeed 'noticed the improvement in several areas', particularly the troublesome East Donegal area.[43] British forces believed the improvement was attributable to the 'change of government and the departure of Neil BLANEY [sic]', whose dismissal from the government in 1970 was earlier noted.[44] While co-operation was deemed to be improving, there were reasons, largely attributable to some of the activities of British security and intelligence personnel, why it was not greater.

The killing of innocent civilians on Bloody Sunday in January 1972 damaged the reputation of the British Army in the Irish Republic. The so-called 'Littlejohn affair' also caused tensions in British–Irish relations. In December 1972, a Dublin city-centre bank was robbed by three British men, Robert Stockman and Kenneth and Keith Littlejohn. In the extradition proceedings which followed, the Littlejohn brothers claimed that British intelligence had ordered them to carry out this robbery, in order to provoke authorities in the Republic to introduce internment against IRA suspects. After initially denying involvement, the British government later admitted that the brothers had been in contact with its intelligence services.[45] The nature of the British extradition proceedings, held *in camera*, contributed to public suspicion about HMG's role in the affair. Indeed, the Foreign Secretary, Sir Alec Douglas-Home, urged Arthur Galsworthy 'not to be drawn on why proceedings were held in camera'.[46] Garret FitzGerald's memoirs claim that the Littlejohn affair was one of the main points of contention in British–Irish relations during this time, along with the behaviour of the British Army in Northern Ireland. This controversy caused a diplomatic rift when the revelations emerged in 1973, at a time when the British government felt that security co-operation from the Republic was slowly, but steadily, improving.

British–Irish security co-operation

The record of a July meeting in London, between the Prime Minister and the Taoiseach, indicates that there was much agreement between the two sides on security policy. In particular, both sides agreed that swift progress towards a political settlement in Northern Ireland was essential to improve security there: '[t]he quicker the progress that could be made with the constitutional processes, the less support there would be for the IRA and other extremists'. Reference was also made to the increase in loyalist violence. Heath noted that 'the security forces were now taking larger hauls of bombs and guns from Protestants than from Catholics'. Cosgrave agreed that it was right to show 'no toleration towards extreme Protestants'.

Heath then raised question of extradition. This was a particularly difficult matter for the Irish government. It was up to the courts to determine what constituted a political offence, and political offences were non-extraditable. Most republican paramilitaries argued that their actions were politically motivated, sometimes avoiding extradition. To combat this problem, the British and Irish governments sought to implement a policy whereby fugitive offenders could be tried in either jurisdiction, for acts allegedly committed in either part of the island. This issue was raised at Sunningdale and, as mentioned, delegated to the body known as the Law Enforcement Commission (LEC).

Heath asked Cosgrave for his views on security. Cosgrave complained that some paramilitaries had eluded the Irish security forces by returning to Northern Ireland, particularly to the Crossmaglen area in Armagh, thus inverting the British argument that the Republic was used as a haven by republicans. He also remarked that there was a 'great increase in the number of arrests made' in the Republic as a result of the two new Irish army units stationed along the Northern Ireland frontier.[47] British authorities privately acknowledged this improvement, but diplomatically noted that 'public tributes would be embarrassing to Dublin'. They also privately acknowledged that there was little that the Irish government could do regarding extradition, 'in view of the separation of powers of the Executive and the Judiciary in the Irish Republic . . . should the Courts decide that an offence is political'.[48] Despite seemingly cordial British–Irish relations, tensions emerged in August 1973. That month, the allegations made by the above-mentioned Littlejohn brothers became public. The Irish government was greatly unimpressed, and expressed its disappointment to Arthur Galsworthy. The Littlejohn affair was not the only matter of concern raised by FitzGerald when he met Galsworthy on 17 August.

FitzGerald highlighted recent advances in British–Irish relations, pointing to Liam Cosgrave's statement recognising the 'British dimension in Irish Affairs', which would have been 'unthinkable' under any of his predecessors. Cosgrave had, on his appointment as Taoiseach, stated that Ireland had 'a European and a British dimension', a statement which earned him the praise of the *Presbyterian Herald*, the official newspaper of the Presbyterian Church in Ireland.[49] FitzGerald also mentioned the coalition's firm action against the

PIRA despite 'recent warnings in the Irish Press (a nationalist newspaper owned by the deValera family) warning [sic] that they had gone too far. Nonetheless they had persisted'.[50]

He told Galsworthy that the 'depressing thing' was that there had been no *quid pro quo* from the British government. In particular, it had not delivered on police reform and release of internees; and the tactics of the British Army in nationalist areas of Northern Ireland also remained problematic. The Littlejohn affair compounded these problems. The British insistence that relations with Dublin were unaffected by these revelations did little to help the situation. With regard to detainees, FitzGerald urged a bloc release of the '40 or so detainees in the Maze [prison] who had forsworn allegiance to the IRA'. A refusal to release these men, he argued, was an example of the British failure to understand the psychology of the Irish. 'The British methods were slow, patient, methodical and plodding. What was important to the Irish was gesture and symbol.' Releasing these men would be symbolically important, and well received by the Northern Ireland minority. FitzGerald also suggested that the British Army either withdraw from republican areas, or curtail activities there. While he recognised such withdrawal 'might lead to "minor recrudescences [sic]"', the resulting security problems would be minor in scale and 'the local people themselves would be able to deal with them'. Galsworthy quickly refuted FitzGerald's contention, saying that he felt 'very sceptical' that any 're-infiltration' of republican areas by the IRA could be effectively 'dealt with by the local people'. He argued that the British experience in Derry did not encourage him to share FitzGerald's 'optimism'. He also dismissed the suggestion of a bloc release of detainees as impracticable. Galsworthy did agree that British methods were slow and plodding, 'but they worked'. Searches of houses in republican areas such as Lower Falls and Ballymurphy 'almost always led to the discovery of arms', despite FitzGerald's point that these searches often antagonised the locals.[51]

Regarding the Littlejohn affair, Galsworthy's response to FitzGerald was uncompromising. He dismissed the brothers' criminal past since: 'the IRA was a criminal organisation and . . . the kind of people who would associate with the IRA were people of that persuasion . . . if he [FitzGerald] asked his own special branch he would surely find that they had informers whose habits and records were none too clean'. The ambassador cited the arms crisis of 1970 as an example of the difficult circumstances faced by British authorities. He argued that agents of the previous Irish government had been engaged in 'organising the supply of money and arms to the terrorists . . . under the general aegis of a number of ministers in the government of the Republic'. Thus it was important for the British to gain information about the IRA by any means possible. FitzGerald then informed him of another potentially sensitive issue which might affect British–Irish relations.

He related that an (un-named) Irish newspaper was carrying out its own investigations into two bombing incidents in Dublin in November 1972, which resulted in 2 deaths and 127 injuries. These bombings occurred on the eve of a vote in Dáil Éireann on an amendment to the Offences Against the State Act (1939). The amendment proposed that a statement by a Garda chief superintendent, that a person was a member of the IRA, would constitute evidence against that person. The bombings caused many deputies, who had originally opposed the amendment, to vote in its favour.[52] The PIRA was originally thought responsible for the attacks, but they were in fact the work of loyalist paramilitaries. FitzGerald informed Galsworthy that the newspaper would allege that 'British agents' were responsible for these attacks. While confirming that he did not doubt Edward Heath's assurance that there was no British involvement had been 'given in good faith', he was concerned that renegade elements in the British security forces may have been involved.

> Not for one moment did he think the British government could conceivably have authorised such acts of violence. But was it not possible that some disreputable characters in our employ or in some way associated with us might have acted on their own authority? If this should prove to be the case, and it came to light, the result would be a total disaster.[53]

The Littlejohn case illustrates the tensions that existed in British–Irish relations. There was still a lack of trust, which prevented the fullest possible co-operation. This point was reinforced to Galsworthy by Professor John Kelly, the Irish government Chief Whip. Kelly argued that his government had been consistently helpful to the British regarding security, but warned that if there was any suggestion the coalition was 'being made a fool of' by the British, they would be '"all back to square one"', and would neither wish nor be able to co-operate with British security forces.[54]

The question of extradition, and the problem of cross-border offences, was again raised at a Dublin meeting between the Prime Minister and the Taoiseach on 17 September 1973. Heath enquired if 'some arrangements could be made to ensure that persons accused of I.R.A. type offences [in the Republic] would not be permitted bail, which enables them to return to the North and continue their activities while awaiting trial'. This was an unrealistic request, given that such cases were dealt with by the courts. Cosgrave diplomatically replied that, despite this obstacle, he would consider Heath's demand. The Taoiseach then pointed to the success of Irish security forces in arresting the PIRA Chief-of-Staff, Seamus Twomey, who had 'been sought in the North by all the forces there, for some considerable time without success'. Heath argued that the two key areas where progress should be made in Northern Ireland were (1) security and (2) the formation of an executive. Whilst bombing attacks in the cities were reduced, sectarian murders were 'now by much the worst problem'. Cosgrave highlighted that 'the statistics indicated that, on a population basis, three times as many Catholics as Protestants were being assassinated'. He criticised some of the statements made by Ian Paisley and William Craig 'which were highly inflammatory' and asked if something could be done about them. Heath agreed that Paisley was 'an extremely shrewd operator. He made statements and allegations which could be without foundation but he could never be caught up with afterwards. At his recent meeting [with Heath] he had produced a shoal of red herring'. No concrete proposals were made on how to deal with the impact of either Craig or Paisley's speeches, however.[55]

Within British Army circles, there was a recognition that the methods used to curtail the PIRA fuelled resentment of the security forces in Catholic areas. While noting that the 'raised army profile' had reduced violence and the number of security force casualties, a report by Brigadier Mostyn of Headquarters, Northern Ireland (HQNI) argued that 'the penalty paid for this profile might be that it drove some people into the Provisionals and for this reason a careful balance in military activity had to be maintained'.[56] This was essentially what the Irish ministers had been saying to their British counterparts for some time.

The matter of the surge in loyalist violence, and the question of how to deal with it, was raised by Whitelaw when, on 12 November 1973, he met the Commander of Land Forces (CLF) and the Chief Constable. He was 'anxious to follow up the proscription of Red Hand Commandoes [sic] and the UFF with some good extreme Protestant arrests'. He added that it would be helpful if these loyalists were 'not subsequently released', since this would 'enhance the SDLP's credibility with the Roman Catholic community and it would also help the pledged Unionists with Protestant opinion'.[57] That month, Whitelaw also met loyalist representatives from Belfast, who informed him about security problems in their locale. They expressed concern that Protestants were being forced out of the area due to intimidation. While this was not happening on a mass scale, 'individual Protestants were being harassed and children were being intimidated on their way to school'. As a solution, the representatives proposed the 'erection of a physical peace-line'. However, Whitelaw 'pointed out that erecting a barrier might act as a focal point for violence and that this would be counter-productive'. The loyalist representatives then asked Whitelaw to ensure that 'houses were allocated only to people of the same religion as those who had left [as] this would remove any incentive for intimidation'. Whitelaw countered that this was a matter for the housing executive, but 'he felt that as far as possible people of the same religion as those who had left should be allocated vacant houses.' He undertook to raise the matter with the housing executive but 'could not in any way commit them'.[58]

In November 1973 Garret FitzGerald discussed loyalist violence at a meeting with Whitelaw. He claimed that while there was some evidence of the Army 'taking it easier in the Catholic areas, there was no evidence that Loyalist violence was either being effectively tackled or seen to be effectively tackled'. Whitelaw denied this, and claimed he was tackling the issue 'in every way he could', but there 'had to be a different style of approach to that used in the Catholic areas'. He was particularly concerned about sectarian murders, and the intimidation of witnesses 'worse on the Protestant than the Catholic side'. Regarding republican violence, Whitelaw confirmed that the PIRA had shifted its emphasis from urban areas and was now primarily operating in border territory, especially South Armagh. He 'jokingly remarked that it was a pity that that area had not been put into the South when the border was being drawn and there were some light-hearted exchanges on the pig-smuggling in the area'.[59] Towards the end of that month (the week preceding the Sunningdale conference), FitzGerald and Whitelaw met again. FitzGerald reassured the Secretary of State that the 'determination of the Irish Government to deal with the men of violence should not be underestimated', but that this was a politically sensitive issue. In particular, there was a danger of Fianna Fáil criticising the coalition's Northern Ireland policy. This was due to 'the considerable pressure on the Leader of the Opposition [Lynch] as a result of a drift towards a more republican line in his party . . . the Government did not want to give a lever to opponents of bipartisanship within the opposition party'.[60] Indeed, the coalition had been heckled by members of Fianna Fáil over the verity of its republican credentials in the Dáil since the summer of 1973. This demonstrates both the emotive nature of Northern Ireland affairs in the Republic, and the ruthlessness of Fianna Fáil in opposition.[61] The extent to which a truly bipartisan approach to Northern Ireland policy existed in the Republic during this period is therefore questionable. There were certainly clear differences in the security policies pursued by the former Fianna Fáil government and those of the coalition, particularly the latter's crackdown on PIRA activity and commitment to cross-border security co-operation.

Security and Sunningdale

Security issues were discussed in detail during the Sunningdale conference in December 1973. To help allay unionist fears, the Sunningdale communiqué declared that the Irish government accepted that Northern Ireland's constitutional status could not be altered without the consent of its people, with a reciprocal declaration by the British government that it would support a united Ireland should a majority so wish. As mentioned, the Irish declaration was de-valued by Kevin Boland's (unsuccessful) challenge in the Dublin courts.[62] It was also agreed that both governments would attempt to effectively deal with cross-border violence.

On 21 December 1973, Paddy Cooney and Conor Cruise O'Brien discussed this issue with Arthur Galsworthy. O'Brien told Galsworthy that the government 'knew the time was coming when there would have to be much more open and overt co-operation over border security', and would have to make some kind of gesture 'to help Brian Faulkner' sell the Sunningdale Agreement to unionists. However, very little open co-operation could be undertaken at that moment, 'for domestic political reasons', particularly Fianna Fáil pressure. Galsworthy was bitterly disappointed by this news, given the impact Boland's court case had on the value of the status declaration. He hoped the Republic could do something to compensate for this. O'Brien stressed that although at least '80% of the people of the Republic were delighted with the Sunningdale Agreement despite Fianna Fáil's sullen and louche attitude towards it', obstacles to co-operation remained

> [I]nevitably members of the Garda and the Irish Army would get shot. This would produce an immediate reaction in public opinion, which would not be what we [the British] expected. Sentimental republicanism was deeply rooted in Irish public opinion, and the reaction would not be to turn against the terrorists, but to accuse the Govt [sic] of bungling and say that at least this sort of thing never happened under Fianna Fáil.

O'Brien argued that the coalition would have to 'be able to point to the Sunningdale institutions in being and not simply in contemplation', a reference to the proposed Council of Ireland. He recognised Faulkner's need for a public gesture on security, and stressed that it would come in time, but immediately 'giving publicity' to such co-operation was politically problematic for the coalition. Given the impassioned debates about state security during the 1973 Irish general election campaign, O'Brien's argument seemed credible. Galsworthy, however, implored the coalition to act on this matter.[63]

Despite these political constraints, the Irish coalition continued its crackdown on cross-border violence and its co-operation with British forces. In November 1973, a British report on border co-operation by Colonel C. R. Huxtable, Headquarters Northern Ireland (British Army) (HQNI), confirmed a major improvement in this regard. Co-operation in most border areas was described as 'good' or 'very good'. Roy Foster has argued that there was continuity in policy on Northern Ireland from Jack Lynch to Garret FitzGerald.[64] However, the archival evidence demonstrates that, where security matters were concerned, there were clear differences between the policies pursued by the Lynch administration and the Fine Gael–ILP coalition. Nonetheless, the image of the RUC remained problematic, and police reform was extensively debated preceding and following the Sunningdale Agreement.

Reform of the police

On 18 September 1973, Ian Paisley, in his role as the moderator of the Free Presbyterian Church of Ulster (FPCU), wrote to Liam Cosgrave, informing him of the intention of his church to stage a peaceful protest against a forthcoming 'ecumenical dialogue' between Catholic and Protestant clerics in Dundalk.[65] Cosgrave replied, indicating that he understood Paisley's letter to be a request for 'police protection'. He assured Paisley that it was 'foreign to the traditions of our part of the country for peaceful protesters to be attacked' and that the Republic's police force was 'an effective and impartial one'.[66] Paisley himself was aware of this, having been afforded the protection of almost 200 Gardaí during a 1972 visit to a County Monaghan Orange Hall.[67] In Northern Ireland, however, the police (RUC) did not enjoy widespread acceptance among nationalists, particularly following its performance (and that of the reserve USC), during the civil rights campaign.[68] Reform of the RUC was thus crucial for nationalists, if any political settlement in Northern Ireland was to work. To that end, extensive discussions on policing took place between Northern Ireland politicians and the British and Irish governments.

The difficulties inherent in the policing question can be seen by comparing two key 1972 policy documents of the SDLP and UUP. The SDLP argued that '[t]he creation of an acceptable security system is the crucial key to providing peace and order and must include a new unarmed police force or forces jointly recruited by both Governments to maintain peace and order'.[69] This clearly implied, at a minimum, the wholesale reform and re-branding of the RUC if not its disbandment. Alternatively, the UUP asserted that policing was 'the task of the R.U.C., supported by the Reserve', and that the force should actually be boosted 'both in numbers and morale . . . by a cadre of localised men, familiar with terrain and clientele, essential to a good police reserve'.[70] To complicate matters further, some unionists believed the RUC should have a specifically Protestant character. The Vanguard Movement organised a strike in February 1973, under the banner of the Ulster Loyalist Council (ULC), which included the UDA and UVF. The strike aimed to end loyalist internment and also to re-establish 'some kind of Protestant or loyalist control over the affairs of the Province, especially over security policy'.[71] However, unionist support for the strike was not universal; Ian Paisley was vocally opposed to it.[72] Nevertheless, the strike demonstrated the underlying sectarian tendencies within Ulster loyalism: religious statues outside a Catholic church in Belfast were smashed, and a Catholic school for children with learning disabilities was attacked during the protest.[73] Loyalist attitudes to policing conflicted with those of the British government, which, far from pandering to loyalist desires, sought to bring policing structures in Northern Ireland into line with those in the rest of the United Kingdom.

A memo on 'Law, Order and Policing' prepared by the NIO in October 1973, stated that '[i]t is the intention that in future no person will be appointed to the office of Chief Constable [of the RUC] who has not served for at least two years in another force', in line with convention in Great Britain. This memo also noted the essential need to increase public support for the police, which, if successful, could lead to the progressive withdrawal of policing duties from the armed forces in some areas.[74] The policy of 'normalising' policing in Northern Ireland had been in place for some time. In March 1973, a letter from the MOD to the Prime Minister proposed making greater use of the Royal Military Police (RMP) in republican 'no-go' areas 'as a first step towards getting [the RUC] back into them'. It was reported that the use of unarmed RMP foot patrols 'throughout the Catholic areas of Londonderry . . . made a major contribution to the improved [security] atmosphere in that city'.[75] In July 1973, Whitelaw confirmed that the government sought to reduce military involvement in policing. He informed the CLF that 'building up the RUC was the crucial security problem', which suggests that the policy of police primacy, later associated with Labour's Merlyn Rees and Roy Mason, had earlier origins.[76]

Throughout this period, the Irish government was highly critical of the RUC, and called for significant reforms to the force. Unlike the SDLP, however, the Dublin coalition did not favour its abolition. In August 1973, Garret FitzGerald discussed the government's concerns about the RUC with Arthur Galsworthy, claiming that the British government had not 'sufficiently grasped' the need for reform. FitzGerald argued the British were naive to 'suppose that all that was necessary was that the present deputy commissioner [Jamie Flanagan] be appointed as commissioner simply because he is a Catholic'. He claimed that his Belfast contacts informed him that, if a number of allegedly corrupt officers were removed from the RUC, this would make it more acceptable to nationalists: 'the highest figure that anyone had given him for the number of "bad men" who must be dismissed from the RUC was 30 . . . Most others had said about 25'. FitzGerald strongly argued that neither Flanagan, nor any other candidate from within Northern Ireland, should be appointed as Chief Constable. He favoured the appointment of an outsider, preferably an Englishman, but wondered if the remuneration 'would be sufficient to attract a really good man for a job that was clearly no bed of roses'.[77] Whitelaw himself had earlier remarked to the CLF that Flanagan 'would not be [a] suitable' Chief Constable.[78] Despite Irish objections, Whitelaw's own doubts, and the British proposal that the Chief Constable serve at least two years in another force, Flanagan was appointed to the post on 1 November 1973. He was the first, and only, Catholic to have held the job.[79] The Foreign Secretary, Douglas-Home, dismissed FitzGerald's complaints, commenting that it might be 'worth reminding the Irish' what HMG were committed to, namely the retention of the law and order powers to the Westminster government, 'a point on which the Irish were quite insistent'.[80] He also noted that the Police Authority was to be re-constituted to include members of the Northern Ireland Assembly, as an integral part of the *Northern Ireland Constitutional Proposals* of March 1973.[81]

Towards the end of 1973, Catholic areas were subject to more regular policing, suggesting that the government's policy was working to some extent. At a meeting between Heath and Cosgrave on 17 September, it was confirmed that the 'R.U.C. [was] going further into Catholic areas and seemed to be meeting with a fair degree of toleration'.[82] This apparent acceptance of the RUC was reflected at a political level among the SDLP. Frank Cooper of the NIO wrote to Whitelaw outlining a discussion he'd had with Sean Donlon of the Irish Department of Foreign Affairs (DFA). Donlon claimed the Irish government had convinced the SDLP to keep talking to the unionists and the British government. He also argued that 'the SDLP would accept the R.U.C. but would want some kind of gesture on policing generally'.[83] This 'gesture' was not specified, but it seems likely that it might have involved the removal of certain RUC officers of allegedly dubious repute; perhaps even those mentioned to Galsworthy by FitzGerald two months previously. This evidence suggests the SDLP had moderated its attitude to law enforcement significantly and was now prepared to support the RUC, subject to some relatively cosmetic reforms. This was a significant change from the party's dogmatic policy enunciated in *Towards a New Ireland*, in which it called for the abolition of the RUC.

As for unionists, the UUP signalled its complete opposition to major reform of the RUC. It was, however, flexible in regard to how policing could be improved. During the executive formation negotiations, Faulkner emphasised the necessity that 'the RUC should be accepted as the police force for Northern Ireland . . . Once this was accepted his party would be willing to discuss ways in which policing could be made more effective'. He did not believe responsibility for policing should be relinquished to any other body – a reference to the proposed Council of Ireland. Roy Bradford agreed, but suggested that the Council might have a useful role to play in co-ordinating RUC and Garda co-operation. As far as the SDLP was concerned, John Hume confirmed that his party aspired to give its full support to the police, particularly if power-sharing was instituted. However, the name and uniform of the RUC caused difficulties for his party. He explicitly called for the 'removal of certain officers who had been involved in improper practices'.[84]

At a British–Irish meeting in Dublin in November 1973, Garret FitzGerald discussed policing with William Whitelaw. The latter confirmed that the name of the police force could not change from 'RUC', since this would result in the loss of '300 of his best policemen'. FitzGerald felt that Whitelaw's security policies were generally sound, but was critical of his decision to preserve the name of the RUC.[85] The Irish government proposed a limited role for the planned Council of Ireland with regard to policing, with northern and southern Police Authorities being responsible to the Council, provided that it was 'an effective decision making body' with 'adequate safeguards ... available to ensure effective policing in the event of deadlock'.[86] Thus, the Irish government eschewed the SDLP line on policing, that is, a common police force for the whole island, responsible to the proposed Council of Ireland. The issue of security in Northern Ireland continued to be the subject of ardent debate after the power-sharing administration took office on 1 January 1974.

Security and the Northern Ireland Executive

The importance of cross-border security was highlighted at an early meeting of the power-sharing executive. Both nationalist and unionist members agreed that further action against the PIRA was essential.[87] Faulkner informed his colleagues that a meeting had been arranged between himself and the Taoiseach, to discuss border security.[88] That meeting took place on 16 January 1974 at Baldonnel military airfield, Dublin. The previous week, Faulkner wrote to Cosgrave to raise a number of security-related issues. He argued that not enough was being done to counter cross-border violence in the Republic (despite evidence from the London files that border security was greatly improved under the coalition government). Faulkner highlighted the existence of 'centres in the Republic where IRA men are known to live and from which they operate, e.g. Buncrana, Lifford and Monaghan. Purposeful, sustained and truly effective action against these people would have an important impact on the security situation'. Incidents such as the arrest and subsequent release of PIRA suspects in the Republic,[89] 'seriously miscarried from our [the executive's] point of view'. These kinds of events were used by unionist and loyalist opponents of the agreement as 'evidence' that the Republic was soft on the IRA.[90] In reply, Cosgrave assured Faulkner that the PIRA was indeed being suppressed. He accepted that there were 'black spots' such as Crossmaglen, but that trouble in this area was 'mainly on the Northern Ireland side of the Border'. Cosgrave then outlined his government's record on security since the establishment of the anti-subversive Special Criminal Court (by the previous government) in 1972: '435 people had been tried and 323 convicted' by this Court, of whom '70 per cent were people from Northern Ireland who had moved to the Republic'. Faulkner was clearly unconvinced by this explanation, arguing that it was irrelevant whether those involved were Northern Ireland citizens or not: '[t]he fact was that they were known to be operating out of Lifford. Buncrana was another notorious place, although possibly not quite so bad'.[91] The Monaghan border was also a trouble spot. The previous month, for example, retired police officer Ivan Johnston was kidnapped in Monaghan and killed by the PIRA. His body was dumped across the Armagh border three days later. An *Irish Independent* editorial castigated the perpetrators, claiming that such actions were 'the very antithesis of our way of life, the essence of which is far more truly reflected in the Sunningdale spirit'.[92]

Following Faulkner's criticisms, the Irish government undertook to reform the Gardaí in border areas, including extra recruitment, and the movement of 'the more experienced men into the Border country'. Cosgrave claimed his government had 'a good record in Border areas', although he acknowledged the problem of 'Northern terrorists taking refuge in the South'. Faulkner urged him to take action against high-profile PIRA members residing in East Donegal. He mentioned that Strabane Assembly member, Ivan Cooper, 'was being approached by people in the Strabane area who were expecting him, now that he was in office, to do something about this intolerable situation'.[93] This suggests that the electorate had not fully grasped that the new Assembly, unlike the Stormont parliament, had no security powers whatsoever. Cooper had written to Faulkner to highlight the problem of known PIRA members operating in the Lifford and Strabane areas. He found it 'hard to understand why Martin McGuinness can have a meal at the Inter County Hotel, Lifford, and not attract the attention of the Garda, who use the premises socially'. He alleged that RUC sources informed him that they had identified arms dumps in the Republic, but that no action was taken by the Gardaí. He did not blame the Irish government or Minister for Justice for this inaction, but questioned the 'loyalty and application of some members of the Garda working in the area'.[94] However, it is unclear from the files in Belfast whether-or-not the information that Cooper's RUC contacts supposedly had about arms dumps was ever relayed to the Lifford Gardaí. Evidence from contemporary newspapers clearly demonstrates the kind of security threats faced in Strabane. The week following Cooper's letter, PIRA members hijacked a helicopter in Donegal, flew to Strabane, and dropped milk-churn bombs on the town. In this bizarre incident, eyewitnesses claimed one of the hijackers, who spoke with a Yorkshire accent, had unconvincingly disguised himself as a woman 'badly needing a bath'.[95] Such a dramatic event again demonstrated the potentially deadly threat facing residents of border towns at the time.

The Alliance Party was also concerned about security co-operation from the Republic. A month before the Faulkner–Cosgrave meeting, the Alliance leader, Oliver Napier argued that the Republic must 'not be allowed to "stab us all in the back". So far they had not agreed to anything substantial e.g., over escaping terrorists or the recognition issue'.[96] At the Baldonnel meeting, Faulkner pressed Cosgrave over Articles 2 and 3 of the Irish constitution, enquiring if it might 'be worthwhile to consider a referendum' to change these Articles, since he did not think many of the Republic's citizens were greatly concerned about the constitution. Cosgrave claimed that 'it would be too risky to deal with Articles 2 and 3 on their own'. He favoured re-drafting the entire constitution, and hoped that an all-party committee could reach agreement on this. However, he acknowledged that if this was impossible, then the coalition would have to consider mooting constitutional change.[97] Archival material demonstrates that Faulkner forcefully argued for more overt security co-operation from the Republic. Such co-operation would have enabled him to challenge the claims of many unionists: that the Republic was not co-operating fully, and would also demonstrate that Sunningdale had been worthwhile for unionism. However, despite political constraints, the Dublin coalition continued to co-operate with British security forces and harassed the PIRA to a much greater degree than the previous Fianna Fáil government.

Cross-border violence: the British Army view and political consequences

On 30 January 1974, a report compiled by a British Army officer for the NIO, confirmed that cross-border violence was increasing. This report by Lt Col M. F. Reynolds stated that 'whilst the level of violence elsewhere in the Province has been significantly reduced since July 1972, the number of incidents attributable to terrorists operating from the Republic has increased'. Border security was thus 'a key issue on both the political and military fronts'. In the three weeks since the Executive took office there were over sixty-one border incidents, the majority of which were 'attributed to terrorists based in the Republic'. Reynolds cautioned that if such violence was not curtailed by the security forces on both sides of the border, it might lead to reprisal raids by loyalists in the Republic. His report placed the blame for this situation on the ineffectiveness of the Irish security forces, since some PIRA members 'spend 95% or more of their time in the Republic (Martin McGuinness and John "Jack" Brogan are typical examples)'. Apart from brief offensive forays into Northern Ireland, such people, Reynolds claimed, could evade capture by British forces. He criticised the Republic for not adopting an 'even-handed approach' to the extradition question.[98] This was a simplistic reading of the situation, ignoring the above-mentioned political and legal constraints faced by the Irish government, although such an analysis from a soldier, rather than a politician, is perhaps understandable. Much of Reynolds's report focused on the Lifford area. The then Secretary of State, Francis Pym, informed the Irish ambassador to London that, although Lifford was 'particularly sensitive', 'cross-border co-operation between the security people is on the whole very satisfactory'.[99] Reynolds's frustration, therefore, whilst understandable, must be placed in the context of the overall improvement in security co-operation. It must also be recognised that the total eradication of violence in border areas was impossible. However, the report echoed the perception of many unionists: that the Dublin authorities were not doing enough to crack down on the PIRA in border regions.

Faulkner was keenly aware that both security problems, and the persistence of ambiguities concerning the Republic's recognition of Northern Ireland's constitutional status, might have electoral consequences for pro-Sunningdale unionists.[100] At his meeting with Cosgrave, he emphasised that 'if an election were called soon and if the question of status and Sunningdale were left with their present ambiguities the whole position could well be hopeless'. He predicted that seven of the twelve Westminster seats could go to 'hard-line unionists'.[101] The results were actually worse than Faulkner feared.[102] When the executive discussed these election results, most ministers agreed that security issues had had a major impact on the outcome. Bob Cooper, of the Alliance Party, claimed that the vote was 'evidence of frustration at the lack of improvement in the security situation'. Interestingly, he thought that if there had been an improvement, 'loyalists would have been more ready to accept Sunningdale and a Council of Ireland'. SDLP members were keen to emphasise that, despite this setback, Sunningdale should be ratified. Unionists were more cautious: they appear to have realised that rapid progress would further isolate unionist opinion. They believed that all aspects of Sunningdale, including the Council of Ireland, could not be implemented without 'evidence of action by the Republic on status, extradition and dealing with violence'. Leslie Morrell, the executive's Minister for Agriculture, said that the blame for the situation should be put 'on the South'.[103] Despite this criticism, there is some evidence that Cosgrave listened to Faulkner's concerns. For example, at the end of January 1974, a number of PIRA members were arrested in Buncrana, one of the towns which Faulkner had complained about to Cosgrave during their meeting earlier that month.[104]

When the members of the executive met the new Secretary of State, Merlyn Rees, for the first time on 26 March 1974, security was the only issue discussed. All the executive parties informed Rees that violence was one of the primary obstacles to political progress. Oliver Napier argued that increased activity by the PIRA was evidence of an attempt to 'bring down the power-sharing concept and force Great Britain to wash its hands of Northern Ireland.' Rees, pondering the issue of violence,

> [R]eferred to the large number of people enjoying an easy life through violence and intimidation in what was virtually a 'Chicago' situation and wondered whether this undercurrent of violence would go on even after internment had been phased out and political institutions firmly established.[105]

Despite an earlier reassurance that the government firmly supported the executive, this remark could have done little to inspire confidence among the executive that Rees planned robust and resolute action to deal with political violence.

British–Irish affairs continued to be dominated by border security. Rees informed FitzGerald, at their first meeting on 7 March, that there was an 'extreme reluctance' among 'Pro-Assembly Protestants' to proceed with the formal ratification of Sunningdale, because they felt the Republic was not doing enough to improve security. FitzGerald stated that the Irish government was prepared to 'get down to a practical discussion' to improve border security. Frank Cooper, who was also in attendance, added that 'the border was long and covered some remote areas where full security was virtually impossible', an admission that the British security forces were not in full control on the Northern Ireland side of the border.[106]

The issue of security was also discussed when Brian Faulkner met Harold Wilson, on 1 April 1974. The mood of that meeting was pessimistic. Faulkner agreed with Wilson that 'it was hard to see what more could be done to improve security', but expressed satisfaction at Gerry Fitt's speech in the House of Commons which 'had come so close to encouragement by the SDLP of support for the security services; this would help produce information from the Catholic areas'. In his speech, Fitt stated his party's opposition to violence, and called on SDLP supporters to 'show the same courage as our leaders are showing at present' to prevent violence.[107] When asked by the Prime Minister what the main issues for the SDLP were, Faulkner 'thought that detention was still the most important single issue. He did not think the Council of Ireland was so important for them [sic], and that members of the SDLP would admit as much in private'.[108] It is likely Faulkner's opinion was influenced by a private discussion with Gerry Fitt the previous month, at which he told the unionist leader that the SDLP 'could not ratify the agreement without some move on detention', whilst neglecting to mention the Council of Ireland explicitly.[109] Fitt's failure to convey the fact that the Council of Ireland was by far the main priority for the party, thus resulted in Faulkner's underestimation of the SDLP's commitment to a strong Council of Ireland.

Later that month, Wilson visited Northern Ireland to meet the executive. He stated that, politically, all the government's hopes rested with the executive. Direct rule had been supported by all the main parties two years previously only as a temporary expedient until some solution could be produced. Any return to direct rule produced by the collapse of the executive would be in radically different circumstances. Oliver Napier warned Wilson that an early ratification of Sunningdale could produce 'a D-Day with violence from both extremes of the political spectrum'. The meeting did reveal that the Republic's security forces had taken effective action against the PIRA. Ivan Cooper confirmed that the 'IRA pocket in Lifford [which he had complained about in January] had been virtually flushed out'. Wilson's contribution to the meeting was ambiguous. He stated that the government backed the Executive, but mentioned that Army morale was a problem:

> In present conditions the Army would have to bear the brunt of the burden . . . There was no question of the Government's determination to end violence. There was, however, a problem of morale in the Army and particularly among Army families and the Government would have to give serious thought to the prolonged use of troops in a police force role in Northern Ireland . . . [Wilson] was against setting a fixed date for the withdrawal of the troops as this could only lead to an escalation in violence. He backed the Executive in what they were trying to do and said he would be caught in an increasingly difficult position should the troops be caught in the crossfire between the two communities as the pressure to pull out completely would be hard to resist.

Wilson's language alarmed some unionists. Roy Bradford expressed concern at Wilson's remarks. He felt it was incumbent on HMG to convince the majority community that it was not in any way attempting to disengage from Northern Ireland.[110]

Throughout April, meetings concerning the ratification of Sunningdale continued. Unionists were aware of the political difficulties inherent in formalising the agreement. Faulkner claimed that if he ratified Sunningdale, he 'would be deserted by all his supporters. If he went ahead and reached that point, he could resign, but that would mean the end of power-sharing'. John Hume stressed the difficulties faced by SDLP members: anything other than a full ratification of Sunningdale would 'look to SDLP supporters like a trick. The SDLP leaders lived right in among their people in a way that the Unionists did not . . . This task was getting more difficult . . . by the lack of progress over "internment"'. Hume mentioned that Paddy Devlin was considering resigning due to a lack of progress on the internment issue. He then posed the question: 'Could Mr Faulkner not take the plunge [,] sign Sunningdale in full, and then reap the benefit over SDLP co-operation on identification with the RUC?'[111] Hume's comment adds weight to the suggestion that policing was not the main concern of the SDLP if it could suddenly 'identify' with the RUC when Sunningdale was ratified. Rather, the proposed Council of Ireland, which required the ratification of Sunningdale, was the most important issue for the party.

Internment, detention, extradition and the report of the Law Enforcement Commission

Internment and detention posed serious problems for the SDLP. Detention was introduced in November 1972, under the Detention of Terrorists (Northern Ireland) Order. Whilst providing more safeguards than internment, it still allowed for a suspect to be held without trial for up to twenty-eight days. If the Chief Constable wished to further detain a suspect, the case had to be referred to a commissioner who determined if the extra detention was necessary. The detained person could appeal the decision within twenty-one days of its enforcement, and the Secretary of State could release the person at his discretion, or refer the case to a commissioner. Under this legislation, a suspect could be detained for alleged commission, direction, organisation or training for the purpose of terrorism. But, despite the improved safeguards, detention was still *perceived* as somewhat arbitrary and open to the same abuses as internment (which remained on the statute books until 1975), particularly among the nationalist community.[112] It is likely therefore that few members of the nationalist community drew any distinction between the two processes.

The SDLP had organised a civil disobedience campaign against internment, which included non-payment of rent and rates. Two executive members, Austin Currie and Paddy Devlin, were participants in the strike. Once the SDLP was in government, however, it called for an end to the strike, even though internment remained.[113] The issues of internment and detention were consistently raised by the SDLP in its meetings with British authorities.[114] On 10 May 1974, Devlin informed Merlyn Rees that the three executive parties did not have common views on all security matters: the 'SDLP members could not agree with the Unionists' on the need for continued use of detention. Austin Currie suggested that the release of some 'Protestant detainees' resulted in an increase in violence on both sides. He suspected there was 'a direct increase in Protestant violence following the releases and this was leading people to turn to the IRA for defence'. Rees assured the SDLP that he supported ending detention as soon as it was safe to do so. Rees also mooted a policy aimed at preventing ex-detainees returning to violence.

Rees planned to start a 'sponsorship' scheme, whereby a member of a former detainee's local community would attempt to guarantee his or her good behaviour. However, this was deemed to be unrealistic and unworkable. Instead, it was suggested that existing voluntary organisations, in the released person's locale, should support the individual after their release. The NIO planned to assist this scheme by providing a 'small grant in aid', if the voluntary organisation participating in the scheme was acceptable to the Secretary of State. It was acknowledged that groups participating in this programme might 'form a personality' of their own and 'become an irritant to the NIO and the Executive'. These disadvantages were thought to be outweighed by the potential prevention of re-offending. There was some division in the SDLP over this proposal. Ivan Cooper opposed it on the grounds that it would, in effect, be a successor to the recently abolished Community Relations Commission, and claimed that the official agencies of the executive were capable of dealing with ex-detainees. Devlin and Currie disagreed, arguing that the executive could not be seen to give preferential treatment to ex-detainees, and claimed the proposed scheme would 'fill a vacuum and play a very important role in the re-settlement of ex-detainees within their communities'. Unionist minister Roy Bradford's concern was that the groups participating in this scheme would become too powerful and publicise their views on detention and release policy. Rees reassured Bradford that, although such groups could make their views known, they would not in any way influence his policies. Frank Cooper further clarified that these organisations would have no right to advise on releases and would have insufficient funding to acquire much political power. They would effectively be 'short-term . . . and [their] functions would be a cross between prisoner's aid, alcoholics anonymous and a marriage guidance council'.[115] Rees's scheme demonstrates that, as Paul Dixon has argued, British policy during this period combined elite and civil society approaches to conflict resolution.[116] Despite the political attention paid to this issue, the SDLP did not secure the ending of detention. The party's termination of the civil disobedience campaign, regardless of the continuance of internment and detention, suggests that these issues, like policing, were not its primary concern.

In May 1974, the LEC finally published its report.[117] The findings were controversial, from a unionist point of view. Instead of extradition, which the British side deemed the most effective means of tackling cross-border violence, it recommended the establishment of an all-Ireland common law enforcement area, since extradition was problematic for the Irish.[118] Michael Cunningham has argued that there was 'no convincing legal impediment' for the Irish position, which was 'a matter of political sensibilities'.[119] However, by omitting to explain the political criticism which the coalition faced from Fianna Fáil, and the way in which the Irish courts determined which crimes were political, Cunningham arguably overstates the Dublin coalition's room for manoeuvre on this issue.

The LEC report was vehemently debated by the executive, with nationalist and unionist ministers differing over its conclusions. Ivan Cooper urged a speedy ratification of Sunningdale, in order that the SDLP could 'urge their constituents to come out fully in support' of the police. John Hume warned against a dilution of Sunningdale because this would be 'a victory for our opponents, both [the] IRA and Protestant extremists'. He argued that once Sunningdale was ratified, 'opposition and violence would collapse. If not the British would pull out and the Protestants would be the long-term losers'.[120] Given that both the OIRA and PIRA opposed Sunningdale, and that loyalist violence was an increasing problem, this was an unlikely argument. However, Hume's comment about a potential British 'pull out' supports the argument of Patterson and Kaufmann that rumours of 'a British "doomsday" plan became rife and were taken seriously by both the SDLP and the Dublin government'.[121]

During this same meeting, the information minister, John Baxter, challenged Hume's view that the SDLP's endorsement of the RUC would have a major impact, particularly on Catholic recruitment to the force. Given the perception among many Catholics, that the RUC was biased, his argument seems convincing. Baxter also claimed that when unionists 'saw the strong case for extradition [in the LEC report] they would not understand why it was not adopted'. Unionist agriculture minister, Leslie Morrell, expanded on the reasons for unionist suspicion over the security aspects of Sunningdale, which included the SDLP's attitude to the police:

> [O]ne of the matters causing the most trouble among Protestants was the lack of support for law and order by some members of the Executive. If they would be able to support after ratification of Sunningdale but could not do so now there must be something very terrible in Sunningdale – that was how the argument ran.[122]

The executive members discussed the LEC report with Merlyn Rees on 10 May. He informed them that there was 'already a great deal of co-operation between the Security Forces of the North and South ... Nevertheless much of the present co-operation was covert, and HMG hoped that the North and South could work openly together in future'. The covert nature of this co-operation, may have contributed to a perception among unionists that it was not happening at all. Rees referred to the matter of the withdrawal of British troops from Northern Ireland. It may be that Rees was trying to pressurise hesitant unionists to ratify Sunningdale. There would, he argued, be a 'slight reduction in the number of troops in Northern Ireland ... [and] although there was a groundswell of opinion in Great Britain that the Army should be brought back from Northern Ireland, there was absolutely no question of a withdrawal of troops. The Army would remain as long as it had a job to do'. Rees understood that, from the Republic's point of view, extradition was not possible, but that it seemed likely that 'the Irish were prepared to ... make the [common law enforcement] system work as effectively as possible'. Faulkner argued that it was 'hard to accept a second best solution' with regard to law enforcement. Perhaps he was also worried about the symbolism that an all-Ireland law enforcement system might have on unionist public opinion. Ivan Cooper, on the other hand, urged HMG and the Executive to 'do their best to emphasise the advantages of introducing a system of extra-territorial jurisdiction'. However, the UK Attorney General, Sam Silkin, warned that he 'could not disguise the disadvantages of this method in comparison to the far simpler process of extradition'.[123]

A week later, the executive again met with Rees. The circumstances were much more difficult, given the commencement of the UWC strike. Roy Bradford argued that the LEC recommendations 'did not meet Sunningdale', since the agreed communiqué stated that the commission would recommend the 'most effective means' for dealing with cross-border violence. He stated that 'the release of the Republic and the SDLP from extradition arrangements could release unionists from their commitment to a Council of Ireland'.[124] Bradford's argument was not valid, since the Republic had never explicitly committed to extradition, and the SDLP could not have committed to it in any case, as it had no power to do so. He contended, however, that 'if extradition was deemed not to be politically possible, other parties to the Sunningdale agreement might have to consider what might not be politically possible for them'. This reaction to unionist public opinion by the Faulknerites was, however, too late. It is clear that the lack of improvement in the security situation, and the (misinformed) perception that the Republic was not co-operating with British security forces, played a significant role in the success of the UWC strike, which brought about the collapse of the power-sharing executive.

Conclusion

Most unionists did not appreciate the differences between the power-sharing executive and the old Stormont government in relation to security matters. The Stormont government had extensive security powers, which enabled it to take firm action against paramilitary violence. The executive, however, had no security powers at all, and relied on the British Army to deal with paramilitaries. Throughout the executive's time in office, levels of violence remained stubbornly high. This increased unionist perceptions that the executive was ineffective, thus reducing the chances that the power-sharing settlement would succeed.

Attempts by British authorities to create a local military force acceptable to the minority community failed; the ill-judged decision to send UDR application forms to ex-members of the USC contributed to this failure and increased the perception among the nationalist community that the security forces were 'Protestant and partial'.[125] Similarly, the government's ineffective attempt to reform the police did little to alter this perception.

Likewise, the behaviour of the British Army, particularly its treatment of residents in republican areas during searches, did not engender nationalist support for the security forces. The continued use of internment and detention was resented by nationalists, as it was disproportionately applied against that community. The British Army's behaviour also damaged the prospects of better security co-operation between the Republic and the UK.[126]

Nevertheless, there was a significant improvement in cross-border security co-operation when the Fine Gael–ILP coalition government took office in March 1973. The British authorities felt that the coalition was much more forthcoming in regard to border security than the previous Fianna Fáil administration. This is confirmed in a confidential British note of March 1974, entitled 'The Coalition and Northern Ireland'. The note authored by Galsworthy contained the statement that Cosgrave's government 'continue[d] to be an improvement on their predecessors. They have better ideas and are trying to put some of them into effect' even if 'many of their efforts have been faltering and fumbling'. The coalition was regarded as 'more active and determined than their predecessors' on all aspects of security co-operation.[127] The extent of this improvement challenges Paul Bew's argument that the British government's 'obsession' with improving security co-operation with the Republic was unrealistic. However, archival evidence confirms his view that such co-operation was never 'decisive', due to the political constraints on the coalition and residual tensions concerning British Army behaviour.[128]

Brian Faulkner underestimated the importance of the Council of Ireland to the SDLP, believing instead that detention and police reforms were the party's main concerns. The SDLP, however, was flexible on security issues, but insistent on a Council of Ireland being established. Bew and Patterson have rightly argued that the lack of any serious changes in British security and internment policy was the reason why the SDLP put so much emphasis on the proposed Council of Ireland.[129] However, it is also likely that the party would have prioritised the all-Ireland aspects of Sunningdale regardless. Similarly, the SDLP paid insufficient attention to unionist fears regarding the ratification of Sunningdale and the devaluation of the Irish declaration on the status of Northern Ireland. Overall, politicians and officials in Belfast, Dublin and London, believed an improvement in security was vital if the executive was to succeed. However, the proposed Council of Ireland was an equally important reason why the power-sharing experiment failed. This issue is examined in the following chapter.

Notes

1 Rees, *Northern Ireland*, p. 318; Lee, *Ireland*, p. 449.
2 Of these, 135 were killed by security forces. Jackson, *Home Rule*, p. 269.
3 S. Swan, *Official Irish Republicanism, 1962–1972* (Lulu.com, 2007), p. 356.
4 H. Patterson, *Politics of Illusion: A Political History of the IRA* (London: W.W. Norton, 1997), p. 166, 278; *Britain's White Paper: Republican Statement and Demands for All-Ireland* (Sinn Féin Official/Northern Republican Clubs Executive, 1973).
5 E. Moloney, *A Secret History of the IRA* (London: Allen Lane, 2002), p. 142.

6 A. R. Oppenheimer, *IRA: The Bombs and the Bullets. A History of Deadly Ingenuity* (Dublin: Irish Academic Press, 2008), p. 28.

7 Lee, *Ireland*, p. 442.

8 Bourke, *Peace*, p. 170.

9 M. L. R. Smith and P. Neumann, 'Motorman's long journey: changing the strategic setting in Northern Ireland', *Contemporary British History*, xix: 4 (2005), pp. 413–35.

10 B. Hanley and S. Millar, *The Lost Revolution: The Story of The Official IRA and the Workers' Party* (Dublin: Penguin Ireland, 2009), pp. 14–21.

11 The Irish government also became increasingly concerned about this possibility after the UWC strike. See chapter 6.

12 H. McDonald and J. Cusack, *UDA: Inside the Heart of Loyalist Terror* (Dublin: Penguin Ireland, 2004), pp. 58–60.

13 The almost exclusively Protestant nature of this force, its association with atrocities against Catholics in the 1920s, and its deployment against civil rights protesters in the 1960s meant it was viewed with hostility and suspicion by most Catholics. For critiques of the USC and the Northern Ireland government see M. Farrell, *Arming the Protestants: The Formation of the Ulster Special Constabulary and the Royal Ulster Constabulary, 1920–27* (London: Pluto, 1983) and *Northern Ireland: The Orange State* (London: Pluto, 1976). Some of those who participated on the attack of the Belfast to Derry March in 1969 at Burntollet Bridge had been identified as off-duty members of the USC. Jackson, *Ireland 1978–1998: Politics and War*, p. 370.

14 C. Ryder, *The Ulster Defence Regiment: An Instrument of Peace?* (London: Methuen, 1991), pp. 59–60.

15 H. Patterson, 'Sectarianism revisited: the Provisional IRA campaign in a border region of Northern Ireland', *Terrorism and Political Violence*, xxii: 3 (2010), pp. 337–56. For debates on the extent to which sectarianism motivated this PIRA campaign, see, S. Bruce, 'Victim selection in ethnic conflict: motives and attitudes in Irish republicanism', *Terrorism and Political Violence*, ix: 1 (1997), pp. 56–71 and R. W. White, 'The Irish Republican Army: an assessment of sectarianism', *Terrorism and Political Violence*, ix: 1 (1997), pp. 20–55.

16 TNA, CJ 4/390, meeting between the Prime Minister and Mr Lynch today in Munich, 4 September 1972.

17 Ibid., note for the record, 23 October 1972.

18 *Irish Independent*, 5 July 1972, 19 August 1972, 5 September 1972.

19 Ibid., 3 July 1972.

20 Ibid., 17 October 1972.

21 Ibid., 20 October, 1972.

22 He ended the thirst strike on 16 January 1973 and was ordered off the hunger strike by the PIRA Army Council. *Irish Times*, 11 January 1973; 16 April 1973.

23 TNA, CJ4/390, note for the record, 24 November 1972.

24 R. Fanning, *Independent Ireland* (Dublin: Helicon, 1983), p. 134, p. 206. Fianna Fáil has been classified as more 'nationalist' than Fine Gael, which has been regarded as a conservative 'law and order' party. See P. Mair, *The Changing Irish*

Party System: Organisation, Ideology and Electoral Competition (London: Pinter, 1987), pp. 12–61. See also K. Boland, *Fine Gael: British or Irish* (Cork: Mercier, 1984).

25 University College Dublin Archives (UCDA), P176/446, Fianna Fáil parliamentary party minutes, 15 January 1957. Lynch himself was absent from that meeting.
26 See J. O'Brien, *The Arms Trial* (Dublin: Gill and Macmillan, 2000). See also D. Keogh, *Jack Lynch: A Biography* (Dublin: Gill and Macmillan, 2008) and T. Ryle Dwyer, *Nice Fellow: A Biography of Jack Lynch* (Cork: Mercier, 2001).
27 TNA, CJ4/391, Duke of Devonshire to Prime Minister, 22 January 1973.
28 B. Arnold, *Jack Lynch: Hero in Crisis* (Dublin: Merlin, 2001). For the Irish government's response to the outbreak of violence in 1968, R. Fanning, 'Playing it cool: the response of the British and Irish governments to the crisis in Northern Ireland, 1968–69', *Irish Studies in International Affairs*, xxii (2001), pp. 57–85.
29 C. O'Donnell, *The Sunningdale Communiqué and Bi-partisanship in the Republic of Ireland, 1973*, Working Papers in British–Irish Studies, no. 81 (2007), pp. 3–4.
30 *Irish Times*, 26 February 1973.
31 *Irish Independent*, 13 February 1973.
32 Ibid., 12 February 1973.
33 The Lifford area is a frontier region in East Donegal and is a major border-crossing point between County Donegal in the Republic and County Tyrone in Northern Ireland.
34 TNA, FCO 87/247, D. G. Allen to Kelvin White (FCO), 1 March 1973. ASUs refers to operational units of paramilitary organisations, primarily PIRA.
35 TNA, CJ4/391, meeting between the Secretary of State for Northern Ireland with Dr G. FitzGerald and Dr D. O'Sullivan, 4 April 1973.
36 *Anglo-Celt*, 27 April, 1973.
37 TNA, FCO 87/225, Galsworthy to United Kingdom Representative (UKREP) Belfast, 10 April 1973.
38 Ibid., White to Galsworthy 11 April 1973.
39 *Irish Times*, 18 May 1973.
40 TNA, FCO 87/263, A. J. Craig (Near and Middle East Department, FCO) to Messrs Parsons and LeQueane, 9 April 1973.
41 *Irish Times*, 4 January 1974.
42 TNA, FCO 87/247, Galsworthy to UKREP Belfast, 14 April 1973.
43 TNA, FCO 87/248, Galsworthy to UKREP Belfast, 6 May 1973.
44 Ibid., report by F. R. G. Williams on the state of links as between security forces in Northern Ireland and Eire, 4 June 1973.
45 FitzGerald, *All in a Life*, pp. 198–204.
46 TNA, FCO 87/204, Douglas-Home to Galsworthy, 7 August 1973.
47 TNA, CJ4/391, note for the record, 4 July 1973.
48 TNA, CJ4/388, background note to Mr Cosgrave's visit, July 1973.
49 *Irish Times*, 2 April 1973.
50 TNA, CJ4/392, Galsworthy to UKREP Belfast, 17 August 1973.
51 Ibid.
52 FitzGerald, *All in a Life*, pp. 106–8.

53 TNA, CJ4/392, Galsworthy to UKREP Belfast, 17 August 1973.
54 TNA, FCO 87/204, for Sir G. Arthur from Galsworthy, 9 August 1973.
55 NAI, AG 2004/1/254, Heath visit, 17 September 1973.
56 TNA, CJ4/509, note for the record of Secretary of State's conversation with Brigadier Mostyn, 8 Brigade HQ Northern Ireland, 1 October 1973.
57 Ibid., meeting between the Secretary of State, the CLF and Chief Constable, 12 November 1973.
58 Ibid., meeting between the Secretary of State and representatives of the Suffolk/Lenadoon area, 27 November 1973.
59 NAI, JUS 2005/24/8, meeting between G. FitzGerald and W. Whitelaw, 6 November 1973.
60 Ibid., meeting between the Minister for Foreign Affairs and the Secretary of State for Northern Ireland, 30 November 1973.
61 *Dáil Éireann: Official Report*, 14 June 1973, vol. 266, col. 583–4. The coalition had been charged by Fianna Fáil members of being 'lackeys of the British', *Irish Independent*, 6 November 1973.
62 See chapter 1.
63 TNA, FCO 87/248, Galsworthy to NIO and HQNI, 21 December 1973.
64 R. F. Foster, *Luck and the Irish: A Brief History of Change 1970* (London: Allen Lane, 2007), p. 93.
65 NAI, AG 2004/1/254, Paisley to Cosgrave, 18 September 1973.
66 Ibid., Cosgrave to Paisley, 19 September 1973.
67 *Anglo-Celt*, 21 January 1972.
68 Bew, *Ireland*, pp. 490–3.
69 SDLP, *Towards a New Ireland* (Belfast, 1972).
70 UUP, *Towards the Future* (Belfast, 1972).
71 Anderson, *14 May Days: The Inside Story of the Loyalist Strike of 1794* (Dublin: Sill and Macmillan, 1994). p. 4.
72 Interestingly, the strike was supported by the Catholic Ex-Servicemen's Association because the strikers also condemned the continued use of internment. See *Irish Times*, 7 February 1973.
73 *Irish Times*, 8 February 1973.
74 TNA, CJ4/331, law, order and policing – note by the Northern Ireland Office, October 1973.
75 TNA, FCO 87/225, from MOD to PM, 30 March 1973.
76 Police primacy is attributed to Rees and Mason, in e.g. P. Arthur, *Special Relationships: Britain, Ireland and the Northern Ireland Problem* (Belfast: Blackstaff, 2000), p. 165; Bourke, *Peace*, p. 232.
77 TNA, CJ4/392, Galsworthy to NIO, 17 August 1973.
78 TNA, CJ4/509, note of a meeting in Stormont Castle, 16 July 1973.
79 *Irish Independent*, 1 November 1973; see his obituary in the Canadian *National Post*, 9 April 1999.
80 TNA, CJ4/392, Douglas-Home to Galsworthy, 23 August 1973.
81 *The Northern Ireland Constitutional Proposals* (HMSO, 1973).
82 NAI, AG 2004/1/254, Heath visit, 17 September 1973.
83 TNA, CJ4/331, Cooper to Whitelaw, 12 October 1973.

84 Ibid., meeting between the Secretary of State, the Alliance Party, the Social Democratic and Labour Party and the Ulster Unionist Party, 16 October 1973.

85 NAI, JUST 2005/24/8, FitzGerald–Whitelaw meeting, 8 November 1973.

86 Ibid., policing, common law enforcement and related matters, [November 1973].

87 See chapter 1.

88 PRONI, OE/2/1A, executive minutes, 8 January 1974.

89 *Irish Independent*, 17 January 1974.

90 PRONI, OE/1/35, Faulkner to Cosgrave, 10 January 1974.

91 PRONI, OE/1/28, meeting between the chief executive of the Northern Ireland Executive and the Taoiseach of the Republic of Ireland, 16 Jan 1974.

92 *Irish Independent*, 17 December 1973.

93 PRONI, OE/1/28, meeting between the chief executive of the Northern Ireland Executive and the Taoiseach of the Republic of Ireland, 16 Jan 1974.

94 Ibid., Cooper to Faulkner 31 January 1974.

95 *Irish Independent*, 25 January 1974. British woman Dr Rose Dugdale, and two Irishmen, were later convicted by Dublin's Special Criminal Court for their involvement in this attack. *Irish Times*, 27 November 1974.

96 TNA, CJ4/509, Secretary of State meeting with Alliance Party 18 December 1973.

97 PRONI, OE/1/28, meeting between the chief executive of the Northern Ireland Executive and the Taoiseach of the Republic of Ireland, 16 January 1974.

98 Ibid., Reynolds to Goddard 30 January 1974.

99 NAI, DT 2005/7/624, O'Sullivan to H. McCann (Secretary at the DFA, Dublin) 11 January 1974.

100 See C. O'Halloran, *Partition and the Limits of Irish Nationalism: An Ideology under Stress* (Dublin: Gill and Macmillan, 1987), pp. 189–93.

101 PRONI, OE/1/28, meeting between the chief executive of the Northern Ireland Executive and the Taoiseach of the Republic of Ireland, 16 Jan 1974.

102 See chapter 1.

103 PRONI, OE/2/10, executive minutes, note of a discussion of the political situation following the results of the general election, 5 March 1974.

104 *Irish Independent*, 29 January 1974.

105 PRONI, OE 1/24, meeting between the Secretary of State and the Northern Ireland Executive, 26 March 1974.

106 TNA, Prime Minister's Office files (PREM), 16/145, record of a meeting between the Secretary of State for Northern Ireland and Dr G. FitzGerald, 7 March 1974.

107 House of Commons (HC) Debates, vol. 871, 1 April 1974, col. 887.

108 TNA, PREM 16/145, record of a conversation between the Prime Minister and the Chief Executive of Northern Ireland, 1 April 1974.

109 TNA, CJ4/512, secret and personal note by N. K. Finlayson, 26 March 1974.

110 PRONI, OE/1/24, meeting of the Northern Ireland administration and the Prime Minister, Stormont, 18 April 1974.

111 TNA, CJ4/512, secret note by M. Reid to S. Orme, 4 May 1974.

112 The Detention of Terrorists (Northern Ireland) Order, 1972. (1972 no. 1632). Quoted in J. Harris, 'The Conservative Government and the Sunningdale Agreement, 1972–74' (PhD dissertation, Queen's University Belfast, 2008), p. 123.

113 Faulkner, *Memoirs*, p. 126.

114 TNA, CJ4/331, meeting between the Secretary of State, the Alliance Party, the Social Democratic and Labour Party and the Ulster Unionist Party, 16 October 1973.

115 TNA, CJ4/512, meeting between the Northern Ireland Executive and the Secretary of State and the Attorney General on the Law Enforcement Commission Report, 10 May 1974. For comment on the scheme, *Irish Times*, 6 April and 19 April 1974.

116 P. Dixon, 'Paths to peace in Northern Ireland (II): the peace processes 1973–74 and 1994–96', *Democratization*, iv: 3 (1997), pp. 1–25.

117 The membership of the LEC was as follows: Mr Justice Walsh, Mr Justice Henchy, Mr T. A. Doyle, and Mr D. Quigley (Irish Republic); and: Sir R. Lowry, Lord Justice Scarman, Sir K. Jones and J. B. E. Hutton (United Kingdom).

118 This was also referred to as the 'extra-territorial method', and allowed for a person to be tried in either Northern Ireland or the Republic for an offence committed anywhere on the island.

119 Cunningham, *Government Policy*, p. 26.

120 PRONI, OE/2/19, executive minutes, 7 May 1974.

121 Patterson and Kaufmann, *Unionism*, p. 175.

122 PRONI, OE/2/19, executive minutes, 7 May 1974.

123 TNA, CJ4/512, meeting between the Northern Ireland Executive and the Secretary of State and the Attorney General on the Law Enforcement Commission report, 10 May 1974.

124 PRONI, OE/1/24, meeting between the Secretary of State and the Northern Ireland administration, 17 May 1974.

125 Foster, *Modern Ireland*, p. 589.

126 The coalition was particularly critical of army behaviour in the Creggan estate, Derry City in August 1974, where 'thousands of people had been harassed in recent weeks.' See TNA, FCO 87/312, aide memoire by Irish embassy to FCO, 8 August 1974.

127 TNA, FCO 87/311, confidential note, the coalition and Northern Ireland, 28 March 1974.

128 Bew, *Ireland*, p. 511.

129 Bew and Patterson, *British State*, p. 60. See also Cunningham, *Government Policy*, p. 16.

3

The Sunningdale Council of Ireland

During the 1972–75 period, the issue of cross-border co-operation in Ireland provoked much political debate. The Sunningdale Agreement of 1973 proposed a Council of Ireland comprising elected representatives from the Northern Ireland Assembly and Dáil Éireann. This Council was to have executive functions and to eventually administer certain public services in both jurisdictions in Ireland. It proved one of the most contentious issues during this time, and was strongly resisted by a large section of the unionist community, who claimed it provided the Dublin government with an undue influence in Northern Ireland's affairs. Many unionists also interpreted this proposal as a stepping stone to a united Ireland. Scholars remain divided over what functions various actors attached to the proposed Council of Ireland, and how it might have developed if established. A number of accounts have retrospectively endorsed the contemporary loyalist claim that the Irish government indeed intended to use the Council to absorb Northern Ireland into the Republic.

Christopher Farrington has argued that the Irish government, in concert with the SDLP, sought a powerful Council with a 'longer term aim of achieving a united Ireland'.[1] '[T]he assumption [on the Irish side] was that a strong council would be an institutional mechanism which would unify Ireland.'[2] Cillian McGrattan has suggested that the SDLP and the Dublin government became 'locked-in to an increasingly narrow policy trajectory, based on maximising gains for the minority community in Northern Ireland', particularly a strong Council of Ireland.[3] The Irish government and the SDLP are classified as 'the two nationalist negotiators'. It is claimed that 'a large degree of unanimity' existed between them, in particular with regard to prioritising the Council of Ireland over power-sharing. Their supposed joint strategy, based on a 'path dependent' approach, hoped to 'achieve maximal concessions in the form of [the] gradual unification [of Ireland]'. Path dependency is defined as 'historical sequences in which later events, outcomes or choices conform in specific ways to initial occurrences or choices'.[4]

However, archival evidence demonstrates that almost all Irish government departments actually opposed giving the Council any significant functions.

The Department of Foreign Affairs (DFA) sought a strong Council with the potential to become an all-Ireland government. The DFA, however, was isolated and to a large extent ignored by the other Irish departments. The evidence also suggests that the proposed Council was not a particularly divisive issue for the power-sharing administration, and that the executive was in no danger of collapsing because of it.

Council of Ireland: historical origins

The idea of a Council of Ireland, which would provide a forum for politicians from Northern and Southern Ireland, long preceded the Sunningdale settlement. It originated in the Government of Ireland Act (1920), which introduced partition. The partition of Ireland was not meant to be permanent. The British government eventually planned to unite both parliaments in Ireland under a single legislature based in Dublin.[5] However, the 1920 settlement was rejected in Southern Ireland. This was evident from the results of the 1921 elections, whereby 124 southern MPs (returned unopposed), pledged their allegiance to Dáil Éireann.[6] This, coupled with the continuation of the War of Independence in the 'South', effectively ended the possibility of a Council of Ireland being established. Sir James Craig and Michael Collins attempted to improve relations between both states, but little came of their efforts.[7]

When the frontier of the Irish Free State and Northern Ireland was formalised in 1925, cross-border co-operation did take root, albeit slowly. Michael Kennedy has shown that, up until 1969, co-operation existed in areas such as transport and electricity generation, but for political reasons it received little publicity.[8] The zenith of cross-border co-operation, from a unionist perspective, was the introduction of internment on both sides of the border, in response to the IRA's 'Operation Harvest' campaign, 1956–62, referred to in the previous chapter. However, the eventual outbreak of the conflict in 1968, and the role played by the British Army in Northern Ireland, made similar cross-border security co-operation difficult for the government of the Republic. Cross-border co-operation was generally conducted at official level, with occasional political meetings taking place. The most famous of these were the Lemass–O'Neill meetings, held in 1965.

Despite these high-profile meetings, institutionalised cross-border co-operation was studiously avoided. Terence O'Neill, speaking on Irish radio in 1965, claimed that despite the recent advances in North–South relations, the timing was not yet right for a Council of Ireland. He wished to 'concentrate on government discussions for the present', and was hopeful that co-operation in the areas of agriculture, physical planning, transport and tourism could be further developed.[9] Despite O'Neill's utterances, there were no further developments in this area until the late 1960s. Files from the Irish

Department of External Affairs show that there was a proposal to resurrect the concept of a Council of Ireland in 1969. The British peer Lord Longford informed Kevin Rush, of the Irish Embassy in London, about a proposed speech in the House of Lords wherein he would advocate 'the resurrection of the Council of Ireland for which provision had been made in the 1920 Act'. Rush confirmed that the idea of an all-Ireland Council had recently been 'floated' within his department. It was later confirmed to Longford that the Dublin government favoured a bilateral Council of Ireland, which could 'provide a start towards the "dialogue" which would have to be undertaken sooner or later between Dublin and Belfast as the situation deteriorated'. Rush also mentioned that Jack Lynch, the Taoiseach, had recently 'spoken of a possibility of a federal solution' to the Northern Ireland problem, and speculated that a bilateral Council might be one of the early ways of achieving this. In general terms, he informed Longford that the Lynch government policy on Northern Ireland revolved around 'the "consultations" aspect . . . that Dublin had a right to be consulted about this fundamental Irish problem, and furthermore [had] a role to play in the solution of it, both long and short term'.[10]

Despite the outbreak of the conflict in 1968–69, officials from Northern Ireland and the Republic continued to engage constructively with each other. In April 1971, civil servants from both states met in Dublin to discuss possible North–South economic co-operation. They recognised that, although both jurisdictions were in competition regarding future economic development, they had a 'mutual interest in the development of the Border areas'. The delegates from Northern Ireland stated that it would be worth examining the possibility of combining a number of towns on both sides of the border to 'form a growth complex which would render the location a more attractive one for a new industry from the point of view of availability of a large number of workers'. The report suggested that additional studies be conducted with a view to further co-operation within the tourism industries; it noted that co-operation between the Northern Ireland Electricity Service (NIES) and the Republic's Electricity Supply Board (ESB) was far-reaching. However, there were no proposals relating to the formation of a North–South Council at this time, and it appeared such a Council was unnecessary for effective cross-border co-operation.[11]

At a meeting between Taoiseach Jack Lynch and Prime Minister Edward Heath in September 1972, it was confirmed that cross-border co-operation had been 'largely unaffected' by the Northern Ireland conflict. The two premiers discussed areas for co-operation similar to those mentioned in 1971. The British argued that successful co-operation was likely to make Lynch 'more amenable', and also had the potential to 'persuade the minority that political progress was more profitable than violence'. Lynch stressed that he was keen to improve cross-border relations during the 'changed circumstances of 1972'. This suggests that, despite the violence in Northern Ireland, there was constant British–Irish contact at governmental and official level, and the relationship does not seem to have been in danger of collapse during this period.[12]

Soon, events in Northern Ireland brought the issue of cross-border relations to the fore of the political agenda. The prorogation of Stormont stimulated wide-ranging discussion about the potential establishment of an all-Ireland institution. As already mentioned, the UUP document, *Towards the Future: A Unionist Blueprint*, proposed a North–South inter-governmental council to discuss matters of mutual interest.[13] However, the UUP sought 'several major contributions' from the Republic before such a body could be established. Among the contributions considered necessary was the 'acceptance by the South of the right of the people of the North to self-determination', formalised in an agreement between the three governments in Dublin, Belfast and London. The UUP also favoured the creation of a common-law enforcement area for the British Isles, in order to combat cross-border violence.[14]

As also mentioned previously, the SDLP proposed an all-Ireland body, the National Senate of Ireland. Its policy explicitly stated that this proposed institution was designed to lead to Irish unification.[15] The differing interpretations of the remit of the Council of Ireland, subsequently proposed at Sunningdale, caused significant difficulties for the nationalist and unionist supporters of that agreement. The precise nature of the powers of the Council was to be finalised between officials and politicians from both parts of Ireland, and it was planned that the Council be established after the final ratification of Sunningdale. The Council of Ireland was the culmination of the British government's acceptance of an Irish dimension in Northern Ireland affairs, as expressed in the 1973 White Paper, *The Northern Ireland Constitutional Proposals*.

Loyalist parties, such as the DUP and VUPP, reacted angrily to the Council of Ireland proposals. The VUPP claimed to be 'disturbed' by these proposals, while simultaneously expressing the hope that 'one day the two states in Ireland can live, work and co-operate as good neighbours'.[16] It did not, however, think the timing for such co-operation was right in 1973. The blame for accepting the Irish dimension was placed firmly on William Whitelaw; one VUPP publication menacingly noted that 'heads have rolled in British history for less'.[17] The DUP was equally critical, claiming that the proposed council was little more than a 'half way house to a united Ireland'.[18] The party further claimed that the British constitutional proposals established 'beyond dispute the disastrous principle – republican violence pays'.[19] It is unclear how valid this claim was, since only nationalists opposed to the IRA were included in the discussions on Northern Ireland's future; and both factions of the IRA opposed the British proposals. However, because of the lack of clarity in the proposals concerning the Irish dimension, loyalist political figures were able to portray the White Paper as a threat to the union, and mobilise unionist opinion against the Council of Ireland.

Political discussions about the proposed Council of Ireland

In January 1973, Brian Lenihan (Irish Minister for Foreign Affairs), and his officials, discussed the potential formation of a Council of Ireland with Sir John Peck, then UK Ambassador to Ireland. According to Peck's record of the meeting, there was a significant difference of opinion between the Minister for Foreign Affairs and one of his senior officials over the functions which should be attached to the council. Lenihan sought a 'very modest structure capable of evolving into something important'. However, Peck alleged that the assistant secretary of the DFA, Bob McDonagh, 'made the same gloomy noises [as usual], stressing how hard it would be to sell anything so modest as we proposed to the Irish Republic'. McDonagh was referring to the British suggestion that a Council of Ireland should be a purely consultative institution. Peck was unsympathetic towards McDonagh, claiming that his argument was 'rubbish, and not the first example of DFA officials thinking they know more politics than their own politicians'.[20] On 15 January 1973, Lenihan met Sir Alec Douglas-Home, the foreign secretary, to discuss the potential functions of a Council of Ireland. Lenihan suggested electricity generation and tourism were areas which might come under its remit, as well as the disbursement of EEC regional development funding. Hugh McCann also suggested that the proposed Council have responsibility for 'other non-contentious issues', such as the environment.[21] It appears, therefore, that Fianna Fáil, traditionally regarded as a more 'republican' party, did not seek to use the proposed Council of Ireland as a means to achieve Irish unity.[22]

In early 1973, British thinking on cross-border co-operation appears to have been influenced by the Northern Ireland civil servant, Kenneth Bloomfield.[23] Given that the government had accepted the principle of the Irish dimension, Bloomfield argued that the Republic should make a declaration recognising the status of Northern Ireland as part of the UK. The existing statutory provision, the Ireland Act, 1949, guaranteed that Northern Ireland would not cease to be part of the UK without the consent of its parliament. Since that parliament had been prorogued in 1972, Bloomfield suggested that the consent instead be vested 'in the *people* of Northern Ireland to be determined at a poll'. He also contended that there should be 'tough bargaining behind the scenes' with the Republic to secure the status declaration. If this happened, then a reciprocal declaration could be made outlining the possibility of establishing all-Ireland institutions of a consultative and advisory nature, with the potential to develop executive functions to improve relations between both parts of Ireland. The following format was suggested.

a. It is hereby declared that Northern Ireland shall not cease to be a part of the United Kingdom without the consent of the people of Northern Ireland as indicated by majority vote at a poll.
b. Provided however that nothing in the above declaration or in this Act shall be construed as inhibiting or impeding the formation of consultative and advisory institutions to further the interests of Ireland as a whole, or as preventing the vesting in such institutions by mutual agreement of the Northern Ireland Assembly and the Oireachtas of specific responsibilities including, if so desired, executive functions.

This would have to be matched by the Republic, either by amending its constitution or 'some other form of visible commitment' recognising Northern Ireland's constitutional status. The Dublin government should be expected to declare 'that, while it remained the national aspiration to secure the unity of Ireland in amity and by consent, it would be the policy of the Irish Republic, for as long as such consent was absent, to participate in co-operative endeavours with the institutions established in Northern Ireland by the Northern Ireland Act, 1973'. This document is significant, since it contains within it some aspects which eventually formed part of the British White Paper and the Sunningdale communiqué.[24] It is also clear that Bloomfield's arguments were taken seriously by London officials. William Nield, permanent secretary at the Northern Ireland Office (NIO), in a handwritten comment on these proposals stated: 'I have as you know some sympathy for thinking on these lines. Please take Mr B's points into consideration in dealing with the Irish dimension in the GEN79 policy series.'[25]

William Whitelaw summarised his Council of Ireland proposals in a memorandum for the cabinet in January 1973. He noted that most Northern Ireland parties made reference to 'some sort of scheme' for institutional co-operation between Northern Ireland and the Republic 'which many described as a Council of Ireland', but that there were differences of opinion as to what role it should have and what conditions needed to be met before its establishment. Whitelaw argued that British policy should be based on the twin principles of not 'arousing the fears of the majority community', by making the Council part of a wider settlement, whilst also satisfying 'the minority community and the Government of the Republic that we really mean business', regarding the Council of Ireland. Like Bloomfield, he argued that the former objective might be achieved if the Irish government gave 'de facto recognition to Northern Ireland'. He discounted the possibility that his future White Paper would contain a fully worked-out plan for a Council of Ireland, since political representatives from both communities in Northern Ireland would have to be consulted in 'determining its forms, functions and proceedings'. He suggested that the forthcoming White Paper might refer to a proposed tripartite conference on the Council of Ireland, following the formation of a power-sharing executive. In any event, this was not included in the White Paper, but it is clear that the idea for a conference resembling that which eventually took place at Sunningdale in December 1973 had been considered in British political circles for a substantial period of time.[26]

An annexe to Whitelaw's memorandum contained an assessment of the British–Irish discussions which had so far taken place, about the proposed Council. Whitelaw criticised Irish DFA officials, stating that 'the discussions have shown how unrealistic and ill-thought out the attitude of the South, at least at official level, is on these matters'. This highlights the difference in thinking between DFA officials and the Irish government on the subject. The institutions envisaged by Irish officials were 'similar in many ways to EEC or the Council for Europe', with a ministerial council, a parliamentary tier, and a supporting secretariat. British officials stressed that it was unrealistic to attempt to impose any such Council, since there 'was a need to win over the people of the North (and particularly the Protestants) to the new institutions'. Irish officials argued that, if a Council of Ireland was not 'set up with full powers', it might be better not to press ahead with the idea. Whitelaw noted that 'there is reason to believe that Ministers in the South are more realistic than their chauvinistic officials'. He stressed that it was not British government policy to inhibit the potential areas in which North-South co-operation could develop. The British government would support institutions having 'the capacity to develop, if North and South so wish, into something real and influential'. However, he noted that it would be counter-productive to British and Irish policy if 'we were to give the impression that the institutions were deliberately designed to pave the way towards unification'. The formula, devised by Bloomfield, on the status of Northern Ireland and an agreed all-Ireland institution with possible executive functions, was included almost verbatim in Whitelaw's document.[27]

The proposed Council of Ireland was discussed by British and Irish officials at a meeting in mid-January 1973. Irish Ambassador to the UK, Dr Diarmuid O'Sullivan, argued that the proposals he had received from British officials amounted to a 'Council without real power'. A body with consultative functions would 'be a talking shop and would become the object of derision.' Sir Stewart Crawford of the Foreign and Commonwealth Office (FCO), accused O'Sullivan of taking 'too discouraging a view of what [the British] had in

mind'. They did not, he contended, exclude a parliamentary aspect to the
Council. The Irish officials took a strong line on the proposed Council in these
early discussions. O'Sullivan pointed out that the Irish government had 'dual
objectives': to 'make the two communities of Northern Ireland accustomed
to living and working together, and to achieve the same rapport between
North and South', with both polities 'put on convergent lines'. McDonagh
(DFA) claimed that the 'Irish were clear what they were aiming at: reunification ... Unless the Council of Ireland contained a promise of movement in
that direction, it, and those who supported it, could be thrown to the wolves'.
He modified this claim somewhat, adding that he 'did not envisage that the
Council of Ireland would govern the whole island from a set date, but he did
think that it might be possible to adopt a programme under which it could
take up some certain functions on set dates, as in the case of the EEC.'
McDonagh then made an interesting remark about North–South co-opera-
tion. He suggested that co-operation in the fields mentioned by the British,
such as electricity supply and tourism, 'could be done just as well without a
Council'. However, 'we had to cater for the Irish dimension. If a Council of
Ireland was not the way, they must find another way'.[28] This suggests that the
DFA's primary concern was securing a role for the Republic in Northern
Ireland affairs, and that the creation of a powerful all-Ireland Council was
seen as the best way of doing so. The stronger the proposed Council, the
greater the Republic's potential influence on Northern Ireland's affairs. The
British side recognised that the Irish 'regarded [their] readiness to establish a
Council with real functions as a test of our willingness to turn the proposed
Irish dimension into reality.'[29]

In February 1973, John Peck wrote to Kelvin White of the FCO concerning
a meeting he had with Garret FitzGerald, then an opposition TD. FitzGerald
argued that the proposed Council should 'have a parliamentary element from
the word Go [sic]'. However, earlier in the conversation, he had referred to the
Irish style of negotiation. He pointed out that the 'British never seemed to
realise that the Irish, whatever their political or religious persuasion, invariably embarked on a negotiation by making an opening bid or adopting a
position which was not intended to be taken seriously'. As an example, he cited
the SDLP which he said was 'horrified when their [sic] proposal for a condominium had been taken seriously'.[30] The view that the British did not understand the Irish mentality was rejected within the FCO. A further letter to Peck
noted that while the Irish were unlikely to cease the practice of opening with
an unrealistic bid, 'the British [had] successfully coped with wily Orientals
who have the same negotiating habits'. The letter also noted that, despite
FitzGerald's claims, John Hume was a strong advocate of a condominium at
the time it was proposed.[31] Further intergovernmental meetings took place
later that spring.

British–Irish Council of Ireland meetings

In March 1973, FitzGerald met Edward Heath, to discuss the proposed council. FitzGerald had replaced Brian Lenihan as foreign minister, when the Fine Gael–ILP coalition took office after winning the general election on 28 February 1973. He stressed that any Council of Ireland should make special provision for the Derry/Donegal region. This should take the form of a 'special relationship with the Council of Ireland . . . with access to Brussels through the Council'. He also discussed the possible evolution of such a Council, and argued that it might act as a safeguard for unionist interests. Heath agreed that a Council with a 'blocking power for the majority' would put unionists back in control of the constitutional destiny of Northern Ireland.[32] However, despite these discussions, the British government did not concede to the Irish request for a Council of Ireland 'with specific, clearly-defined functions'.[33]

FitzGerald met with William Whitelaw in April 1973. The issue of the Republic recognising the status of Northern Ireland was discussed. FitzGerald stated that 'previous Irish governments had always tacitly recognised the North but there were great emotional difficulties in amending Article 2' of its constitution. As will be seen, the issue of status was of central importance to the discussions of the Northern Ireland Executive. FitzGerald apparently failed to grasp the obvious potential for significant unionist antipathy towards a Council of Ireland. Perhaps he was downplaying the prospect of such resistance in discussions with the British. He argued that the 'majority in the North would do better relying on their Irish compatriots in the South than HMG "across the water"', a statement which many unionists would have found disagreeable. Whitelaw, however, stressed that he had 'no objection to such an argument as long as it did not foster the idea in majority minds that an independent Ulster could survive'.[34] FitzGerald was perhaps ignoring the advice of his fellow minister, Conor Cruise O'Brien, who warned that Dublin should be aware of the possibility of a loyalist backlash over its involvement in Northern Ireland's affairs. O'Brien advised against placing too much importance on the advice of Northern Ireland nationalist politicians. 'John Hume in particular was inclined to scoff at the whole idea of a Protestant backlash as 'bluff'. Vestiges of this thinking remain.'[35] Despite FitzGerald's rather grandiose vision for North–South relations, the Irish government did not try to establish a Council with many significant functions; rather, it thought that a Council should start small and evolve over time. In May 1973, Declan Costello, the Irish Attorney-General, offered a realistic appraisal of what the Council might entail. 'Obviously at the beginning, the functions which it will be possible to give it will be extremely limited and the hope will be that, in the course of time, fuller functions may be devolved to it.'[36] The type of Council it proposed, therefore, suggests that the re-unification of Ireland was not the principal policy of the Dublin government.

The reports of Irish government departments on Council functions

In June 1973, a number of internal meetings took place between representatives from various Irish government departments; their purpose being to establish what functions might be transferred to a Council of Ireland. The archival evidence highlights just how little the Irish departments were prepared to consider devolving to the Council. For example, officials from the Department of Agriculture reported that they 'had not yet given the matter a great deal of thought. It should be borne in mind that many decisions in the field of agriculture were now taken in Brussels'. Noel Dorr, an official from the DFA, stressed that they 'should not exclude the view of a Council of Ireland as an embryo government of Ireland which would one day represent the entire island in the EEC institutions'. Despite Dorr's suggestions, however, officials from the Department of Agriculture were only prepared to recommend that an 'all-Ireland advisory service' on agriculture and fisheries be assigned to the Council.[37]

Discussions by the Inter Departmental Unit on Northern Ireland (IDU) with officials from the departments of health, labour and social welfare, produced comparable proposals. Social welfare officials thought that a Council would have no role to play with regard to social welfare benefits. They pointed out that there might be 'some merit' in harmonising rates of benefit in Northern Ireland and the Republic; however, the Republic's social benefits were significantly lower than those in Northern Ireland, and the 'global cost to the South of bringing its benefits up to those of the North would be about £100 million'. The poor economic position of the Republic meant that this was never a realistic option. Despite Bob McDonagh's appeal to 'include rather than exclude' areas which might be passed to the Council of Ireland, the primary suggestion from the social welfare officials was the establishment of an independent appeals commissioner, under the aegis of the Council.

The department of health, in its submission, outlined the existing high level of cross-border co-operation between the health boards, particularly in the sphere of emergency medicine. It felt that attempting to 'institutionalise' such arrangements would be problematic, particularly how to manage the 'allocation of limited resources'. Health officials avoided advocating any definite plans.[38] Comments made by the department of transport and power were almost identical to those of the health officials, highlighting the cordiality of existing relations and 'considerable co-operation' between Northern Ireland and the Republic in this area. It also envisaged problems in attaching any of the existing areas of co-operation to the proposed Council.[39] The responses from these departments, coupled with reports from the departments of defence and justice, that no function relating to the armed forces or the police should be placed under the control of a Council, adds weight to the suggestion that the Irish government did not seek, in practical terms, to use the Council to pursue Irish political unity.[40]

The above discussions appear to have prompted the DFA to take a more realistic approach to the proposed Council. A DFA memorandum, authored by Garret FitzGerald, written in July 1973, was much more cautious concerning the Council than previously. The document noted that '[b]ecause of the complexity of the issues . . . discussions with departments have not succeeded in producing a clear-cut picture of the functions which a Council of Ireland might have'. While this memo advised 'identifying the structures and functions which would maximise the role of a Council of Ireland', it also recognised that the 'portents for a maximum-type Council [were] not very encouraging'. The memo cited hostile unionist opinion as the reason why such a strong Council was unlikely to materialise, omitting to mention the restrictions placed on the transfer of functions by the Irish departments themselves. FitzGerald argued that the Council should have a three-tier structure, based on the EEC model, comprising ministerial, parliamentary and secretarial bodies. One example of the DFA's slight change of approach was evident in comments regarding the parliamentary body which 'will not in the foreseeable future have anything like the status of a normal parliament. It could, therefore, be rather unreal to give real decision making powers to an Executive committee of that body'. Associating particular ministers with certain portfolios was also thought problematic, since this could 'smack too much of the "Government of Ireland" approach to be politically acceptable to the Unionists'. FitzGerald argued that the proposed Council assembly should have the potential to evolve in the direction of an all-Ireland parliament, but that it was 'unrealistic, even as a negotiating position, to advocate such a status for it in the short run and it must be accepted that it can only have a lesser role for the foreseeable future'. This included providing a forum for politicians from both parts of Ireland to 'get to know and understand each other [and] . . . debate and make proposals' on matters within the competence of the Council. It was thought that the EEC might also restrict the Council's evolution. The common EEC membership of Northern Ireland and the Republic, FitzGerald stated, impinged on 'many of the functions which are appropriate for transfer to a Council of Ireland'.[41]

Further negotiations, July–December 1973

The Prime Minister met the Taoiseach on 2 July 1973 to discuss political developments in Northern Ireland, including the proposed Council of Ireland.

Heath stated that once an executive was established, it would be possible to proceed with the Council discussions. He also said that both governments had 'already agreed that its terms of reference should be open ended, so that it could add further subjects to its remit when it was ready to do so'. A united approach to the Council would diminish the possibility of a split in the executive when it came to discuss the issue on a tripartite basis. Cosgrave, however, was more cautious. He argued that there was a danger that northern unionists would think both governments were 'ganging up against them', and that the SDLP would resent not being consulted about these issues. Both premiers agreed that this problem might be resolved by maintaining strict confidentiality. However, Cosgrave's remark highlighted the difficulties faced by both governments in trying to find a solution acceptable to both communities in Northern Ireland. Heath then mentioned that the question would arise as to 'whether the Irish Government could in some way formally recognise the status of Northern Ireland', and include the concept that its status could only be changed should the majority there so wish. Cosgrave replied that an agreement from the Irish government to 'meet representatives of Northern Ireland on an equal footing in a Council of Ireland would constitute *de facto* recognition of the status of Northern Ireland'. He pointed out the problems involved in amending the Irish Constitution and argued that such formal recognition might cause more problems than it would solve. He did not express any reservation about the *de facto* recognition *per se*, merely the way such recognition might be publicly perceived.[42]

In September 1973, Galsworthy, the British ambassador to Ireland, in a letter to the NIO in Belfast, argued that the Irish government took a 'package deal' approach to the Council of Ireland. He wrote that the Irish government stated that the SDLP required the establishment of a Council of Ireland before agreeing to participate in an executive. Galsworthy replied that the SDLP had indicated to the British that it would join an executive before the formation of a Council, provided there was a clear commitment to its establishment. He strongly suspected that the DFA had attempted to influence the Irish government by arguing that establishing the Council was essential if progress was to be maintained. The DFA wanted 'an elaborate and far-reaching' Council of Ireland, which Galsworthy claimed was 'an obsession with them'. He also feared that the DFA would pressurise the SDLP to insist on the establishment of a Council of Ireland before the formation of an executive.[43] However, there is no archival evidence to support the suggestion that the DFA pressurised the SDLP in this way, and, in any case, the SDLP accepted the formation of an executive before a Council was established. Even if the DFA secretly urged the SDLP to follow its line, that department did not necessarily represent the views of the Irish government (or other Dublin departments).

At a British–Irish meeting on 21 September 1973, the Taoiseach stated that 'unless there was a commitment to a Council, the position of the SDLP would be much weakened'. He did not state that such a Council had to be formed before an executive. This suggests that the policy of the Irish government was simply that there should be a commitment in principle to a Council by the British government. The Taoiseach also added that it was 'important to convince the Unionists that they were not being submerged and it was important to convince the SDLP that there was a firm commitment to a real Council . . . they had shifted on other things but would not shift on the question of a Council'. Heath assured Cosgrave that the British government 'meant business insofar as a Council was concerned'. As outlined in chapter 2, the SDLP was quite flexible on matters such as police reform, but the establishment of the Council was of primary importance to them. The only strong objection expressed by Heath to the structure of the proposed Council was the 'suggestion that the Parliamentary Assembly in the Council could have the say on how a Council should evolve . . . this was a matter for the respective governments'. Little more was said on the subject, and the meeting moved on to security issues, leaving substantial discussion on the matter to another time.[44]

The previous week, officials at the FCO met with Northern Ireland politicians to discuss the Council of Ireland issue. During the meeting with pro-Assembly unionists, Faulkner expressed concern that Heath might say something about a Council which would 'make it impossible for the Unionists to take part in an Executive . . . [they] could not accept a Council of Ireland which had executive powers. All measures to be taken would have to receive the approval of their national parliaments'.[45] This suggested that Faulkner was not fundamentally opposed to executive functions, merely a Council which could act without first consulting both parliaments. Officials also held meetings with members of the SDLP. The latter argued for a Council of Ireland 'with 50:50 representation between North and South' which it thought would be acceptable to unionists. The party admitted that it 'saw the force of the argument that a Council could not meet until an Executive was formed'.[46] This admission adds weight to the earlier suggestion that the SDLP was not influenced by the Irish DFA on this issue.

In early October, Kelvin White wrote to Philip Woodfield commenting on the SDLP's relationship with the Dublin government. He referred to his conversation with the Irish Ambassador to the UK, Diarmuid O'Sullivan. According to White, O'Sullivan spoke of his frequent exasperation with the SDLP; he had tried to 'sow seeds of doubt about the SDLP in Dublin, and he thought Dublin [was] beginning to learn'. He thought the Dublin–SDLP relationship was on a better footing, despite the fact that 'Paddy Devlin and Conor Cruise O'Brien still loathed each other'.[47] O'Sullivan informed White that the detail of the nature of the relationship between the SDLP and Dublin government was unimportant provided the former was 'conscious of some movement between London and Dublin on a Council of Ireland'. The archival evidence does not seem to support the argument of Bew and Patterson that by September 1973 'any significant differences of approach' between the SDLP and the Dublin government on the Council of Ireland had been eliminated. They have argued that, following a series of visits by SDLP leaders to Dublin in September 1973, the Irish government came to support the SDLP's vision of a Council of Ireland with 'substantial powers'.[48] However, as shown in chapter 2, the Irish government had clear differences with the SDLP on policing, and as far as the Council of Ireland was concerned, it was reluctant to devolve substantial powers to that body. It was by no means fully supportive of the SDLP, which sought the creation of a federal, united, 'new Ireland'.

On 26 October 1973, Irish government officials visited Brian Faulkner, at his County Down residence, to relay Dublin's views concerning the Council of Ireland. The officials stressed that the Irish government wished to reconcile people on both sides of the border. The Council could provide contacts between both states, and help 'remove the basis of support for politically motivated violence'. Faulkner recorded his opposition to a parliamentary body attached to the Council, arguing that the 'wreckers on both sides would make it totally unworkable, no matter what voting system was devised.' Given the obstructive behaviour of the hard-line unionist and loyalist members in the Northern Ireland Assembly, his concerns were not without foundation. He also claimed that the Irish 'use of the words "reconciliation" and "Council of Ireland" would not make it any easier for him to sell the concept of a Council to his supporters'. From a unionist viewpoint, '"reconciliation" was seen simply as another word for "reunification" and "Council of Ireland" was inevitably linked with the concept of a council contained in the Government of Ireland Act, 1920'. Faulkner also asked that the Irish government reduce unionist fears by refraining from visiting Northern Ireland, since 'a series of visits by [Dublin] Ministers at the moment would tend to give the impression that the take over from Dublin had already begun',[49] highlighting the problem of how innocuous political events might be perceived by the electorate.

In November 1973, during a meeting between Garret FitzGerald and William Whitelaw, unionist political difficulties were among the matters discussed. Whitelaw was concerned that the SDLP might 'push their [sic] luck too far', resulting in the isolation of Faulkner. It was essential, he argued, that Faulkner's party should have a majority on the executive. The unionist leader had previously informed Whitelaw that he could not form an executive if his party did not have this majority. However, Whitelaw claimed that he 'could, and probably would, give on the mechanics of a Council of Ireland and would, for example, agree to a parliamentary tier'. As noted above, Faulkner thought that a parliamentary tier might be subject to disruption by his loyalist opponents, but he did eventually agree to it. How the proposed Council might be financed was also discussed, and Whitelaw stated that this area 'might not present a great problem' and that all sides should 'not get too excited about it until the details emerged'. However, he pointed out that 'he had to keep reminding people that HM Treasury could not finance every idea proposed by a Council'. FitzGerald replied that the Irish government 'certainly did not regard the U.K. as a "milch cow for the whole of Ireland"'.[50]

The week preceding the Sunningdale conference, discussions in London focused on the Council of Ireland. Whitelaw again emphasised the importance of a declaration on the status of Northern Ireland by the Republic: 'If Brian Faulkner got this he would be very relaxed as he was interested to see an effective Council of Ireland set up.'[51] This meeting was one of Whitelaw's last as Secretary of State for Northern Ireland; he was replaced by Francis Pym on 2 December.

The Irish government considered how the proposed Council might be financed. On 2 November 1973, FitzGerald presented a memorandum to the government, adopting a somewhat unrealistic approach to the issue. He argued that more emphasis should be placed on 'political possibilities and ideals' rather than 'economic and financial strictures'. It stated that the allocation of grants to the Council might not be enough to give it the financial powers necessary to be effective. FitzGerald suggested that the Council might receive motor vehicle duties, a percentage of VAT, or duties from a potential 'wealth tax'.[52] Tax increases, at a time of already high taxation in the Republic, were unlikely to have been popular with the electorate, whatever their views on Irish reunification. The memorandum reflected the importance the DFA placed on the establishment of a strong Council of Ireland compared to their colleagues in other government departments.

The following month (December 1973), all attention focused on the Sunningdale conference, which took place from 6 to 9 December. It is important to note that a Council of Ireland, with executive and harmonising functions, was agreed to by all parties. When the Northern Ireland Executive took office in January 1974, officials from both parts of Ireland considered what executive functions might be transferred to this proposed Council. As well as internal discussions, the officials held meetings on a North–South basis. The deliberations of the Northern Ireland officials did not bode well for proponents of a strong Council of Ireland.

Northern Ireland attitudes to the Council of Ireland

On 4 January 1974, Brian Faulkner resigned as UUP leader, following the Ulster Unionist Council's (UUC) rejection of the Council of Ireland proposals. Faulkner informed the executive that the UUC vote demonstrated the

'great concern among unionists over a Council of Ireland'. The members of
the executive agreed that Faulkner should write to the Taoiseach outlining the
'dependence of the Sunningdale agreement on action by the Republic', with
regard to the status of Northern Ireland and paramilitary violence.[53] Faulkner
expressed these views in person to Liam Cosgrave at a meeting in Dublin on
16 January 1974. He claimed that the result of the UUC vote meant that there
was no hope of his ratifying the Sunningdale Agreement until 'the question
of status was cleared up', and more firm action by the Republic against the
PIRA was forthcoming. He informed Cosgrave that, as far as the SDLP was
concerned, John Hume was the most vocal advocate of a Council of Ireland,
but 'he had the feeling that Gerry Fitt and Paddy Devlin had not got the same
enthusiasm for it'. Faulkner 'agreed that a Council of Ireland was a good thing
for both North and South', but that it should proceed slowly lest it 'smash up
"the whole thing" [Sunningdale]'.[54] Despite his concerns, the meeting with
Cosgrave 'satisfied [him] that there [would be] no going back on the Sunningdale declaration about the status of Northern Ireland' by the Dublin
government.[55]

The Dublin government recognised the potential problems for Faulkner in
proceeding too quickly with the ratification of Sunningdale. The Dublin official Muiris MacConghail noted that the problems for unionists, regarding a
Council of Ireland, would necessitate the government having to 'go somewhat
slower on the Council idea'.[56] This was confirmed by Faulkner, who wrote to
Cosgrave in February 1974, urging greater caution on the Council of Ireland.

> The concept of setting up a Council of Ireland with both a ministerial and
> parliamentary tier creates the impression of an all-Ireland parliament in embryo
> . . . It would be a great pity to see the whole project founder because of an
> insistence on creating the whole structure at once . . . the Council of Ireland is
> proving an obstacle which, if wrongly handled, could bring down the whole
> affair.[57]

It appears that even the nationalist members of the executive recognised this.
One week previously, the executive agreed that there would be 'unacceptable
risks to the stability of the Executive in pressing ahead with a Council of
Ireland in advance of progress on all the other points'.[58]

Following the defeat of moderate unionism in the UK general election on
28 February, Faulkner wrote to the Irish government, commenting on its
apparent inaction regarding paramilitary violence. He stressed his continued
personal belief that a Council of Ireland could make a worthwhile contribution to cross-border relations, and recognised its symbolic importance for 'the
Catholic community' in Northern Ireland. A lack of improvement in the
security situation was the primary reason for this anti-Sunningdale sentiment.
Such sentiment was not confined to proletarian loyalists, but also '[t]he most

sensible and well-balanced people in the professional and business community'. He was implicitly critical of the SDLP which was pressing for a full and prompt ratification of Sunningdale as 'a *sine qua non* for their continuance in the Executive', believing that this might have serious consequences for the executive itself: 'if we cannot find a means to secure for the Council a broader basis of acceptability then the power-sharing experiment is doomed'. This, he argued, would be 'a tragic situation', with incalculable consequences.[59] A draft of Faulkner's letter urged the Taoiseach to push for further action against some specific high profile members of the PIRA by the Republic: 'action against notorious individuals is very important; one Martin McGuinness is worth six "unknowns"'.[60]

Cosgrave replied to Faulkner, expressing the view that postponing the Council's establishment might cause a loss of 'credibility in the Sunningdale package'. The proposed parliamentary tier of the Council posed no threat to unionists, since co-operation between both states could only be conducted at inter-governmental level. 'In view of its minimal functions, and in particular the absence of any financial and legislative powers, the Assembly lacks the features that would make it, in any real sense, a[n all-Ireland] parliament in embryo. It is, as its title implies, a *consultative* body'.[61] While Cosgrave was correct in his assessment, it did not change the fact that unionists perceived it as something more sinister than this: their 'perennial fear was the threat of Irish unification'.[62] Unsurprisingly, the SDLP did not share Faulkner's anxious assessment of the Council of Ireland proposals. John Hume was the most vocal and consistent advocate of a strong Council, and the speedy ratification of Sunningdale. Despite the implications of the February general election results, Hume argued that the time had come to press ahead even more rapidly with the Council of Ireland idea, claiming that support for it would inevitably follow its establishment.[63] This was a serious underestimation of the strength of unionist feeling against a Council of Ireland, as demonstrated in the February 1974 general election. It is questionable whether Hume himself believed this, or if he was merely trying to pressurise the Faulknerite unionists into ratification. However, it is also possible that Conor Cruise O'Brien was correct to assert that Hume was inclined to 'scoff' at the idea of a 'Protestant backlash'. Hume's views regarding Sunningdale were often challenged by Roy Bradford. The latter was genuinely in touch with grassroots unionist feeling and contributed pragmatically to the discussions, tempering the aspirations of the less cautious SDLP members. Bradford was highly suspicious of the southern state, the place of his birth.[64] When the executive met with Merlyn Rees to discuss the general election results, Bradford was pessimistic about the prospects for a Council of Ireland.[65] He argued that the fact that voters who, 'would in normal times be labelled "liberal" or "moderate"', and who now voted for the United Ulster Unionist Coalition (UUUC), should be taken as a signal by the executive to 'put the brakes on political developments until there had been some success on the security front'.[66] His remarks illustrate that, for unionists, progress on a Council was linked to improvements in security and the recognition of the status of Northern Ireland by the Republic, whereas for nationalists, the establishment of the Council was an aim in itself.

As April progressed, the Irish government apparently recognised the potential difficulties faced by Faulkner regarding the Council, and was prepared to accept its gradual, phased introduction. At a meeting in London later that same month, the Tánaiste, Brendan Corish, who was in attendance, informed Harold Wilson that Faulkner faced, many difficulties regarding the formation of the Council of Ireland, and risked losing the support of important allies such as Roy Bradford.[67] Three weeks later, British officials heard from Brendan Halligan, general secretary of the ILP, confirming that Dublin would accept a Council implemented in phases.[68]

During this time, although the ratification of Sunningdale was still unsettled, the executive continued working, despite the divergence of views among its members regarding the effects of the ratification upon the security situation. Roy Bradford, supported by Oliver Napier of the Alliance party, argued that progress would have to be slow if loyalist violence was to be averted. Herbie Kirk, the finance minister, expressed doubt that either a full or partial ratification would have 'any different effect on terrorists who were ... to a large extent internationally motivated'. John Hume, however, continued to apply pressure for early ratification, even though his arguments at times appeared contradictory. On the one hand, he claimed that although Sunningdale could not achieve a reduction in violence, its implementation could enable his party to support the police; on the other hand, he argued that 'if Sunningdale were ratified opposition and violence would collapse'. This demonstrates that unionists were reluctant to ratify Sunningdale before nationalists supported the police, while nationalists were not prepared to support the police before Sunningdale was ratified. The damage resulting from this lack of support was noted by both Brian Faulkner, and the SDLP's Ivan Cooper. Cooper recognised that his party's refusal to publicly support the security forces was 'a real impediment in the minds of Protestants' to moderating their attitudes to the Council of Ireland. Faulkner concluded the meeting with his thoughts on what was necessary to make progress on Sunningdale. His recommendations highlighted the importance of public perception to the prospects of political progress: '[the] SDLP must be enabled to demonstrate that they are not selling out and [the pro-] Assembly Unionists must be able to show that they are not bringing [Sunningdale] about by stealth'. Despite these potential difficulties, Faulkner recommended that the executive aim to settle the matter 'by the end of this month'.[69]

The previous month, at a meeting with Harold Wilson, Faulkner had suggested that there might be a possibility that the SDLP would agree to 'a scheme . . . designed not (he said) to replace the Council of Ireland, but to work towards it more gradually . . . a "Fabian approach"'.[70] Faulkner was proved correct when the SDLP's executive members agreed to a phased implementation of the Council of Ireland on 13 May.[71]

That same day, a scheme to implement the Council of Ireland in phases was devised by members of an executive sub-committee. It recommended holding a meeting with Irish ministers by the end of May to agree 'upon the phases by which, and conditions in which, the Council of Ireland provisions of Sunningdale can be implemented'. This proposed meeting would precede a tripartite conference where the formal agreement would be ratified, including the Dublin government's declaration recognising the status of Northern Ireland. Minimal reference was to be made to the Council of Ireland: 'It was agreed that a Council of Ministers [should] be initially established and the Council of Ireland subsequently developed on the basis agreed between the Irish Government and the Northern Ireland Executive.'[72] The following day, the Assembly voted on a motion calling for a renegotiation of the Sunningdale Agreement, unaware of the executive's decision to phase the implementation of the Council of Ireland. This motion had originally been tabled in March by John Laird, who represented the West Belfast Loyalist Coalition.[73] The anti-Sunningdale motion was easily defeated, but the vote was to have serious repercussions for the longevity of the power-sharing executive. Loyalist opponents of the agreement, organising themselves under the banner of the Ulster Workers' Council (UWC), called for a halt to industrial activity in protest at the result of the vote. The UWC was unaware that a decision to implement the Council of Ireland agreement in phases had been reached by the executive, since no public announcement to this effect had been made. The strikers controlled the main electricity generating station at Ballylumford. Its workforce was almost exclusively Protestant. Intimidation of workers by loyalist paramilitaries was also widespread.[74] On 28 May, the executive collapsed, after the unionist members tendered their resignation. Loyalist opposition to the Council of Ireland was the primary reason for its downfall.

How the Council of Ireland might have evolved has been the subject of much debate. According to Alvin Jackson, despite the inherent safeguards, the Council was 'an impressive step towards reunification'.[75] Richard Bourke has argued that the Council proposed in 1973 was 'a new look version of the old [1920] Council of Ireland'.[76] The 1920 Council was explicitly designed to create a single Irish legislature. Thus, the implication is that the 1973 Council had similar aspirations. Alternatively, Michael Kerr has emphasised the unionist veto with regard to the development of the Council: '[i]ronically, while [the

Council] was seen as being a vehicle towards a united Ireland, constitutionally it was nothing of the sort and, as it stood, it could become no such thing'.[77] The Council's potential to evolve into an all-Ireland government will now be examined.

Northern Ireland proposals for Council of Ireland functions

In January 1974, Kenneth Bloomfield wrote a memo concerning potential Council of Ireland functions. He saw the Council as having executive functions and a consultative role. The consultative role would pose few problems, since there had been much ongoing co-operation in areas such as railways and fisheries. However, Bloomfield foresaw difficulties with the Council having any 'harmonising functions'. This was due to the difference between the economic positions of Northern Ireland and the Republic. The latter was notably less wealthy than its northern counterpart. Unless Northern Ireland was to 'break its parity links with Great Britain, hold back development, or even to reduce its standards, such harmonisation can in various fields only be achieved by a more rapid development on the Southern side'. Given that public services were of a noticeably lower standard in the Republic, his caution seems entirely logical.

His paper defined 'executive functions', which could be interpreted in two possible ways, 'Pattern A' and 'Pattern B'. Pattern A functions were '[e]xecutive decisions', on certain matters agreed by the Irish government and the Northern Ireland Executive which a Council of Ministers would take for the whole of Ireland 'which are now taken separately by the two governments'.[78] 'Pattern B', referred to 'executive actions', whereby certain services should become the direct executive responsibility of the Council of Ireland. For example, 'the staffs engaged in tourist work in the Department of Commerce and its Dublin counterpart would transfer to the Council and conceivably then, or at a later stage, the staffs of the two tourist boards'.[79] However, Northern Ireland departments had, '*at this stage* comparatively little to recommend by way of Pattern B'. Northern Ireland officials sought to continue the existing co-operation with the Republic, without formalising or centralising it. Bloomfield's paper demonstrates that Northern Ireland officials sought to avoid the Republic gaining a significant say in their affairs. They were also ill-disposed to transfer executive functions to the proposed Council. The report of the Northern Ireland Department of Health and Social Services (DHSS) on potential Council of Ireland functions was broadly representative of the proposals made by other Northern Ireland departmental officials. These reports confirm the disparity in the standards of public services between Northern Ireland and the Republic. Few officials exaggerated these disparities, with the possible exception of the Northern Ireland agriculture department.

The memo noted that the Northern Ireland health department 'decided some years ago [before EEC membership] to provide free emergency services on a "Good Samaritan" basis for residents of the Republic taken ill or involved in accidents while visiting Northern Ireland'. However, the Republic did not reciprocate this gesture, or even acknowledge it. It was only with the advent of EEC membership that there was 'some degree of reciprocity' in respect of these services. The document observed that, 'since Northern Ireland's health services are generally much more highly developed than the Republic's, the South has hitherto looked to the North for help rather than vice versa'. The health officials were not opposed to future co-operation, but highlighted the considerable damage to Northern Ireland's interests which the 'harmonisation' of health services on an all-Ireland basis might have wrought. Bloomfield noted that there was 'still such a wide disparity between social security systems and benefits in the two countries as to severely restrict the scope for reciprocity'. As we have seen, a similar point was made by officials from the Republic. However, the DHSS officials thought co-operation could occur regarding 'super-specialities in the hospital field' on an island-wide basis, 'joint ventures' on industrial development in border areas and 'the common (but small) problem of itinerants on both sides of the border.' These rather humdrum functions were unlikely to have been what most Northern Ireland nationalists envisaged for a Council of Ireland. Northern Ireland officials were keen to maintain the higher levels of services they enjoyed, equivalent to those in Great Britain. Only one department appears to have been reluctant to co-operate with the Republic for ideological reasons. This was the Northern Ireland agriculture department. Northern Ireland and the Republic were competitors in the export market, which may partially explain this reluctance. However, the northern agriculture officials claimed, in apparent sincerity, that that cross-border co-operation might be hindered by the 'climatic and geographical differences' between the Republic and Northern Ireland. The officials did, however, suggest that the Council may have a role to play in the sphere of agricultural research.

A further memorandum authored by Bloomfield, Sir David Holden and K. R. Schmield, mentioned the disagreements between Northern Ireland and the Republic concerning potential Council functions. There were some differences regarding the issue of electricity generation. Northern Ireland officials strongly argued that electricity generation should not be devolved to the Council, and that each government should 'retain through its appropriate department the ability to intervene to deal with emergency or deadlock situations.' The chairman of the NIES feared that staff on both sides of the border would object if the proposed Council was made responsible for electricity generation. It was also feared that 'the public in the North who are opposed to a Council might take the excuse to withhold payment of bills'. Northern

Ireland officials believed that members of the Dublin steering group had received 'a firm political directive in general terms to push as much as possible into the area of executive action without adequate thought being given to the practical difficulties'. They also commented that it seemed unusual 'for the "generalists" on the Southern side to take up again [sic] points which their own "specialists" (i.e. those who had detailed experience of the subjects under consideration) had for the most part conceded in discussions'. It is probable that the 'generalists' were officials from the Irish DFA. Bloomfield, Holden and Schmield stressed that they were not suggesting that greater cross-border co-operation was 'undesirable ... [but] ... commitment in principle to new institutions, the implications and problems of which have not been thought through ... would work against and could destroy the development of that co-operation between the two parts of Ireland which is the objective of the present discussions'.[80]

In March 1974, Brian Faulkner wrote a memo to his executive colleagues concerning potential Council functions. It is likely that his thinking was influenced by the results of the February general election. Faulkner's memo concluded that the Council of Ireland must be implemented in stages, and its functions were likely to be limited.[81] Northern Ireland officials and unionist politicians were therefore cautious about the proposed Council. The SDLP advocated a powerful Council, but was forced to agree to its phased implementation. However, the Republic of Ireland was also reluctant to devolve too many executive functions to the Council. During the 1973–74 period, this reluctance became increasingly apparent. Eventually, Dublin decided that the Council of Ireland should be little more than a symbolic institution with few executive powers.

The Republic of Ireland's Council proposals

In April 1973, a memorandum from the Department of the Taoiseach, considered a fundamental question regarding this institution from an Irish point of view: 'Why do we want a Council?' Three basic aims were suggested.

(a) To provide for harmonious common action in certain limited matters where the interests of North and South overlap – such as fisheries, tourism and railways.
(b) To act as a symbolic North–South link to induce the bulk of the minority in the North to accept political structures which are now to be created in the area; and sufficient to allow Dublin to accept the new settlement.
(c) To involve the common interests of North and South in pragmatic projects of mutual benefit ... in this way to promote reconciliation on both parts of the island on a converging path ... without ultimately specifying the ultimate shape or timetable for possible unity between them.[82]

Proposal (a) was considered the most acceptable to unionists, whilst proposal (c) was the policy of the previous Fianna Fáil government. This was to remain the coalition government's policy, but the 'emphasis [was] now on the process rather than the results'. The government's policy, therefore, was to pursue reconciliation between North and South. The memo stated the government should work 'towards an indeterminate form of unity by consent over an unspecified period'. This was a somewhat ambiguous phrase, lacking in clarity. The memo further suggested that, if the government was serious about creating a '*Council of Ireland*' rather than a '*Council of Northern Ireland*', 'an embryo institution which we hope will develop towards unity in Ireland', it must take political risks by granting 'substantial functions', to the Council.[83]

> As a minimum general principle we should certainly try to ensure that all areas of co-operation in practical matters between the administrations North and South come *explicitly* under the aegis of any Council – even if there seems to be no practical need for such formal sponsorship in particular cases.[84]

However, by early 1974, Dublin departments were less enthusiastic about the creation of a powerful Council of Ireland. A government study group, established in December 1973, noted that officials from Northern Ireland were likely to oppose every area of cross-border co-operation which the Republic suggested. The report stated that the Irish government had instructed the officials 'to have as many executive functions as possible examined for possible transfer to the proposed Council'. However, these assessments did not necessarily correspond with a desire to transfer significant functions. Indeed, Irish officials had already ruled out important matters from possible transfer, reducing the powers of the Council to 'negligible proportions'. Consequently, it was concluded that 'the only powers which could be transferred . . . would be general powers of government in relatively unimportant areas'. This report also recognised that 'the Council was sometimes seen as an unnecessary intervention between the relevant departments, both in the Republic and Northern Ireland', given the fact that co-operation already existed at official level between departments in both jurisdictions, a point which was also made frequently by Northern Ireland officials. Therefore, the responsibilities which the Republic was prepared to concede to the Council were not particularly important. The department of health, for example, 'decided before Sunningdale that the main business carried out under the Department . . . ought not to be transferred to the Council of Ireland at this stage'. Furthermore, no timetable was suggested as to what stage such business might be transferred in future. The department of industry and commerce was equally reticent towards the Council. Indeed, because of the politically sensitive nature of attempting to administer 'industrial development planning on an all-Ireland basis', the department could only recommend that the establishment of an all-Ireland film industry, and development co-operation in border areas be put under the aegis of the Council.[85]

A joint report by northern and southern officials noted the potential difficulties involved in devolving the powers of local authorities to a Council of Ireland. Both sets of officials realised that 'the provision of houses for people in Kerry and Antrim for example is an activity which can be administered best in Kerry and Antrim'. Potential problems were also envisaged regarding civil servants reluctant to move to other parts of the island, 'particularly if the transfer involves movement to somewhere like Armagh'.

Whilst the Irish were reluctant to give the Council significant powers, the officials had 'from the start acted on the assumption that the Government wish [was] that the Council should be more than just a consultative forum'. This implied that the Council should have some decision-making powers. However, it did not imply that the government sought to use the Council as a means of bringing about Irish unity. Indeed, since the Council's powers to make decisions would be confined to relatively uncontroversial areas, its potential to evolve into anything resembling an all-Ireland government was negligible.[86] Thus the vision of a Council of Ireland, with extensive functions, as contained in the April 1973 document, had, by February 1974, been replaced by a decidedly more banal, moderate one.

This moderation of Irish government policy was complete by February 1974, when the government accepted that any Council of Ireland must only have limited powers. Like their Northern Ireland counterparts, Irish officials ruled out 'certain major functions' from being transferred to the Council on the basis that 'it would be impracticable to transfer them to the proposed Council as executive functions'. These included housing, road construction, and health and social security services.[87] Excluding key areas of government policy from transfer does not suggest that the Irish government desired to use a Council of Ireland as a means to politically reunite the island. It could also be argued that excluding these functions represented a realistic assessment of what the Irish government could afford in the challenging economic climate of the 1970s. Yet, Irish governments of various hues seldom avoided using irredentist rhetoric regarding partition, so this exclusion of functions can be regarded as significant. Furthermore, it highlights the difference between the united Ireland ideology of the Republic and the realities of the practical policies pursued by the Irish government. Therefore, despite the stated policy in the Irish government's April 1973 memorandum, promoting reconciliation leading to the 'convergence' of both states, the policies actually *pursued* by the Dublin government, in the crucial year of 1974, were different. By 1974, the Irish government had accepted any Council must only be a symbolic institution with relatively insignificant powers. Thus, the Irish government did not attempt to use the Council of Ireland as a means towards achieving reunification, and was reluctant to cede any of its sovereign responsibilities to such a Council.

Conclusion

The evidence presented herein illustrates the problematic nature of Farrington's claim that the Dublin government sought to use the Council of Ireland to advance the cause of Irish unity.[88] If unification was indeed the policy of the Dublin coalition, it would presumably have sought to devolve as many important functions to the proposed Council as possible. However, the issue was complex, and there were distinct limits to the policy the Irish government could pursue, since its government departments did not wish to cede any significant functions to the Council. The functions recommended for transfer by the Irish departments were akin to those advocated by their Northern Ireland counterparts. In fact, the British government arguably had fewer objections to what powers could be transferred to the Council than the Irish government. As shown above, the British government was flexible towards the Council, but was cautious regarding its financing. However, in contrast to the Irish government, the only areas excluded from consideration by the British government were in the fields of health and security.

Any early enthusiasm for a relatively strong Council of Ireland, particularly among DFA officials, was negated by the attitudes of other Irish departments. By February 1974 the limits imposed on the Council of Ireland by the Dublin authorities were clearly visible. Also, since unionist consent was required to allow the Council to become more powerful, its potential to bring about reunification is questionable. However, of perhaps even greater importance, is the fact that the responsibilities the Dublin government were prepared to transfer were minor. This raises the question of the extent to which civil servants and permanent officials act as restraining influences on government ministers. DFA officials appear to have attempted to drive a particular, pro-Irish unity policy forward, despite the reticence of other Irish civil servants and politicians. Indeed, it seems clear that few Dublin ministers pressed for a strong Council of Ireland. The influence of officials and civil servants might have been stronger in Northern Ireland, where the nationalist members of the executive were in favour of a strong all-Ireland body. The Northern Ireland officials' recommendations mirrored the proposals of unionists. This is primarily explained by self-interest (due to the poor standard of public services in the Republic), rather than any inherent unionist bias on their part.

The contention that the Dublin government, in concert with the SDLP, sought a strong Council of Ireland due to a path dependent approach to the issue, as argued by Cillian McGrattan, is also problematic.[89] Firstly, by treating both the SDLP and Dublin government as a single entity, it assumes that both had the same policy goals. However, contemporary documents clearly demonstrate how widespread the differences between the SDLP and the Irish government were. There was no question of the SDLP's conception of an all-Ireland body, similar to its proposed National Senate, being accepted by the Dublin government. Secondly, this path dependent approach only allows for the evolution of policy in one direction, and not for changes which result in a moderation of original aims, as was the case regarding the significant diminution of the Republic's conception of the Council of Ireland over the 1973–74 period.

The proposed Council of Ireland was designed as a mechanism whereby the SDLP, and other Northern Ireland nationalists, could operate within the framework of the new constitutional arrangements for Northern Ireland. Officials within the DFA sought to transfer all existing areas of co-operation to the Council of Ireland, and were the most favourably disposed to the Council becoming more powerful over time. This disposition was influenced by their wish to see the institutionalisation of an 'Irish dimension'. A Council of Ireland was considered the most effective means of securing this goal, but the DFA was flexible in this regard, and was prepared to consider other options if this was not the best way to guarantee a role for Dublin in Northern Ireland affairs.

The prospect of a very powerful Council of Ireland being formed was curtailed by a lack of will on the part of officials from both northern and southern states to devolve significant executive powers to that body. Effectively, it could only make decisions on mundane and uncontroversial matters, on the basis of strict unanimity. Therefore Farrington and McGrattan overstate the importance of a strong Council of Ireland to Irish government policy, and the extent to which the Dublin coalition was committed to Irish unity. Too much emphasis is placed on archival material written by DFA personnel, and not enough attention is paid to the material from other Irish departments. The powers which the Irish government was prepared to devolve to the Council of Ireland did not include power to alter the constitutional relationship between Northern Ireland and the UK without unionist consent and, as such, this could hardly be construed as an attempt to form an embryonic all-Ireland government. Some unionists, however, genuinely believed the Council's attempted establishment represented the first step in the process of a gradual diminution of British sovereignty in Northern Ireland. The perception of what the Council had the potential to become, and its power to mobilise the forces working-class loyalism, resulted in the aforementioned UWC strike and the demise of the power-sharing executive. Had loyalists been aware of the private discussions concerning the Council, it might have seemed less threatening, although it may not have been received any more favourably, following the February general election results. The loyalist slogan 'Dublin is just a Sunningdale away' captured unionist emotions, and crystallised their fears. However, it was ultimately an erroneous characterisation of the importance of the Sunningdale Council of Ireland to Irish government policy.

Notes

1 See C. Farrington 'Reconciliation or irredentism: the Irish government and the Sunningdale Communiqué 1973', *Contemporary European History*, xvi: 1 (2007), pp. 89–107.
2 Ibid., p. 98.
3 C. McGrattan, 'Dublin, the SDLP and the Sunningdale agreement', pp. 61–78.
4 Ibid., p. 69.
5 Bew, *Ireland*, pp. 395–6.
6 Lee, *Ireland*, p. 47.
7 Jackson, *Ireland*, p. 341. For Craig, the Free State and the Council of Ireland, see P. Buckland, *James Craig: Lord Craigavon* (Dublin: Gill and Macmillan, 1980), pp. 57–59.
8 M. Kennedy, *Division and Consensus: The Politics of Cross-border Relations in Ireland, 1925–1969* (Dublin: Institute of Public Administration, 2000). See also E. Tannam, *Cross-border Co-operation in Northern Ireland and the Republic of Ireland* (Basingstoke: Palgrave Macmillan, 1998).
9 *Irish Independent*, 19 February 1965.
10 This department was re-named the Department of Foreign Affairs in 1971. NAI, DFA 2000/14/444, memorandum by K. Rush, 7 October 1969.
11 TNA, CJ4/390, report on North–South discussions on possibilities for economic co-operation, 20 April 1971.
12 Ibid., Prime Minister's meeting with Mr Lynch, Munich, 4 September 1972.
13 UUP, *Towards the Future* (Belfast Ulster Unionist Party, 1972). See chapter 1.
14 This was deemed preferable to an extradition treaty by the UUP.
15 SDLP, *Towards a New Ireland* (Belfast: SDLP, 1972).
16 *Victory for Democracy, Law and Justice* (Belfast: VUUP, 1972). The other loyalist groups associated with this publication were the Ulster Loyalist Council (ULC), Loyalist Association of Workers (LAW), and the Ulster Defence Association (UDA).
17 Ulster Vanguard, *Government without Right* (Belfast: Ulster Vanguard, 1973).
18 *1973 Assembly Election Manifesto*.
19 Ibid.
20 TNA, CJ4/390, Sir J. Peck to UKREP Belfast, 4 January 1973.
21 TNA, CJ4/391, meeting between Mr Lenihan and Sir A. Douglas-Home, 15 January 1973.
22 See Mair, *Irish Party System*, pp. 12–61 and Boland, *Fine Gael*.
23 See chapter 1.
24 TNA, CJ4/391, minute by K. P. Bloomfield, 'The status of Northern Ireland and North/South relations', 17 January 1973.

25　Initialled 'WN 31/1/73'. TNA, CJ4/391, minute by K. P. Bloomfield, 'the status of Northern Ireland and North/South relations', 17 January 1973. GEN79 was the Northern Ireland policy committee of the British government.

26　Ibid., memorandum by W. Whitelaw, 'Cabinet: Northern Ireland. Council of Ireland', 24 January 1973.

27　Ibid., memorandum by W. Whitelaw, annexe to 'Cabinet: Northern Ireland. Council of Ireland', 24 January 1973.

28　Ibid., 'Council of Ireland: second meeting with Irish government representatives', 23 January 1973.

29　Ibid., 'Council of Ireland: preliminary discussions with the Irish government', 14 February 1973.

30　TNA, FCO 87/228, J. Peck to K. White, 5 February 1973. See chapter 1 for analysis of SDLP's condominium proposals.

31　Ibid., F. F. Steele to J. Peck, 7 February 1973.

32　NAI, DT 2004/21/2, meeting between the minister for foreign affairs and the Prime Minister Edward Heath, 15 March 1973.

33　Ibid., 'Memorandum delivered to the British Government, 15 March 1973 on the instructions of the Government re British White Paper on Northern Ireland to be published in March, 1973'. The British White Paper did not accede to the Irish demands.

34　TNA, CJ4/391, note of a meeting in London, 4 April 1973.

35　NAI, AG 2004/1/254, memorandum by C. Cruise O'Brien, 'The North', 22 March 1973.

36　Ibid., D. Costello to G. FitzGerald, 30 May 1973.

37　NAI, DT 2005/7/653, preliminary consultations with Departments. Agriculture, Fisheries and Lands, 15 June 1973.

38　Ibid., preliminary consultations with Departments. Social Welfare, Labour and Health, 11 June 1973.

39　Ibid., preliminary consultations with Departments Transport and Power, 8 June 1973.

40　NAI, Department of Justice (JUS) 2005/24/8, preliminary consultations with Departments of Defence and Justice, 18 June 1973.

41　Ibid., memorandum for the government, Department of Foreign Affairs, report by minister for foreign affairs on the possible structures and functions of a Council of Ireland, 30 July 1973.

42　TNA, CJ4/391, note for the record, 2 July 1973. Emphasis as original.

43　TNA, CJ4/392, Galsworthy to NIO Belfast, 18 September 1973.

44　NAI, AG 2004/1/254, Heath visit, 21 September 1973.

45　TNA, FCO 87/228, meeting between the PUS [Permanent Under Secretary] and members of the Unionist Party, 11 September 1973.

46　Ibid., meeting between the PUS, Mr Fitt, Mr Hume, Mr Devlin and Mr McGrady, 10 September 1973.

47　Ibid., White to Woodfield, 4 October 1973. The letter concludes with the observation that O'Sullivan had been written off by the 'younger element' within the DFA for being too 'pro-British', which, White observed, may be read as a 'synonym for "honest and ineffective"'.

48 See Bew and Patterson, *British State*, p. 58.

49 NAI, DT 2005/7/624, meeting between S. Donlon (DFA) and D. Nally (DT) with B. Faulkner, 26 October 1973.

50 NAI, JUS 2005/24/8, meeting between G. FitzGerald and W. Whitelaw at the NIO, London, 8 November 1973.

51 Ibid., meeting between the Minister for Foreign Affairs and the Secretary of State for Northern Ireland, 30 November 1973.

52 Ibid., memorandum for the government [by Minister for Foreign Affairs]. 'Council of Ireland – Financing', 2 November 1973.

53 PRONI, OE/2/1A, executive minutes, 8 January 1974.

54 NAI, DT 2005/7/653, Cosgrave and Faulkner meeting, 16 January 1974.

55 PRONI, OE/2/3, executive minutes, 18 January 1974.

56 NAI, DT 2005/7/651, minute by M. MacConghail, 5 January 1974.

57 PRONI, OE/1/35, Faulkner to Cosgrave, 6 February 1974.

58 PRONI, OE/2/6, executive minutes, 28 January 1974.

59 PRONI, OE/1/35, Faulkner to Cosgrave, 31 March 1974.

60 Ibid., draft of letter from Faulkner to Cosgrave.

61 Ibid., Cosgrave to Faulkner, 13 February 1974. Emphasis as original.

62 A. F. Parkinson *Ulster Loyalism and the British Media* (Dublin: Four Courts Press, 1998), 35.

63 PRONI, OE/2/10, executive minutes, 5 March 1974, note of a discussion on the political situation following the results of the general election, 28 February 1974.

64 Bradford was born in Rockcorry, Co. Monaghan.

65 Rees replaced Pym as Northern Ireland secretary following Labour's victory in the February general election.

66 PRONI, OE/1/24, executive minutes, meeting between the Secretary of State and the Northern Ireland Executive, 26 March 1974.

67 TNA, PREM 16/145, meeting of the Prime Minister and Mr Cosgrave, 5 April 1974.

68 TNA, PREM 16/144, minute by K. C. Thom 'Anglo-Irish Affairs', 26 April 1974.

69 PRONI, OE/2/19, executive minutes, 7 May 1974.

70 TNA, PREM 16/145, record of a conversation between the Prime Minister and the Chief Executive, 1 April 1974.

71 See chapter 5 for the details of this agreement.

72 PRONI, OE/2/21, executive minutes, annex – Sunningdale – outline scheme, 13 May 1974.

73 Jackson, *Home Rule*, p. 278.

74 See chapter 5.

75 Jackson, *Home Rule*, pp. 272–3.

76 Bourke, *Peace*, p. 213.

77 Kerr, *Imposing*, p. 64.

78 PRONI, OE/2/6, executive minutes, 28 January 1974, executive memorandum (EXMEMO) 13/74. Council of Ireland: Memorandum by the Secretary to the Executive, 28 January 1974.

79 Ibid.

80 PRONI, OE/2/19, memo by K. P. Bloomfield, D. C. B. Holden and K. R. Schmield. executive minutes, 7 May 1974.

81 PRONI, OE/2/9, EXMEMO 77/74, The Sunningdale Agreement, A. B. D. Faulkner, 8 March 1974.

82 NAI, DT 2004/21/2, Council of Ireland memorandum, 16 April, 1973.

83 Ibid. Emphasis as original.

84 Ibid.

85 NAI, DT 2005/7/665, proposals for Northern Ireland Settlement, transfer of functions to the proposed Council of Ireland, [January 1974].

86 Ibid., discussions between officials of the government of the Republic of Ireland and officials of the Secretary of State for Northern Ireland, 18 December 1973.

87 Ibid., transfer of functions to the proposed Council of Ireland, report by Irish Officials, February 1974.

88 Farrington, 'Reconciliation or irredentism', pp. 89–107.

89 McGrattan, 'Dublin, the SDLP and the Sunningdale agreement', pp. 61–78.

4

Social and economic policy and the executive in office

A wide range of socio-economic policy matters were discussed by the power-sharing executive, despite its brief tenure. Issues such as job creation and educational policy were subjects of particularly high priority for the power-sharing administration. The downturn in both the regional and world economies at the time, created a particularly challenging environment for an executive that desperately needed a popular social and economic programme in order to build support for power-sharing in the wider community.

Ian McAllister has noted that the predominance of the constitutional issue in Northern Ireland had resulted in the 'tendency to relegate discussion of socio-economic matters to a secondary role'.[1] The records of the executive, however, show that social and economic policy making was considered of primary importance by parties from both sides. Analysing the executive's socio-economic proposals will help to establish to what extent ideological differences affected the executive's ability to agree on these policies. It might be assumed that the UUP – with its historic connection to the British Conservative Party – would be less inclined to favour high public spending and extensive social welfare provision than the professedly socialist SDLP. Analysis of contemporary party political literature and archival material, however, demonstrates that this was not so. What emerges, with some minor exceptions, is a broad cross-party consensus with regard to socio-economic policy. Ideological differences between the nationalist and unionist parties on the executive do not appear to have adversely affected its ability to agree on the parameters of an extensive socio-economic programme.

The economic context of the time will also be taken into consideration. The executive took office during a period of economic difficulty in the United Kingdom and the wider world. In considering this wider economic context, it will be shown that the executive was keenly aware of the fiscal constraints facing its proposed socio-economic programme and believed that, while necessary for Northern Ireland's development, some aspects of the plan might not meet with the approval of HM Treasury in Whitehall.

The economy of Northern Ireland in historical context

A discussion paper entitled *Northern Ireland: Finance and the Economy* was published in 1974 by the NIO. It stressed the 'economic interdependence of Northern Ireland and Great Britain', and argued that the state of the economy in Northern Ireland, at any given time, was 'much influenced by the overall state of the United Kingdom economy and by the direction of economic policy at Westminster'.[2] Given that Northern Ireland was an integral part of the United Kingdom, it might reasonably be assumed that this observation was superfluous. However, on closer inspection the inclusion of this rather obvious statement seems justified. Fifty years of devolved government in Northern Ireland had led to an allegedly widespread belief that the region was, somehow or other, financially autonomous of Westminster. The financial relationship between Stormont and Westminster was complex; many political figures did not understand how it worked. Indeed, Merlyn Rees noted, in a September 1974 memorandum, that there was widespread ignorance among the region's politicians about Northern Ireland's economic state. He hoped that the publication of *Finance and the Economy* might engender more economic 'realism' among Northern Ireland's politicians.[3] This was particularly true of those in the unionist community who were given to favour independence for Northern Ireland, or some form of Dominion status.

Given that some politicians struggled to grasp the realities of the economic relationship between Great Britain and Northern Ireland, confusion among the electorate regarding how Northern Ireland paid for its public services was understandable. The confusion over the nature of the economic connection between the Treasury and the Stormont government is another example of the difference between how the public perceived a political process and how it functioned in reality. The authors of *Finance and the Economy* sought to dispel some of the myths concerning Northern Ireland's finances. The paper illustrated that the relationship between Northern Ireland and Great Britain, during the 1970s, was characterised less by interdependence, and more by the almost absolute dependence of Northern Ireland on grants-in-aid from Great Britain.[4] Historically, this pattern of dependence on monies transferred from Westminster began early in the life of the northern state.

Alvin Jackson noted that 'there was never any lasting and coherent formula which governed the financial relationship between Belfast and London'.[5] This view was corroborated in the work of James Mitchell, who characterised the financial relationship between London and Stormont as one of 'ad-hocery' (sic) and inefficiency.[6] However, it is clear that, at the time of the enactment of the *Government of Ireland Act*, it was expected that Northern Ireland would be more solvent than proved to be the case. For example, the British government originally expected the Northern Ireland government to contribute

£7.92 million per annum from its revenues to help pay for services provided to Northern Ireland by the British government, such as the defence of the realm. This was known as the 'imperial contribution'. However, this contribution was gradually reduced to a residual charge in the token amount of £500,000 per annum and abolished completely under the terms of the *Northern Ireland Constitution Act* in 1973.[7] This occurred because the Northern Ireland government was increasingly unable to generate enough revenue to pay for its internal public services, much less an additional imperial contribution. Northern Ireland's lack of resources, however, did little to engender a culture of thrift among successive governments in the region. Whenever Northern Ireland administrations were short of revenue, the British government of the day consistently responded with a series of measures guaranteeing that these shortfalls would be met by HM Treasury in London, provided that Northern Ireland's taxation and social benefits were of the same rate as those in Great Britain. Arguably the most significant accords between the Northern Ireland government and HM Treasury occurred in 1946 and 1954 respectively. The 1946 arrangement established the principle of parity in taxation and services while the 1954 agreement was designed to allow the Northern Ireland government 'leeway' to spend more on such services as public housing, standards of which lagged significantly behind the rest of the UK.[8]

One reason why successive Stormont administrations struggled financially was due to the high level of unemployment in the region, which was consistently among the highest in the United Kingdom. This forced the Stormont government to spend increasing amounts of the region's revenue on unemployment benefits. However, despite the region's small size, there were significant geographical differences in the numbers of people out of work. Unemployment rates tended to be much higher in Catholic areas and in the western counties of Northern Ireland.[9] *Finance and the Economy* highlighted these striking geographical anomalies in the jobless rates. For example, unemployment in unionist dominated Larne was only 3.3 per cent. However, in the predominantly nationalist town of Strabane, situated on the western border of Northern Ireland, unemployment reached a demoralising 17.7 per cent, a level that was to rise significantly over the following decade.[10] Graham Walker has claimed that the discrepancies between Protestant and Catholic employment rates 'cannot be reduced to naked sectarian exclusiveness', as factors such as the location of industries and the focus on industrial apprenticeships in many Protestant schools were also important.[11] Low pay among those who had work was also a significant problem, and the proportion of those receiving family income supplement was five times higher per capita in Northern Ireland than in Great Britain. Stormont's ever-increasing welfare bill was one of the primary reasons why HM Treasury's financial subsidy to Northern Ireland increased over the years. The amount of the Westminster subsidy to

Northern Ireland rose most sharply after 1966. In that year, the financial subsidy to Northern Ireland was £51 million. By 1974 it reached £313 million.[12] Northern Ireland's dependence on financial aid from Great Britain was therefore abundantly clear. The task, faced by the executive, of tackling social problems (particularly job creation), was formidable. This might have mattered less if the executive had been formed at a time of general prosperity, but 1973 proved to be a year of financial uncertainty not only for the UK but also for the world economy as a whole.

The global economy faced two serious crises in 1973. Firstly, the Bretton Woods agreement collapsed in that year. This agreement, set up in 1944, established a system of fixed exchange rates, using the US dollar as the world's reserve currency. The dollar was itself convertible into gold, and countries that held supplies of dollars could exchange these for gold, at a fixed rate of $35 per ounce. The system depended largely on prudent monetary policy within the USA. However, during the 1970s spending in the US grew significantly, inspired by foreign policy commitments and rising defence costs, particularly the prolonged war in Vietnam. This led to rising inflation, and, due to fixed exchange rates, threatened other major economies. It also resulted in 'balance of payments' deficits for many countries, including the United Kingdom.[13] Fearing a run on its gold reserves, the USA suspended the dollar's convertibility into gold in 1971. In that year, sterling was floated, and by 1973 the Bretton Woods system collapsed entirely, as other major economies floated their currencies.

Secondly, the Organisation of Petroleum Exporting Countries (OPEC), declared an oil embargo in October 1973. The embargo was instigated during the Yom Kippur War between Israel and a coalition of Arab states led by Egypt and Syria (including Iraq and Jordan).[14] The Arab oil producers targeted the embargo at nations friendly to Israel, particularly the US.[15] The OPEC action resulted in the quadrupling of the price of oil within a matter of months, increasing the cost of industrial production and distribution. The oil crisis thus produced a concurrent rise in inflation, which reached 'unprecedented levels' after 1973, and also produced a rise in unemployment.[16] The effects of the crisis might have been less dramatic in Britain, had not the country's coal miners been involved in a pay dispute with the government. During this dispute, the NUM instituted an overtime ban, which drastically reduced the supply of coal. In December 1973 the government had to introduce a three day working week to cut down on the use of energy.[17] *Time Magazine* reported that over 700,000 workers were forced to claim benefits due to lay-offs in industry.[18] The strike eventually resulted in the calling of the February 1974 general election which had serious political consequences for the power-sharing executive. Northern Ireland, however, did not share the same hardships as Great Britain. It was spared the introduction of a three day week, for which Lord Dunleath of the Alliance Party expressed his gratitude in the Assembly in December 1973.[19] Economic output in Northern Ireland actually peaked in 1973, but witnessed sharp falls thereafter.[20] Despite state support, high levels of unemployment remained one of the key economic problems in the region. The Assembly held a Private Member's debate on the subject in November 1973, although this had to be suspended following violence by some of the loyalist members.[21] To these general economic problems were added many social problems, one of these being the lack of good quality housing. That being so, what policies did the Northern Ireland political parties espouse to tackle the serious difficulties facing the region?

The economic and social policies of the Northern Ireland political parties

Despite their differing ideological outlooks, there was a significant degree of accord among the Northern Ireland parties on many socio-economic issues. By analysing the election literature of the various parties, it is possible to identify the three main issues that were given most attention. These were: the debate within unionism concerning the economic implications of the union with Great Britain; the high levels of unemployment in the region; the attitudes of the various parties towards the EEC.

The largest party, the UUP, strongly favoured a devolved regional government in Northern Ireland. Following the prorogation of Stormont, it advocated a Bill of Rights, to ensure fair treatment for all sections of the community in such areas as education, employment, free speech and freedom from discrimination on the grounds of religious belief.[22] This pro-devolution stance was reinforced the following year in the UUP's *Fundamental Principles* pamphlet. The party was not prepared to countenance any scheme that would 'take Northern Ireland out of the United Kingdom', such as a Unilateral Declaration of Independence (UDI), a federal UK, federal Ireland or negotiated independence.[23] However, following Faulkner's decision to share power with the SDLP, there were a number of anti-Sunningdale unionists, such as John Taylor, who were prepared to consider a form of negotiated independence for Northern Ireland.[24] However, there was little appetite for independence within the UUP, even among those who opposed power-sharing.

The overwhelming opposition to independence by most of the UUP was in marked contrast to the ambiguous attitude of the Ulster Vanguard movement, which later became the VUPP. The VUPP never had a clear political programme. It more closely resembled a coalition of individuals opposed to any reform of the old Stormont system, particularly anything involving power-sharing with nationalists. Its lack of clear policy goals is evident from its attitude towards the economic benefits of the union with Great Britain. Vanguard's publication, *Community of the British Isles* (1973), seems to suggest that some form of independence might be economically beneficial to Northern Ireland. The pamphlet, the authorship of which has been erroneously attributed to David Trimble, quotes the Director of the Centre for the Analysis of Conflict at University College London as saying that, 'the smallest of areas can be viable as a state, e.g. Tonga, provided it is part of a wider economic system'. The document argues that Northern Ireland, as part of the EEC, or 'merely as a unit in the international trading system, would be as viable as any other state'.[25] In general, however, Vanguard opposed the EEC. One reason for this opposition was that EEC membership would mean that the *Safeguarding of Employment Act* would only be allowed to continue for a further seven years. The Act prevented 'uncontrolled immigration into Northern Ireland and [was] a security against large inflows of Irish immigrants dedicated to the annexation of the state by the Irish Republic'. Similarly, Vanguard's *Dominion of Ulster* document claimed that Northern Ireland's lack of resources would not necessarily prevent it from economic success. It asked how the State of Israel prospered, which, when it was established, possessed 'little more than a few drought plagued citrus groves'.[26] (The pamphlet's author was presumably unaware of the Deutsche Mark (DM) 3 billion in Second World War reparations paid to Israel by the Federal Republic of Germany (FRG) after 1953.)[27]

However, evidence of Vanguard's inconsistency on the question of the economic arguments for the union is apparent in its 1973 election manifesto, *Power for the People, Power for Our Land.* Here, the VUPP made the case for a federal UK, with 'up to a dozen state or regional parliaments sharing the primary powers of government'. The example of post-war West German federalism was cited as a positive exponent of that system. It was thought that a federal system would be more beneficial to Northern Ireland's future prosperity.[28] Federalism was also supported by the loyalist micro-party, the Volunteer Political Party (VPP), which was associated with the UVF. It argued that in a federal system, poorer parts of the UK would form alliances to defend the interests of peripheral regions.[29]

Unlike other unionist parties, the DUP focused exclusively on the constitutional question in its electoral literature during this period. The DUP was also unique among unionist parties in its explicit support for the total political integration of Northern Ireland with the rest of the UK. Any diminution of the link with Great Britain was thought to be potentially damaging to Northern Ireland, particularly from a financial point of view. The party leader was highly critical of the VUPP for espousing a federal system or independent Northern Ireland. If the link with Britain was broken, Paisley argued, 'we are finished economically'.[30] The party political literature clearly shows that most unionist parties deployed economic, as well as ideological, reasons in support of the union with Great Britain.

The issue of unemployment was also highlighted by almost all the political parties in the region. In general, the Northern Ireland parties, whether nationalist or unionist, supported interventionist policies to stimulate the economy and maintain high levels of employment. The non-sectarian, pro-union, Alliance Party argued that as many as 34,000 new jobs had to be created to tackle the unemployment problem in the region. To help create these jobs, it was suggested that the state should provide financial assistance to industry. In return for this support, it was proposed that the state would take ownership of the companies it assisted 'and would receive most of its profits'. These profits would then be reinvested to create new jobs.[31] The government actually pursued similar policies to those advocated by Alliance, such as the heavy subsidisation and subsequent nationalisation of the Harland and Wolff shipyard, in order to prevent mass unemployment in loyalist East Belfast.

The VUPP favoured similar policies to Alliance, supporting state investment in industry to tackle the unemployment problem.[32] The UUP placed less specific emphasis on its policy to deal with unemployment, but it does not appear to have differed greatly from the other parties in terms of the details of its policy. Its attitude to unemployment is perhaps best summarised by the remarks of Roy Bradford in a 1973 television interview. He argued that the question of job creation in Northern Ireland was not a 'doctrinal' one. Public and private industry had to be used in concert if the problem was to be tackled effectively, since the market alone would not solve Northern Ireland's economic problems. Northern Ireland was, in Bradford's view, pioneering a 'new type of mixed economy', with the finance to do so coming from the British government in the form of grants or loans.[33] Marc Mulholland has shown that Bradford and his unionist colleague on the executive, Herbie Kirk, had argued in the 1950s and 1960s that Northern Ireland should have an 'autonomous economic strategy from Britain'.[34] These views were thus consistent with the UUP's devolutionist approach to the union: devolution recognises not just differing identities within a polity, but a devolved government can pursue policies which take regional problems into account.[35] There was also an element of localism evident in the UUP's attitude to the provision of employment. The party argued that 'jobs in Northern Ireland should, if possible, be filled by Northern Ireland people.'[36] It might be surmised that this was a muted reference to people from the Republic seeking work in Northern Ireland. Given the UUP's links with the British Conservative Party, it might be assumed that there would be significant differences between its unemployment policies and those of the more explicitly left-wing parties. Closer examination, however, shows that policy differences in this regard were not particularly pronounced.

Despite the SDLP claiming that it planned to promote and adopt 'radical socialist policies', the economic and social themes that it stressed were markedly similar to those highlighted by the pro-union parties.[37] Like those parties, unemployment was the main socio-economic concern of the SDLP. It criticised successive Stormont governments for subsidising capital intensive industries as a means of creating employment, such as those which required large factories with expensive machinery. It argued that corporations merely exploited these subsidies, and that not enough jobs were created to justify the investment.[38] The party favoured subsidising labour intensive industry which required less expensive plant and equipment. Thus the SDLP only differed from the pro-union parties on how industrial subsidies should be targeted, not on the subsidies themselves.

Poor housing, one of Northern Ireland's most significant social problems, was seen by the SDLP as an opportunity for economic growth in the region.[39] It planned to control urban land prices and make low interest capital available to the housing executive to enable it to build 25,000–30,000 housing units a year until 1975. These plans involved a 'radical expansion of the construction industry', which the party felt would lead to a significant increase both in employment and economic output in general. Some elements of 'economic nationalism' were evident in the SDLP's policies. Because of the importance of the agricultural sector in both Northern Ireland and the Republic, the party advocated an all-Ireland agriculture spokesman within the EEC to ensure the case for Ireland's farmers was heard in Brussels. The attitudes of the Northern Ireland agriculture department to cross-border co-operation, mentioned in the previous chapter, suggest that this was an unlikely prospect.

The other democratic socialist party in Northern Ireland, the Northern Ireland Labour Party (NILP), produced some detailed socio-economic plans during the 1973 Assembly election campaign. The party argued that Northern Ireland needed 16 per cent economic growth per annum, over an unspecified period of years, to bring its standards up to the EEC average. The party asserted that 'Northern Ireland has been governed throughout its history by Tories and therefore by the economic philosophy of Toryism'.[40] This is debatable on two points. Firstly, while Northern Ireland Prime Ministers were all members of the UUP, which had historic links with the Conservative Party, Northern Ireland was ultimately subordinate to Westminster, which at different periods in history had Tory, Labour and coalition governments. NILP's argument also ignored the post-1945 consensus between Labour and the Conservatives on the desirability of high levels of employment, using public funds to do so where necessary.[41] Secondly, the subsidies that were paid to Northern Ireland throughout the years, suggest that there was little attempt made to curtail public spending in the region, and the UUP was not ideologically averse to using public money to stimulate the economy. Despite periodic electoral successes, the NILP's political approach ultimately failed to capture the electorate's imagination.

The most radical of all economic policies was advocated by anti-Sunningdale republican parties. Only one of these, OSF, was legal and could stand for election. PSF was illegal at this time, and could not do so, but it did produce literature outlining its socio-economic aims. In Northern Ireland, OSF was known as the Republican Clubs. Both northern and southern branches of the party followed the line espoused by party leader, Tomás Mac-Giolla. The Republican Clubs professed radical socialism, but it has been argued that it was a 'communist party pretending it wasn't a communist party'.[42] To tackle unemployment on the island of Ireland, OSF's 1973 party conference called for the nationalisation of Ireland's banks and natural resources, and the establishment of Soviet-style collective farms to increase agricultural productivity.[43] Unsurprisingly, the Republican Clubs' policies were electorally unpopular, and the party received only 1.8 per cent of the vote in the 1973 Assembly election.[44] OSF also fared badly in the elections in the Republic that same year. Research carried out among Dubliners in the period 1972–73 regarding their attitudes to various social groups found that out of seventy categories, 'communists' were sixty-ninth in order of popularity, ahead only of 'drug pushers', which may partially explain the party's poor performance in the southern state.[45] PSF's economic policies were markedly similar to those of OSF. The former's publication, *Éire Nua* (1971), stated that the wealth of Ireland belonged to the Irish people, who should control the means of production, distribution and exchange.[46] Given that PSF's economic policies were similar to the Republican Clubs, it is highly unlikely the party would have attracted much electoral support, had it been able to contest the Assembly elections.

Another major theme, which emerges from contemporary electoral literature, is the attitudes of the parties to the socio-economic advantages and disadvantages connected to EEC accession. Of the pro-union parties, Alliance was the most supportive of the UK's entry into the EEC. It believed that Northern Ireland's status, as a peripheral and economically disadvantaged region of the UK, meant that Northern Ireland would receive significant structural funds from Brussels to develop its infrastructure. Alliance also believed that EEC membership would mean increased economic support for local agriculture, which the party considered was in need of financial investment.[47] Little mention is made of the EEC in the UUP literature. Faulkner's memoirs, for example, appear to be neutral on the subject.[48] Until 2009, the UUP sat with the Europhile European People's Party (EPP) in the European Parliament. Following a merger with the British Conservative party, however, it joined the Eurosceptic European Conservative and Reformist (ECR) group.[49]

The party most in favour of the EEC was the SDLP. As mentioned, it believed that Ireland should have a common agriculture spokesman in

Brussels. Apart from the economic advantages of the EEC, the SDLP argued that membership might provide a possible stimulus for Irish unity, as the importance of national borders diminished over time.[50] The SDLP's support for the EEC made it unique among nationalist parties: both wings of Sinn Féin were strongly opposed to the EEC, seeing within it the features of capitalism and imperialism. The SDLP's position contrasts sharply with that of the VUPP, which generally opposed EEC membership.[51] The other main loyalist party, the DUP, avoided mention of the EEC, but it is known from subsequent events that Ian Paisley was strongly opposed to it, seeing the 'hand of the Vatican at work' in Brussels.[52] A 1992 DUP pamphlet expressed scepticism at an EC dominated by German premier Helmut Kohl, French President François Mitterrand and EC Commission President Jacques Delors: 'all faithful R[oman] C[atholic]s'.[53]

It is clear that Northern Ireland faced significant economic problems in the 1970s. The economy of Great Britain and the world economy in general performed poorly during that time. In this context, how did fiscal and other constraints affect the social and economic policies of the Northern Ireland Executive? Were there signs that ideological and personal differences within the executive, and pressure from higher civil servants on its members, might have placed restrictions on its socio-economic policies and prevented it reaching agreement?

Constraints on the socio-economic policies of the Northern Ireland Executive

There were, on paper, few significant differences in the socio-economic policies of the three executive parties. It appears that the ideological differences between the governing parties had little impact on their ability to formulate these policies. It has been suggested that *Steps Towards a Better Tomorrow*, the executive's social and economic plan, was primarily the work of John Hume and Paddy Devlin. The document was apparently accepted by the unionist and Alliance members of the executive with little amendment. McAllister contends that this demonstrates 'how little socio-economic thinking had been undertaken by the other two parties prior to the Executive's formation'.[54] Perhaps this is so, but as the examination of the political party literature demonstrated, there were remarkably few differences between the three executive parties on these issues anyway. It is therefore likely that the general acceptance of Hume and Devlin's proposals reflects the overall similarities between the parties on non-constitutional issues, rather than a lack of imagination on the part of the pro-union parties. Maurice Hayes, then an official in the Department of Health and Social Services, has stated that what was surprising about *Steps Towards a Better Tomorrow* was that it was 'less radical than might have been expected'.[55] Hayes's view was undoubtedly influenced by the scale of the social problems facing Northern Ireland at the time. Robert Ramsay, Faulkner's former Principal Private Secretary, noted that social problems were 'so deep-seated and the means at the disposal of the various individual agencies trying to deal with them so inadequate, despite the vast total costs of the alleviating programmes overall'.[56] In these circumstances, Hayes expected more radical policies to have been formulated by the executive, and concluded that its proposals reflected the general political conservatism that was at the heart of the political culture in Northern Ireland. According to Hayes, the executive's policies were:

> [V]ery much in the nature of social policy in those Butskellite days when both Labour and Conservative governments resided in the middle ground, and there was little difference between them in their ability to use public money for social engineering or to buy their way out of trouble, and nothing in their manifesto so radical as to cause a reaction.[57]

There were two good reasons why the executive would not have wished to cause a reaction in publishing its policy proposals. Firstly, the executive was unpopular enough without advocating social policies that could be deemed too radical by the Northern Ireland electorate. Indeed, many loyalists believed that the pro-Sunningdale unionists were radical enough in accepting a Council of Ireland and the SDLP as coalition partners. If the executive focused on popular issues such as improving health services, housing and employment, then its policies were less open to criticism from its opponents. Secondly, and just as importantly, the executive was cognisant of the difficult fiscal climate in which it had to operate. Its 'Statement of Social and Economic Aims' stressed that the 'economic climate in the world as a whole, and in the United Kingdom in particular, is bound to influence the rate [at] which we make progress'.[58] A memorandum for the executive recognised that it would have to be accepted that 'the UK government must retain control over public expenditure' and that the executive could not expect more than the amount allocated to it by Westminster for its services.[59] Despite this, the executive's proposals involved extensive public spending, including the construction of 20,000 new houses over a five-year period.[60] This kind of expenditure was unlikely to have been welcomed by HM Treasury. A memorandum prepared by officials from the Northern Ireland Department of Finance suggested that even if the cost of the executive's socio-economic programme was cut by a quarter, it would still require an additional payment from Westminster of £410 million over the five-year period of its implementation from 1974 to 1979. It was reported that unofficial warnings from the Treasury, and the NIO, suggested that such a large additional sum of money was unlikely to be granted. Faulkner's memoirs, however, claim that London officials made clear to the executive that 'within reasonable limits, money was no obstacle'.[61] It is therefore difficult to judge the extent to which financial constraints may have affected the executive, had the latter lasted longer. Ideological differences, however, did not hamper its ability to agree on a programme for government to any significant extent.

Most accounts of those who were part of the executive, or officials closely associated with it, emphasise the good relations that existed between the executive parties and the overall effectiveness of its ministers. Robert Ramsay has argued that, despite their lack of experience in government, John Hume, Paddy Devlin and Austin Currie were 'competent performers . . . at operational level'; 'the new administration was a success'.[62] Unsurprisingly, Ramsay's view is supported by Devlin, who has highlighted the executive's competence and efficiency. Later, Brian Faulkner would provide a more balanced account. Although generally complimentary about the administration, he stressed that its efficiency had sometimes been exaggerated by its supporters.[63]

Faulkner thought that achieving consensus between members of the executive was essential if the administration was to survive.[64] Ministers therefore operated on the principle of 'collective responsibility'. This required that all members of the administration be responsible for executive decisions. Any member who disagreed with a decision should request that the issue be discussed again by the executive. If no consensus was possible, that minister would then resign from office. Ministers also undertook not to publicly criticise each other for any policy decisions that they disagreed with.[65] Faulkner went to a great deal of effort to ensure that good relations developed between the unionist and SDLP ministers. At a personal level, this included pretending to understand Gerry Fitt's jokes, which were 'invariably scabrous'. Fitt, for his part, attempted to defuse tensions whenever they arose during executive meetings, supporting Faulkner wherever possible.[66] Although serious interpersonal issues existed between Roy Bradford and Paddy Devlin, these did not include socio-economic issues, and mainly concerned the implementation of the proposed Council of Ireland.

The continuation of the rent and rates strike by members of the nationalist community was a potential source of tension within the executive regarding socio-economic policy. The unionist finance minister, Herbie Kirk, began pressurising Currie to encourage tenants to end the strike voluntarily. Those who refused would have payments deducted from social welfare benefits, and would be subject to an additional collection charge of twenty-five pence per week to cover administrative costs.[67] Paddy Devlin, himself a former participant in the strike, would be responsible for deducting benefits. There is no archival evidence that the SDLP ministers threatened to refuse to co-operate with Kirk. Neither is there evidence that Devlin objected to the collection charges scheme until the UWC strike began in May. Three days into the strike, Devlin informed the Secretary of State that he would resign unless action on ending detention was taken. However, following the Dublin and Monaghan bombs, the resignation was never tendered (and the money was never collected) since the UWC strike made the executive focus its attention on the issue of the ratification of Sunningdale and maintenance of essential services.[68]

Assessing the extent to which civil servants influenced the policies of the executive is difficult, for a number of reasons. The influence of civil servants on policy formulation would probably have been more visible if the executive had held office for a longer period of time. Paddy Devlin has suggested that during the executive's tenure, Stormont civil servants were to the fore in producing new policy initiatives which they had been unable to do under the previous unionist government.[69] However, Devlin also argued that some of the senior Northern Ireland civil servants, who had spent their careers under successive unionist governments, made 'no secret of their scorn for [the SDLP] and doubts about our capacity to do the job'. When Devlin arrived at the Ministry of Health and Social Services, on his first morning in charge, he recalled that his desk had been piled high with files, 'an old trick to deter a new minister'. Austin Currie has similarly claimed that he felt that some senior officials had difficulty accepting him. However, this did not include the two most senior officials in Devlin and Currie's departments.[70] Ken Bloomfield's recollections are more favourable to senior civil servants than those of Devlin; in Bloomfield's interpretation these officials displayed only a 'guarded wariness' towards the SDLP in government, after having previously only worked with a single party.[71] Overall it does not appear that these minor tensions caused significant problems for the new administration. If any officials were to exert significant influence on the executive's policies, it is likely that they would be British officials at the NIO. Since August 1969, the London government had been scrutinising the Northern Ireland administration more closely, and had established the position of a UK Representative to Northern Ireland (UKREP), whose role was to advise the Stormont government as to whether or not its policies would be acceptable to Westminster.[72] Whilst the 1973 Northern Ireland Constitution Act restored devolved government, Northern Ireland became more financially integrated with the rest of the United Kingdom when the act became law, with overall levels of spending determined by Westminster. Any special increase in spending in the region would have to be justified to HM Treasury.[73] Given the state of the UK economy as a whole, the Treasury would understandably have been reluctant to accede to these demands. However, Faulkner's argument that, within reason, the money would have been found, must also be considered. Overall, it remains difficult to judge the extent to which Whitehall might have restricted the scope of the executive's socio-economic programme due to the latter's brief term of office.

The policies of the executive in office

The legislative output of the Assembly was 'fairly meagre': twelve measures (legislative proposals) were introduced, of which only four went through all stages. Two of these were financial measures.[74] However, the records of the executive show that the administration had planned a wide range of socio-economic initiatives. At an early stage, the executive decided to take steps to assist more vulnerable members of society, and struggling enterprises affected by the increased price of fuel due to the OPEC action. The DHSS planned to offer an additional payment of twenty-five pence per week to those in receipt of family income supplement to assist them with the increased cost of heating oil. Similarly, the Department of Commerce planned to assist electricity and gas companies to offset the deficits incurred by them as a result of statutory price controls.[75] These measures were unanimously approved by the executive, and it appears that, from the outset, there was an attempt to balance progressive social welfare policies with support for private industry, where necessary. Such an approach was consistent with the various pre-election commitments of all the executive parties. This may have been regarded as populist, but it would undoubtedly have alleviated some hardship for the unemployed and those on low incomes.

One of the more ambitious initiatives of the executive concerned education policy. The minister responsible, Basil McIvor, planned to introduce an expansive nursery schools programme, and also the provision of non-denominational or 'integrated' schooling for older children in an effort to tackle sectarianism in the region. It was envisaged that nursery schooling would be available to every child in Northern Ireland, before commencing primary school. The project was capital intensive, as it was thought necessary that nursery schools should be purpose-built on suitable sites. It would have been inappropriate to attempt to attach nursery schools to existing, denominational or state primary schools since this 'would militate against integrated nursery education in the areas concerned'.[76] The plan also proposed that children with learning disabilities would not to be segregated from the wider student body. Officials at the Ministry of Education thought that 800 nursery teachers, and the same number of assistants, would have to be employed to administer the system. The cost of providing this service was estimated at £6.5 million. There was general approval for the nursery education plans in the Assembly, especially among pro-executive parties. Faulknerite unionist Ronald Broadhurst supported the proposal citing the 'Jesuit dictum that a youth is made in the first seven years of his life'.[77] The plan is perhaps typical of the policies of the executive: socially progressive, but arguably unrealistic in terms of delivery. Even more ambitious was the executive's plan to introduce integrated education at primary and secondary levels as an optional alternative to the existing state and voluntary schools.[78] These 'shared schools', run by the state, would have representatives from both Protestant and Catholic churches as members of the boards of management. McIvor recognised that any church involvement might be open to objection, but what was important was to get the scheme underway, as he did not think it would 'get anywhere by trying to fight all battles at once'. He also acknowledged that the plans were likely to cause considerable controversy, since integrated education had long been a contentious matter in Northern Ireland. However, he thought that this might actually benefit the executive, since the policy was 'put forward to give practical support to the spirit of power-sharing and the development of community harmony', and to encourage inter-faith co-operation on schools policy.[79] How realistic this goal was, during a period of polarisation among the communities in the region, was questionable. The February general election results could have done little to encourage notions that community harmony was an imminent possibility. While recognising that the scheme would only 'touch on the edge of the [sectarian] problem', it was thought worthwhile to continue on the basis that new attitudes might be created throughout the schooling system. It was also thought desirable that the executive should be seen to show an example in respect of cross-community initiatives. The Alliance party supported the ending of religious segregation in schools in its 1973 Assembly election manifesto. Further evidence of the executive's plan to tackle sectarianism can be seen in its moves to ban the tattooing of minors, some of whom were being tattooed with 'sectarian and political markings' which were deemed to be 'a real danger to them'.[80]

McIvor also informed the executive that he wanted to abolish the '11 plus' selection examination for grammar schools, not because he was against academic selection *per se*, but 'to remove the concept that is unfortunately attached to it as "failure" of those . . . not selected for grammar schools'. Both Alliance and the VUPP supported the idea of abolishing this selection test.[81] However, the proposed schemes on integrated and nursery education, and plans to abolish the '11 plus' examination, were not implemented by the power-sharing administration, due to its premature collapse. It was not until 1981 that Northern Ireland's first integrated school opened, with McIvor as its founding chairman. Although the plans were probably too expensive to have been approved in full, they demonstrate the executive's awareness of the sectarian problem in Northern Ireland, and a willingness to take extensive steps to minimise the problem over time. They also demonstrate the executive's desire to take action on integration at the earliest possible opportunity in a child's lifetime, in a bid to stop sectarian attitudes taking hold at a young age.

Despite the adverse world economic climate, the executive did enjoy some success on the job creation front, and succeeded in attracting some foreign investment to Northern Ireland. John Hume announced in the Assembly that Strathearn Audio, a Belgian manufacturer, would establish a factory in Belfast, thereby creating 1,500 jobs. The investment was made possible with the assistance of state grants from the Northern Ireland Finance Corporation (NIFC).[82] Unfortunately, Strathearn never achieved its target, closing a few years later, despite a government investment of over £10 million.[83] In 1974, The German firm Grundig, which already had a base in Northern Ireland, planned to create 400 new jobs in Newry. Its chief executive, and honorary consul of the FRG, Thomas Niedermeyer, was kidnapped by the PIRA in December 1973.[84] Brian Faulkner sent wishes of support to Niedermeyer's family at the time and thanked 'German industries and nationals' for all they had contributed to 'the economy and life of Northern Ireland'.[85] As a result of Niedermeyer's abduction, however, Grundig decided not to open an additional Northern Ireland plant at Newry.[86] There is evidence that paramilitary intimidation affected other German industrialists based in Northern Ireland. Niedermeyer's successor as honorary consul of the FRG, and swimwear factory boss, Jürgen Gradel, was confronted at gunpoint by paramilitaries at his home.[87]

While unemployment in Northern Ireland was above the UK average, some areas of the region actually suffered from a shortage of labour. An Assembly debate heard that Craigavon was one such region. John Hume attributed this to the unstable security situation in the region, and the fact that people were generally afraid to move outside their own communities. 'There is little doubt that people generally in Northern Ireland, largely because of unsettled conditions, have not been willing to move from their own areas and there has been a reluctance to move to Craigavon. There is no doubt about that'.[88] Overall, in co-operation with the Central Planning Unit, staffed by Northern Irish and British civil servants, 4,000 new jobs were created in the first half of 1974.[89] It is likely that many companies planned to create these jobs before the executive took office, and it is therefore difficult to quantify the success of its job creation policies. However, it seems clear that Hume as Minister of Commerce energetically attempted to attract new investors to the region, and may well have achieved success given more time.

Conclusion

This chapter has shown that the ability of the Northern Ireland Executive to implement its proposed social and economic programme was severely curtailed by the world economic climate, and the economic circumstances of the United Kingdom at the time. The executive's programme may have been too expensive to have been implemented in full, given that it had to be paid for by the British government at a time when the Treasury was understandably seeking to economise. Despite this, the government appears to have been generally sympathetic to the aims of its socio-economic programme. Its social and economic programme was progressive in general, although the subsequent fall of the executive, after only five months, makes it difficult to allow for a definitive judgement on its policies. There was also an element of populism in the executive's socio-economic policy plans. While not necessarily admirable, this was understandable as a means of creating a broader base of support for the power-sharing institutions. The executive also aimed to take steps to tackle sectarianism, although it collapsed before these schemes were introduced.

The complex financial relationship between Northern Ireland and the government in London has also been outlined. Successive Westminster governments, of various political persuasions, provided generous grants to the devolved government in Belfast when it became clear that this was necessary to ensure that living standards in Northern Ireland would not fall too far behind those of other regions in the United Kingdom. One of the main reasons for the subsidies paid by HM Treasury was the high unemployment rate in Northern Ireland. The government's economic policy towards Northern Ireland was in the broad sense Keynesian, in that it used fiscal policy to maximise employment creation.[90] Peter Hall has argued that British economic policy from 1970 to 1989 was marked by the move from 'Keynesian to monetarist modes of macroeconomic regulation', where control of inflation replaced full employment as government's primary economic priority.[91] However, this was not the case where Northern Ireland was concerned. Indeed, the rate of British subsidy increased hugely over that period, from £313 million in 1973 to £565 million in 1975–76. Public money was also poured into job creation schemes regardless of their long-term sustainability.[92] This illustrates how the region was financially dependent on Great Britain and demonstrates that an independent Northern Ireland would not have been financially viable. Despite these figures, there were those who believed that an 'independent Ulster' could survive and indeed prosper, mainly those with VUPP sympathies. In general this view was not widely held among unionist politicians or indeed loyalist paramilitaries. It might be the case that a minority of loyalists were prepared to accept a fall in living standards, if it meant a return to the old Stormont system and the end of the Council of Ireland proposal. They may even have shared the sentiments of VUPP Assemblyman and UDA leader Glen Barr of Londonderry, who was apparently 'prepared to live on spuds and salt for this Province'.[93]

Despite the generally adverse economic climate in Northern Ireland, one industry continued to flourish. Health minister Paddy Devlin reported to the Assembly that he was conducting investigations into the plethora of massage parlours which were recording an increasing trade in the Belfast area. The matter was raised in the Assembly by Lord Dunleath.

> Lord Dunleath: [Can the Minister confirm that the] increased number of massage parlours are not under the umbrella of his Department . . . [and] would he not consider it his duty to sample personally some of them and report back to this Assembly?
> Hon. Members: Hear, hear.[94]

Devlin accused Dunleath of attempting to 'rub him up the wrong way', before stating that no money would be 'spent by me personally or by the Department' on such services. On Devlin's advice, action taken by the authorities ensured that most of these premises were permanently shut down.[95] Devlin was subsequently praised for his performance as a minister by Faulkner, who particularly admired his commitment to the most vulnerable in society.[96]

In economic matters, Northern Ireland politicians, of various parties, were not overly constrained by ideological dogma. Generally, if an initiative helped to bring much needed employment to the region, it mattered little whether it was done by private enterprise, state investment or a combination of the two. The economic attitudes of Northern Ireland politicians of all parties, whether pro-or-anti-Sunningdale, were perhaps best summed up by Armagh SDLP Assembly member, Seamus Mallon.

> We cannot afford to say, 'Is this industry private owned, because if it is not then, as a good Conservative, I cannot have it?'; nor can we afford to say, 'Is this industry state owned, because I am a socialist and it must be state-owned?' What we want is industry. We are not terribly worried at this stage who owns it.[97]

Public money was used to temporarily alleviate unemployment, such as the government training scheme in Dungannon, County Tyrone, profiled in a 1973 British television documentary, which provided unemployed men in the area with one year's industrial employment at a local factory. It was hoped that a private company would eventually take over the factory and create permanent jobs. However, the men who participated in the scheme were pessimistic about their prospects. When asked what the unemployed people of the town did, the men offered a bleak insight into the lives of out-of-work people in Northern Ireland at the time – although there was also an element of black humour in some of their remarks.

> Well, you have a wide selection . . . you have the bookies shop, you have a choice of seventeen pubs in the town . . . [If] it's a big day you go to chapel or church on a Sunday and it's a big outing, you know. Or sometimes it was an electric

bacon slicer going in [to a shop] . . . everybody goes out to look at it, you know . . . apart from that there's nothing.[98]

It appears that there were few departures from the general principles espoused by the executive parties in their election manifestos and the policies pursued while in government. Archival evidence illustrates the lack of ideological dogma in economic and social matters among most parties, as well as the similarity between many of the social and economic policies of the nationalist and unionist parties. Tensions within the executive, while occasionally pronounced, tended to be related to political or security matters, rather than socio-economic differences. Paddy Devlin's threat to resign was a political decision based on the continuation of internment, and should not be read as a sign that the executive was inherently unstable. Overall, the relationship between the governing parties was good and, under the chairmanship of Faulkner, ministers usually managed to reach consensus. Equally, the relationship between the executive and the civil service does not appear to have been under any significant strain, the only tensions being minor ones between some SDLP members and officials with unionist sympathies. These tensions were of insufficient magnitude to affect the day-to-day work of the administration. There is no compelling documentary evidence that the executive was ever irreconcilably divided on matters of economic or social policy during its tenure. Had the UWC strike not occurred, it would appear that sufficient consensus existed within the executive to implement a coherent social and economic programme, albeit perhaps a more limited one than initially envisaged, due to adverse financial circumstances. The UWC strike, and its aftermath, is examined in the following chapter.

Notes

1 I. McAllister, *The Northern Ireland Social Democratic and Labour Party: Political Opposition in a Divided Society* (London: Macmillan, 1977), p. 62.

2 *Northern Ireland: Discussion Paper. Finance and the Economy* (London: HMSO, 1974), p. 1.

3 TNA, CAB, political situation in Northern Ireland, memo by Secretary of State, 6 September 1974.

4 *Finance and the Economy*, p. 19.

5 Jackson, *Home Rule*, p. 205.

6 J. Mitchell, 'Undignified and inefficient: financial relations between London and Stormont', *Contemporary British History*, xx: 1 (2006), pp. 55–71.

7 Jackson, *Home Rule*, p. 205; *Finance and the Economy*, p. 19.

8 *Finance and the Economy*, p. 16.

9 Ibid., p. 8; Jackson, *Home Rule*, p. 221; B. Rowthorn and N. Wayne, *Northern Ireland: The Political Economy of Conflict* (Cambridge: Polity, 1988), p. 70.

10 *Finance and the Economy*, p. 5.

11 G. Walker, 'The Protestant working class and the fragmentation of Ulster Unionism' in M. Busteed, F. Neal and J. Tonge (eds), *Irish Protestant Identities* (Manchester: Manchester University Press, 2008), p. 367.

12 *Finance and the Economy*, p. 19.

13 P. Subacchi, 'From Bretton Woods onwards: the birth and rebirth of the world's hegemon', *Cambridge Review of International Affairs*, xxi: 3, p. 352.

14 A. Sela, 'The 1973 Arab war coalition: aims, coherence and gain distribution' in P. R. Kumarswamy (ed.), *Revisiting the Yom Kippur War* (London: Frank Cass, 2000)' p. 42.

15 J. Amuzegar, *Managing the Oil Wealth: OPEC's Windfalls and Pitfalls* (London: I. B. Tauris, 2001), p. 32.

16 D. Wass, *Decline to Fall: The Making of British Macroeconomic Policy and the 1976 IMF Crisis* (Oxford: Oxford University Press, 2008), p. 16; T. A. Knoop, *Recessions and Depressions: Understanding Business Cycles* (Santa Barbara: Praeger, 2nd edn, 2010), p. 86.

17 P. Clarke, *Hope and Glory: Britain 1900–2000* (London: Penguin, 2nd edn, 2004), p. 338.

18 *Time*, 14 January 1974.

19 *Northern Ireland Assembly: Official Report of Debates*, vol. 1, col. 1895, 18 December 1974.

20 *Northern Ireland Assembly: Official Report of Debates*, vol. 2, col. 143, 24 January 1974.

21 Ibid., col. 1221, 21 November 1974.

22 *Towards the Future: A Unionist Blueprint* (1972), pp. 13–17.

23 *The Unionist Party: Fundamental Principles* (1973), p. 1.

24 *Newsletter*, 11 April 1974.

25 *Community of the British Isles* (Belfast, 1973), pp. 15–16. Trimble was Vanguard's North Down Publications Officer in 1973. The pamphlet was apparently the work of Stewart O'Fee, see D. Godson, *Himself Alone: David Trimble and the Ordeal of Unionism* (London: HarperCollins, 2004), pp. 36–41. Trimble's historical writings are discussed in H. McDonald, *Trimble* (London: Bloomsbury, 2000), pp 87–91.

26 *Dominion of Ulster*, pp. 9–10.

27 N. Balabkins, *West German Reparations to Israel* (New Brunswick: Rutgers University Press, 1971), p. 129.

28 *1973 Election Manifesto: Power for the People, Power for Our Land.* (Belfast, 1973).

29 Volunteer Political Party, *Manifesto: October 1974 Election*.

30 *Union with Great Britain*. Extract from speech by Ian R. K. Paisley, Northern Ireland Parliament, 22 March 1972 (Linen Hall Library, NIPC P1370). See also *Consistent or Inconsistent* (Newtownards: Ulster Democratic Unionist Party, 1972), for criticism of the VUPP's ambiguity on the union with Great Britain.

31 *The Policies of Alliance* (Belfast: Alliance Party, 1972).

32 VUPP, *1973 Election Manifesto*.

33 Transcript of BBC TV *Business as Usual*, 29 June 1973. NIPC P10132.

34 Mulholland, 'Assimilation versus segregation', p. 288.

35 V. Bogdanor, *Devolution in the United Kingdom* (Oxford: Oxford University Press, 2nd edn, 2001), pp. 1–18.

36 *Unionist Local Government Manifesto, 1973*, pp. 17–19.
37 *SDLP: Second Annual Conference* (1972).
38 *SDLP Manifesto: Assembly Elections. A New North, a New Ireland* (1973).
39 The Stormont government's lack of a proactive housing policy has been criticised in D. Birrell and A. Murie, *Policy and Government in Northern Ireland: Lessons of Devolution* (Dublin: Gill and Macmillan, 1980), p. 211. See also Mulholland, *Northern Ireland*, p. 42, which argues that between 1964 and 1969, housing completions were ahead of targets set by the Wilson report of 1965.
40 *NILP: The Way Ahead. Second Manifesto: Assembly Election, June 1973*, pp 3–12.
41 R. Rose, *The Prime Minister in a Shrinking World* (Cambridge: Polity Press, 2001), p. 145.
42 Ray Kavanagh, former ILP General Secretary, quoted in S. McDaid and K. Rekawek, 'From mainstream to minor and back: the Irish Labour Party, 1987–1992', *Irish Political Studies*, xxv: 4 (2010), p. 635.
43 *Sinn Féin* (Official) *Ard Fhéis* (Dublin: Sinn Féin, 1973).
44 1973 Assembly election results. ARK website. Available: www.ark.ac.uk/elections/fa73.htm.
45 Quoted in Gallagher, *Irish Labour Party*, p. 9.
46 *Éire Nua* (Dublin, 1974), pp. 3–4.
47 *Alliance: Assembly Election Manifesto* (1973).
48 Faulkner, *Memoirs*, pp. 93, 140, 233, 241, 249.
49 BBC News, 22 June 2009. Available: http://news.bbc.co.uk/1/hi/uk_politics/8112581.stm.
50 SDLP, *Assembly Election Manifesto* (1973).
51 *Dominion of Ulster* (Belfast, 1972), p. 10. This pamphlet carried the disclaimer that the views expressed were not necessarily those of the Vanguard movement, however, the VUPP's other publications were generally suspicious of the EEC.
52 Jackson, *Ireland 1798–1998*, p. 409. Jackson also observed that Paisley's antipathy to the EEC did not stop him consistently topping the poll in Northern Ireland's European elections.
53 DUP, *The Surrender of Maastricht: What It Means for Ulster* (1992).
54 McAllister, *Social Democratic and Labour Party*, p. 133.
55 Hayes, *Minority*, p. 170.
56 Ramsay, *Ringside Seats*, p. 136.
57 Hayes, *Minority*, p. 173.
58 PRONI, OE/2/2, executive minutes, 15 January 1974.
59 PRONI, OE/2/9, executive minutes, 12 February 1974.
60 M. Wallace, *British Government in Northern Ireland: From Devolution to Direct Rule* (Newton Abbot: David and Charles, 1982), p. 107.
61 PRONI, OE/2/18, EXMEMO 66/74, financing, executive minutes, 30 April 1974; Faulkner, *Memoirs*, p. 241.
62 Ramsay, *Ringside Seats*, p. 125.
63 Faulkner, *Memoirs*, p. 242.
64 Ibid., p. 242.
65 Ibid., p. 240. See also PRONI, OE/2/2, EXMEMO4/74, collective responsibility, executive minutes, 15 January 1974.

66 Hayes, *Minority*, p. 169, 177.

67 PRONI, OE/2/8, executive minutes, 5 February 1974.

68 Currie, *All Hell*, p. 258. See chapter 5 for the UWC strike. Devlin's resignation, had it happened, would have been related to British security policy, and not any socio-economic policy agreed by the Executive.

69 Devlin, *N.I. Executive*, pp. 2–3.

70 Devlin, *Straight Left*, pp. 214–15; Currie, *All Hell*, p. 244.

71 Bloomfield, *Stormont*, p. 205.

72 Hennessey, *Northern Ireland*, p. 286. For criticism of the UKREP's advice on policy towards the IRA see H. Patterson, 'The British state and the rise of the IRA, 1969–71: the view from the Conway Hotel', *Irish Political Studies*, xxiii: 4, pp. 491–511.

73 Birrell and Murie, *Policy*, pp. 76–7.

74 Ibid., p. 79.

75 PRONI, OE/2/3, executive minutes, 18 January 1974.

76 PRONI, OE/2/13, EXMEMO 30/74, nursery education, executive minutes, 19 March 1974.

77 *Northern Ireland Assembly: Official Report*, vol. 2, col. 1391, 6 March 1974.

78 It was not planned at that stage to alter the overall schooling system in Northern Ireland, which was divided between state schools and predominantly Catholic maintained schools.

79 PRONI, OE/2/18, EXMEMO 65/74, integrated education, executive minutes, 20 April 1974.

80 PRONI, OE 2/20, tattooing of minors, EXMEMO 72/74, 8 May 1974.

81 *Policies for Reconstruction* (Belfast: Alliance Party, 1973); *1973 Election Manifesto: Power for the People, Power for our Land* (Belfast: Ulster Vanguard, 1973), pp. 6–8.

82 *Northern Ireland Assembly: Official Report of Debates*, vol. 2, col. 92, 22 January 1974.

83 PRONI, Central Secretariat (CENT)/1/10/18. J. Barnett to R. Mason, 17 July 1978.

84 *Die Zeit*, 4 January 1974. Available: www.zeit.de/1974/02/Konsul-entfuehrt.

85 *Northern Ireland Assembly: Official Report of Debates*, vol. 2 cols. 124–5, 24 January 1974.

86 Devlin, *Straight Left*, p. 223.

87 *Die Zeit*, 4 December 1981. Available: www.zeit.de/1981/50/Gettos-Gewalt-Gewinn. Thanks to Dr Matthias Euler for assistance.

88 *Northern Ireland Assembly: Official Report of Debates*, vol. 2, col. 294, 30 January 1974.

89 Devlin, *Straight Left*, p. 223. Economic planning in Northern Ireland had assumed a greater importance since the premiership of Terence O'Neill. See Birrell and Murie, *Policy,* pp. 294–6; Mulholland, *Northern Ireland*, pp. 31–4.

90 The definition of Keynesianism draw from that of J. Tomlinson, 'Tale of a death exaggerated: how Keynesian policies survived the 1970s', *Contemporary British History*, xx: 4, p. 431.

91 P. A. Hall, 'Policy paradigms, social learning and the state: the case of economic policymaking in Britain', *Comparative Politics*, xxv: 3 (1995), pp. 275–96.

92 *House of Commons Debates*, vol. 221, cols 497–8, 22 March 1993.
93 *Northern Ireland Assembly: Official Report of Debates*, vol. 1, col. 147, 15 October 1973.
94 Ibid., vol. 2, col. 1991, 26 March 1974.
95 Devlin, *Straight Left*, pp. 219–20.
96 Faulkner, *Memoirs*.
97 *Northern Ireland Assembly: Official Report of Debates*, vol. 2, col. 422, 15 October 1973.
98 Transcript of BBC TV *Business as Usual*, 29 June 1973. NIPC 10132.

5

The UWC strike and its aftermath

The power-sharing executive collapsed in the face of a two-week political strike organised by the Ulster Workers' Council (UWC). The UWC opposed power-sharing and the Irish dimension. The fall of the executive has been much debated by both politicians and academics, with the literature divided between those who believe the British government could have taken firmer action to defeat the UWC, and those who claim the executive would have collapsed regardless. Michael Kerr, for example, has argued that the Labour government chose to abandon the power-sharing executive, refusing to challenge the UWC.[1] This view is shared by Brendan O'Leary, who accused the Labour government of 'abject spinelessness' when confronted by the strike.[2] John Hume's memoirs claimed the British government 'backed down to the strike instead of standing firm as they should have done'.[3] Alternatively, Alvin Jackson, Frank Wright and Don Anderson have stressed that firmer action against the UWC may not have been effective, given the widespread support for the strike among the broader unionist community. In view of this support, such action may actually have galvanised the resolve of the strikers and their supporters, and may not have preserved the executive's life.[4] Bew, Gibbon and Patterson have argued that more direct action against the UWC might have broken the strike, but not necessarily have saved the executive. However, they claim that Wilson's government had in any case decided that the executive would fall, following the February general election results.[5] The intractability of this question is perhaps best demonstrated in the work of Anthony Craig. He has argued that the UWC 'seized authority from the state during their strike, and no one could have stood in their way', whilst also claiming that the strike 'could and would have been controlled', had the government not feared a 'Protestant backlash'.[6]

Official responses to the UWC strike were primarily characterised by political impotence. Both the executive and the Westminster government were in a weak position *vis-a-vis* the strikers, albeit for different reasons. The executive had no security powers of its own, since these were exercised by the London government. The latter, however, appears to have lacked the resources to ensure the maintenance of essential services. The British Army also feared that it could not maintain order in a situation where it had to confront both the PIRA and loyalist paramilitaries.[7] There is insufficient evidence that the Army could have generated and distributed requisite amounts of electricity to maintain essential services. The strike also forced the Prime Minister to consider radical constitutional options in the case of a total breakdown of law and order in the region. However, the significance of Wilson's 'Doomsday' proposals have been exaggerated in the existing literature, and there is no evidence that withdrawal, or any other radical solution, such as Dominion status, were ever government policy. In fact, the evidence suggests that both the cabinet, and the civil service, would never have countenanced withdrawal, and that the Doomsday document offers little more than an insight into one facet of Wilson's thinking at the time.

The origins of the UWC and intra-unionist politics, 1972–74

The UWC emerged from the rubble of the Loyalist Association of Workers (LAW), whose membership consisted of loyalist trades unionists and paramilitaries. It was involved in a number of anti-civil rights marches. According to David Fogel, a former leading UDA member, LAW was a front organisation for the UDA.[8] It had close connections with the Ulster Vanguard movement and was involved in organising protest marches in Northern Ireland throughout 1972 and 1973, including the Vanguard rally at Belfast's Ormeau Park in March 1972.[9] While Ulster Vanguard continued to develop politically throughout 1973, LAW went into decline, and eventually ceased to exist due to internal disagreements. However, many former members maintained contact with each other and the Vanguard organisation. In October 1973, many of its former members attended the first meeting of the UWC at the East Belfast headquarters of the VUPP, an event which attracted little notice at the time.[10]

As already mentioned, unionist politics was rife with division in the aftermath of Stormont's collapse.[11] The UUP was particularly badly hit, with Craig's Vanguard movement (which became a party in its own right the following year), and Harry West's branch of un-pledged unionists seriously undermining Faulkner. He, in turn, was forced to rely on SDLP support in order to form an executive. Faulkner's Assembly grouping actually represented a minority of the unionist electorate. Anti-agreement unionists could thus legitimately claim that an executive led by him did not fully represent unionist opinion. Despite these difficulties, support for Faulkner from the SDLP and the (moderate unionist) Alliance party ensured that the pro-power sharing groups could comfortably control the legislative programme of the Assembly. Therefore, despite causing much high-profile disorder in the chamber, the anti-agreement unionists gained little momentum until January

1974. In that month, the UUC rejected the Sunningdale settlement, forcing Faulkner to resign as UUP leader. Despite his resignation, he remained as chief executive. The UK general election of February 1974 weakened Faulkner's position further, with the UUUC winning eleven of Northern Ireland's twelve seats. Despite forming an electoral coalition, however, anti-Sunningdale unionism was itself riddled with political divisions during this period.

Harry West's faction of the UUP favoured the return of the old Stormont system. Clearly, having rival factions claiming to represent official unionism was untenable. Following a conference at Portstewart in early May 1974, Faulkner's group decided to sever its links with the anti-Sunningdale UUP. Faulkner's grouping styled itself the 'Unionist Party'.[12] One notable absentee from the Portstewart event was Roy Bradford, who Faulkner retrospectively argued was 'repairing his fences' with the West-led UUP.[13] Within the VUPP, opinion was divided, with some supporting the return of Stormont and others an independent Northern Ireland. In April 1974, the UUUC held a conference at Portrush, attended by the controversial British politician Enoch Powell. It published a policy statement calling for a federation of Northern Ireland and Great Britain, which Faulkner referred to as a 'half baked' idea.[14] Despite party differences, there was one issue that the UUUC could agree on, which clearly separated it from the Faulkner unionists: that there should be no Irish involvement in Northern Ireland's affairs, and therefore no Council of Ireland. Ultimately, it was this issue that led to the outbreak of the UWC strike in May 1974.[15]

The UWC strike 14–28 May, 1974: the executive response

As mentioned, the UWC strike was called on 14 May, following the Assembly's acceptance of the executive's amendment to the UUUC's motion calling for the renegotiation of Sunningdale. An *Irish Times* article, written three weeks previously by David McKittrick, argued that any enforced loyalist strike against Sunningdale 'would be universally unpopular'.[16] Initially, McKittrick's assessment seemed correct, as few among the Protestant community appeared to support the UWC. On the first morning of the strike proper, only 10 per cent of the workforce failed to report for duty.[17] During the first days of the stoppage, it was reported that many who supposedly supported the strike were simply 'out for the stout', viewing the strike as a social occasion.[18] However, two days later, events took a more sinister turn. Gangs of loyalist paramilitaries erected barricades on the streets and harassed those going to work.[19] These included 'human chains', primarily comprising women and children, making them more difficult to deal with from a security perspective.[20] It was only when this intimidation occurred (much of which was carried out by the UDA), that the strike gained momentum.[21] Neither the RUC, nor the Army, robustly confronted the paramilitaries in the early days of the stoppage.[22] Emboldened by this 'stand-off' approach by the security forces, the UWC assumed control of the distribution of some goods and services, issuing passes to workers which it deemed essential, predominantly medical staff and civil servants responsible for disbursing unemployment benefits. Most importantly, the UWC also had control of the main electricity generating station at Larne (Ballylumford), which had an almost exclusively Protestant workforce, that supported the actions of the UWC.

The majority of political parties in Great Britain and the Republic of Ireland condemned the strike, although there were some (predominantly hard-left) exceptions. The Dublin based Communist Party of Ireland (Marxist–Leninist faction), called on its members to 'support the struggle of the working class in the North against the imperialist imposed Sunningdale agreement'.[23] Support also came from Tom Kyne, ILP TD for Waterford, who claimed the UWC strike was 'a breath of fresh air'. He favoured an independent Northern Ireland, since 'as long as there were British soldiers in the North, there would be trouble'.[24] Kyne, however, was not representative of the ILP as a whole. This left-wing support, for what some members of the British and Northern Ireland Labour parties described as a fascist led strike, might be regarded as unusual, given William Craig's notoriously hostile attitude towards the trade union movement.[25] However, given that the real power in the UWC came from the working classes and the trades unions, the basis for such support is understandable.

Kenneth Bloomfield has argued that allowing the UWC to control essential services led to confusion within unionism and loyalism as to where real authority lay, since, 'when people see that . . . de facto authority . . . has passed into hands outside government, support for lawful authority can rapidly ebb away'.[26] Overt middle-class unionist support for the strike certainly increased as time progressed. Joe Lee has contended that there was little hostility to the strikers within that class to begin with, since, 'when the crunch came, they all belonged to the same community'.[27] Roy Bradford, writing in the aftermath of the strike, put it slightly differently, but his point essentially supports Lee's argument. Bradford felt that the strike succeeded, not from lack of action by the British government, but because 'from the start it had widespread latent support through most of the Protestant community'.[28] It is clear that a majority of Protestants, of all social classes, opposed any role for the Republic in Northern Ireland's affairs, and that the middle classes were prepared to support a strike enforced by loyalist paramilitaries to thwart this development.

The UWC claimed that the primary motive for staging the strike was a demand for fresh Assembly elections, as a result of the general election in February that same year.[29] However, analysis of the UWC's *News Sheet*, printed during the strike, suggests other factors were also important. Issue 15 of this news sheet criticised the British government for always supporting 'Eire', and instanced the 1916 rising during the Great War, and Irish neutrality during the Second World War, as examples of Irish treachery. It went on to remind readers that Northern Ireland was 'the last bastion of the Protestant Faith left in Europe, and thats [sic] what it all is really about'. The UWC urged the loyalist community to persevere in the hope that a 'glorious future, free from the shackles of Rome' might be achieved.[30] A later issue stated that loyalists should remain aware of the fact that their main enemy was the PIRA who wished to 'destroy our constitution, liberty and our Protestant way of life'.[31] It is therefore evident that the UWC attempted to harness any latent sectarian sentiment within the Protestant community in support of its anti-Sunningdale agenda.

Initially, the executive was not greatly perturbed by the UWC, and was sceptical that a strike would actually take place. At a meeting on 14 May, it 'discussed the situation which might result from the threat by the Ulster Workers Council to call a general strike . . . It was agreed that the Minister of Commerce [John Hume] should not make any advance statement, but be prepared to react to the situation as, and if, it actually developed'.[32] There was good reason for this optimism. In February 1973, a strike organised by the ULC collapsed following the eruption of widespread loyalist violence. The strike, supported by Vanguard's William Craig, was called over the decision to intern loyalists and had the expressed aim of establishing 'some kind of Protestant or loyalist control' over security policy.[33] It was thought unlikely that the bulk of the unionist community would support another strike involving loyalist paramilitaries. However, as the 1974 UWC strike progressed, its members used intimidation, rather than explicit violence, as a means to secure the 'co-operation' of the workforce. On 17 May, three days after the strike commenced, John Hume reported to his colleagues that he had received threats from the UWC stating that the power stations would be shut down, and petrol supplies restricted, if its demands were ignored. The executive authorised Hume to set up emergency depots for petrol should the need arise. Hume left the meeting to liaise with Merlyn Rees, the Secretary of State for Northern Ireland. On his return, Hume informed the executive that Rees was completely firm in his attitude towards the strike and 'prepared to take alternative steps to ensure minimum supplies of electricity if the system should break down completely'.[34]

The control of the power stations was crucial to the success of the strike. There is conflicting information as to what the Army could have done to produce the necessary electrical power, in the event of a walkout by the workers in the power stations. For example, on 20 May, a situation report compiled by Northern Ireland official Maurice Hayes, and presented to the executive, stated that in the event of a complete breakdown of power supply, essential services could be maintained for between two and fourteen days without serious risk to public health, but at some risk of life to the elderly and infirm.[35] As shown below, there was considerable doubt about the Army's capacity to effectively produce and distribute electricity. However, confusion on the issue could have been the result of the poor communication of information between the London and Belfast administrations.

During the early days of the strike, there was little sign of division within the executive: all agreed that there should be no deal with the strikers, and that collectively it should 'try to reach agreement on Sunningdale as a matter of urgency'. Given the opposition of loyalists to the Council of Ireland, this is surprising. However, minutes of a meeting of the executive record one member remarking that support for the UWC strike was based on 'a false understanding of Sunningdale'. He suggested that once this had been removed by a clear statement from the executive, 'support for the strikers would diminish'. No counter-argument was recorded in the minutes, suggesting the executive was still optimistic about the prospect of the strike collapsing of its own accord.[36] At this stage, five days into the stoppage, this was a serious misreading of the threat faced by the executive. Support for the strike was actually increasing.

However, the atmosphere seems to have altered the following day (21 May). Roy Bradford called for the opening up of a dialogue with the strikers because of their 'very wide support'. He received no backing for this proposal from other ministers, including his unionist colleagues. Bradford was pragmatic in his attitude, especially since there were threats that the main power station at Ballylumford (Larne) would be shut down if the station at Coolkeeragh, County Londonderry (which had a predominantly Catholic workforce) was allowed to operate at full power. However, all that was agreed was that a statement on the phasing-in of Sunningdale be issued by the executive after some 'action on security', namely the removal of loyalist roadblocks, by order of the Secretary of State.[37] This implementation of Sunningdale-in-phases was a concession on the part of the SDLP; the party originally sought to put Sunningdale into effect as quickly as possible.

The statement, however, upon which the executive seemed to place a great deal of importance, proved difficult to agree on in practice. At a meeting on 22 May, the SDLP leader Gerry Fitt argued that publishing the agreement to phase-in Sunningdale should be delayed on the grounds that its immediate release would appear as a capitulation to the UWC and lead to further demands from the strikers. It emerged that the UWC had taken charge of the distribution of food and some petrol supplies. Legitimate businesses were also turning to the UWC for help. Kenneth Bloomfield informed the executive that the Confederation of British Industry (CBI) and the Ulster Bank had negotiated with the UWC in respect of the availability of certain services. This was a clear sign that the business community had lost confidence in the ability of the executive to govern effectively. Both the Alliance party and Faulkner unionists favoured issuing the executive's statement on Sunningdale immediately. At this point, Fitt asked to be excused, in order to consult with SDLP backbenchers, to see if agreement could be reached, as many of its members were opposed to an immediate release of the statement. Upon his return, he reported that the position of his party was unchanged. The first vote in the executive's history was then taken, resulting in seven votes in favour of issuing the statement to four votes against. However, two hours later, following discussions between SDLP back-benchers and Stanley Orme, the Minister of State at the NIO, this vote was negated. Fitt returned to inform his colleagues that the SDLP was 'now in a position to accept the proposal and it could be regarded as carried unanimously'.[38] Despite this agreement, little further action seems to have been taken by the executive to reassert its authority, although there were signs of some action the following day.

On 22 May the executive approved, in principle, John Hume's plan, which made provision for the distribution of oil and petrol, under the supervision of the Army. This measure, known as the Oil Contingency Plan, was based on an earlier civil service scheme to distribute oil and petrol in the event of a breakdown of law and order resulting from increased PIRA activity.[39]

During its second week, the strike received the active support of the main anti-Sunningdale political leaders. Paisley was initially loath to support the strike. At the time of its announcement, he was in Canada to attend a funeral. Upon his return, when the strike appeared to be gaining momentum, he took his place on the UWC committee, despite being 'ill-received' by the strike leaders. William Craig of the VUPP, who had been sympathetic towards the strike from the outset, also took a seat on the committee.[40] Therefore, not only was the strike supported by loyalist paramilitaries and loyalist trades unionists, but also the political representatives of a significant section of the unionist electorate, thus making the task faced by the executive extremely difficult.

In view of this formidable opposition, it was decided that the above-mentioned oil distribution plan should be adopted 'as a clear policy of the Executive', to attempt to restore its authority. The Army had informed Hume that the plan was feasible 'provided the necessary troops were made available, legal implications were examined, and the possibility of sabotage was considered'.[41] The plan was enacted on 27 May, as it had earlier been agreed that there was 'no acceptable alternative to this demonstration of the executive's will and determination to govern'.[42] Archival evidence indicates that the executive intended to continue governing Northern Ireland. In the midst of the UWC strike, decisions were taken to continue bringing forward measures on reform of solicitors' practices and public lending, which suggests that the executive itself expected to survive the UWC strike.

As the strike continued, Brian Faulkner actively sought more support from the London government which had appeared to have done little to support the executive. A meeting took place at Chequers, attended by Faulkner, Fitt and Alliance leader Oliver Napier. The Prime Minister appeared firm in his determination to defeat the UWC strike, emphasising its sectarian character. He stated that the British government 'would not accept a political and sectarian strike against Sunningdale. The Constitution Act would stay; the Executive would stay, and Sunningdale, as announced, would stick'. When asked by Wilson about the level of support for the strike, Faulkner replied that this was difficult to assess. Such support, he argued, was largely due to intimidation, 'but as time went on with no break in their hold of the situation, the public was tending to turn on the Executive rather than the strikers'.[43] He claimed that one reason the UWC could attract middle-class support was its avoidance of direct, violent confrontation with the troops. There were reports that the Army had attempted to provoke the loyalist paramilitaries into 'having a go' at them, so that they might be able to act more forcibly against the UWC, and turn the middle classes against the strikers.[44] Wilson then considered the issue of the power stations, and reported that there was no guarantee that putting troops in the stations would result in the maintenance of electricity supply. Faulkner argued that there was not really a choice: '[o]ne had to face the possibility of such a reduction [of power supplies] . . . it would be preferable to depending on concessions from the people involved in the strike'. In order to maintain power supply at the stations, it was believed the Army needed the assistance of senior management, but that this could not be guaranteed due to loyalist paramilitary intimidation. To counteract this, Wilson asked 'whether it might be possible to exert some pressure on the senior people to remain in their posts, as for example by threatening forfeiture of their pension rights', a somewhat unrealistic suggestion. The meeting concluded pessimistically, with the Prime Minister noting that 'these people [the UWC and its supporters] would only be satisfied when they achieved an independent Protestant Northern Ireland, virtually fascist in character'.[45] Following this meeting, Faulkner informed the executive that he had 'gained the clear impression that Mr Wilson was firm in his desire to do whatever was necessary, and within his capability, to stand by the Executive'.[46]

Meanwhile, the strikers' grip on essential services tightened. Power cuts became more frequent, and stockpiles of baby food and supplies for diabetics were gathered in case of further breakdowns in public services. At this stage, Faulkner finally faced the fact that 'if it became a choice between talking [to the UWC] and allowing the economy of the Province to collapse the Executive could be forced to talk from a weaker position'. He suggested that an intermediary be dispatched to assess the attitudes of the UWC to negotiation, but this proposal was not taken further at this stage. The meeting heard further evidence that the strike was causing a breakdown in the authority of the executive. It was reported that in the Falls area of West Belfast, the IRA had taken over the distribution of food. However, with no control over security policy, there was very little the executive could do to tackle the problems posed by either the PIRA, or the loyalist strikers.

Later intervention by the Prime Minister actually strengthened the resolve of the UWC.[47] During the strike, Wilson made a speech which highlighted the massive financial burden that Northern Ireland represented to the British exchequer, and condemned the UWC and its supporters for 'sponging on Westminster' and British taxpayers.[48] Glen Barr, a leading UDA figure and Assembly member for Londonderry claimed that he couldn't have written a better speech himself, and suggested Wilson be made an honorary UWC member.[49] Joe Lee described the 'sponging' remark as juvenile.[50] It was certainly ill-judged, and a politician of Wilson's experience should have known better than to make it, regardless of his personal views concerning the UWC.

The following day, 28 May, the executive finally collapsed. Faulkner told his colleagues that it was becoming increasingly clear that the executive faced a 'prolonged stalemate with unacceptable hardship to the population and some damage to the economy', a situation he could not accept. His pro-Sunningdale unionist colleagues also opposed sacrificing the economic life of Northern Ireland in order to maintain a position which was increasingly untenable. They argued that the proper course would be to seek agreement from the Secretary of State to initiate discussions with the UWC through approved intermediaries. The Finance Minister, Herbie Kirk, suggested the former Governor of Northern Ireland, Lord Grey, or the industrialist Sir Frederick Catherwood as possible candidates. Leslie Morrell, the agriculture minister, emphasised the need to act quickly, given the extent of the strikers' grip on the region: 'time was not available for further thinking and talking . . . food supplies, milk production and basic services such as water and sewage were in danger. All these were in the hands of the UWC'. Education minister, Basil McIvor, added that talking to the strikers would be a sign of responsible action, while Roy Bradford, who had advocated talking to the UWC early in the stoppage, claimed it had been a 'disastrous misjudgement to have thought the strike could have been broken'. He argued that the executive had urged the Secretary of State to take a strong line towards the UWC 'and the result had been a pan-Protestant strike', that could not be broken by the Army. He advocated talking immediately, lest Northern Ireland 'slide into anarchy'.

The unionist members were supported by the Alliance Minister for Law Reform, Oliver Napier. Napier favoured the use of the Army to keep as many essential services going as possible, and believed that mediation should begin 'whether the Secretary of State liked it or not'. Such a move might, he contended, 'turn the tide towards the Executive, especially if the Executive were to be seen as not intransigent'. However, these views were not shared by the SDLP. Gerry Fitt stressed that the executive should remain loyal to Merlyn Rees, since it had requested action from him in relation to the oil plan, and he had responded. Breaking with the Secretary of State would result in 'a very hostile United Kingdom – no Harland and Wolff, no Short and Harland [aerospace company] . . . He did not want to see Northern Ireland dragged down into the mire'. Both these companies were heavily subsidised by the UK taxpayer, and primarily employed Protestants. Perhaps Fitt mentioned these companies in order to persuade the unionist members to support his argument, and to continue the policy of non-negotiation. He also stated that he felt there was a 'vast residue of people who wanted to work and wanted to support the Executive' and a vast 'number of Protestants who did not want to live under Craig and Paisley', despite the strike's increasing support base. John Hume also opposed negotiations, arguing that the executive, having been assured 'of the Army's capacity to follow through with any consequentials [sic] should stand firm'.[51] Hume had earlier been informed by Rees that the latter 'had taken the necessary measures to ensure that adequate power supplies would be maintained' in the event of a collapse in service, which suggests that there was conflicting information about the Army's capacity to run the power stations.[52]

Hume further stated that 'there were fundamental principles not only for the authority of the executive, but for British authority in Northern Ireland'. He argued that there was a possibility the public would go back to work if the executive was seen to reassert control, and stated that he would not resign. Housing minister, Austin Currie, agreed with him, and argued that negotiation was capitulation to the strikers, although 'the use of intermediaries might make that appear not quite so blatant'. He compared the UWC strike 'with the Germany of the Weimar Republic'. He feared the UWC's goal was 'a fascist takeover and reassertion of the Protestant ascendancy'. This would, he contended, drive the minority population 'into the arms of the IRA'.[53] Despite the SDLP objections, the majority view within the executive was that negotiations through intermediaries should commence. The meeting adjourned to allow Faulkner to communicate that request to Merlyn Rees. Rees, however, was not prepared to accept this, and Faulkner immediately tendered his resignation and those of his unionist colleagues. Although the SDLP members did not resign, they were aware that Rees would immediately terminate the executive, as was his prerogative under the Constitution Act. The records show that ministers exchanged good wishes and regretted that, on their last meeting, they had not been able to act in complete unity.[54] After only fourteen days, the UWC achieved its primary objective: the collapse of the power-sharing executive, and the demise of the Sunningdale agreement. The UWC was jubilant, expressing its satisfaction in verse on the pages of its *News Sheet*.

Evil men have tried again, this land of ours to sell;
But we said NO, Sunningdale must go, and your Council of Ireland as well.
Because we don't want, indeed we can't, accept your Popish way;
for we are Ulster Protestants, and shall remain so, all our days.
So once again, loyal Ulstermen have stood up to defend her;
And this they did, with the help of God, and their war-cry –
NO SURRENDER.[55]

Overall, the response of the executive to the UWC strike was not particularly proactive. This was less an indictment of the executive politicians, than a reflection of how little power they actually held, especially regarding security policy. Only the British government could have taken firm action against the UWC. Whether this would have defeated it, remains a matter of conjecture. The Westminster government's response to the strike will now be considered.

British responses to the UWC strike

Whether the British government could, or should, have done more to assist the executive remains a hotly debated question. Much of the debate centres on the government's security response to the UWC. The success of the strike depended, in large part, on the actions Protestant paramilitaries, particularly the UDA, the largest of these groups. In assessing British responses to the UWC strike, it is useful to consider British policy towards the UDA before the strike, and take into account whether this policy was followed, or abandoned, during the events of May 1974.

British security policy towards the UDA was drafted in November 1972 following the growth of vigilante activity in working-class areas of West Belfast. There was to be a joint security policy towards both the UDA and the Catholic Ex-Servicemen's Association (CESA), a vigilante group which ostensibly operated to protect Catholic areas from loyalist attack. Both the UDA and CESA were involved in setting up roadblocks for the purpose of 'screening' traffic entering their localities. Security force policy thus aimed to 'diminish their status as self-appointed protectors of the community'. However, the security forces planned to target only 'their criminal and extremist elements', whilst 'maintaining good relations with the moderate law-abiding citizens' in both groups. It was therefore advised that contacts be maintained with paramilitary leaders with a view to persuading them to act sensibly during tense occurrences. Furthermore, security forces were ordered to tolerate 'unarmed, locally resident vigilante type patrols . . . provided they do not break the law'. However, they were not to tolerate 'marauding patrols', road-blocks, or 'the harassment of drivers or other members of the public'.[56] Given the intimidation that occurred during the UWC strike, and the ubiquitous paramilitary roadblocks throughout Northern Ireland,[57] it is clear that the security forces were not following their own directives against the paramilitary vigilantes of the UWC. However, the document did not consider this issue in the context of widespread civil disobedience of the kind organised by the strikers.

The control of electricity by the UWC was the key reason for the success of the strike. As already mentioned, most of the workers at the main generating station at Ballylumford were Protestant; the same was true of the Belfast headquarters of the NIES.[58] It was more likely that sections of the workforce at these sites would sympathise with the UWC demands, and that those who were indifferent, would be susceptible to loyalist intimidation.

However, Merlyn Rees was initially optimistic that the strike would be easily defeated. With hindsight, this appears surprising, but seen in the context of the previous unsuccessful record of loyalist strikes in Northern Ireland, Rees's optimism was understandable. He informed the Prime Minister that the 'industrial action' in Northern Ireland was 'a last fling by the Protestants', and that the government's policies 'were closer to success than they had ever been'. Rees felt that, if the government 'stood up to this Protestant action', that he would be in a strong position to 'make proposals to the Prime Minister about a date for ratifying the Sunningdale Agreement'.[59] It was apparent that, during this discussion, the implementation of Sunningdale was a priority for the government. This evidence challenges the recent arguments of Michael Kerr, who has claimed that the Labour government was considering how it could 'disengage' from the Sunningdale agreement, whilst, at the same time, 'avoid being blamed for the collapse of the Sunningdale process'.[60]

Conscious of the threat to essential services, Rees informed Wilson that he had 'put on notice troops capable of running the power stations', and, at short notice, troops capable of running sewage plants. He noted that there would be enough power for at least twenty-four hours, but that it might be necessary to send troops in the following day (17 May), the third day of the strike.[61] However, he did not send troops to run the stations at that time, or at any time throughout the strike.

In a further conversation with Wilson on 17 May, Rees informed the Prime Minister that he had 'brought to readiness [on] the other side of the water all the people who would come here and run the power stations'. When asked if he could get enough troops to operate the stations, Rees replied in the affirmative. However, when asked what capacity of power the troops would be able to maintain, he replied 'that is another matter', and stressed that soldiers would be unable to maintain all the generating stations. Rees's conversation with the Prime Minister also raised an interesting point about the attitude of the MOD to events in Northern Ireland. It appears that Rees believed there might have been little awareness within the MOD of the level of threat posed by the UWC to essential services and security in Northern Ireland, as that ministry might have been more concerned with events elsewhere.

> Secretary of State: I havn't [sic] spoken to Roy Mason this morning. I am going to shortly. I would like to feel . . . that the Ministry of Defence are firmly aware that there is a crisis. There is a tendency sometimes – you know when I switched on the news now Middle East comes first and at home nobody is bothered but you know I simply point out that if Ministry of Defence were made aware that there is a problem, it would be helpful.
> Prime Minister: Yes, O.K. I will see that done.[62]

Further discussions in London also focused on the issue of the power stations, and to what extent the troops could generate enough electricity. The Prime Minister suggested that investigations be made into the possibility of a nuclear submarine being sent to Belfast and used to provide power, in the event of a shutdown by the UWC. Such a vessel could produce power, but in the absence of suitable conversion equipment, it was not compatible with the grid in Northern Ireland. A conventional naval vessel, for example HMS *Bristol*, could have provided 6 megawatts (MW) of power, if suitable conversion equipment was available. Because the Belfast power station alone usually produced over 360 MW this would clearly have made little difference, and the decision not to attempt this was, on balance, correct.[63]

Early in the strike, however, Rees seemed more optimistic regarding the issue of electricity services and supply. On 17 May he informed security chiefs that, in the event of a breakdown of these services, 'the supply could be restored to a survival level within 24 hours, and full restoration achieved within three days of a resumption of operations'.[64] That same day, he also informed the executive that he had 'taken the necessary measures to ensure that adequate power supplies would be maintained'.[65] It was known, for example, that hospitals in the region had enough oil to power standby generators for three to seven days.[66] However, as events transpired, following a secret reconnaissance on 19 May at the Ballylumford plant,[67] troops were not put into the stations, as the Army concluded that they would be unable to generate electricity without the help of senior management.[68] In any case, it was by no means certain that senior management could be relied upon to co-operate if troops entered the stations, an outcome which Rees considered highly likely.[69] It is not explicitly clear that he communicated this information effectively to the executive at the time, which may explain why there was confusion among members regarding the Army's capacity to run the stations.

There were also potential political and security risks associated with introducing troops into the power stations. Earlier that week, Stanley Orme, received a delegation led by Ian Paisley and William Craig. Paisley alleged that some of the workers had been 'locked out' of the power stations by the management, and told Orme that the loyalist people 'did not want Sunningdale'.

Both he and Craig 'vehemently denied that there had been any intimidation' of those attempting to go to work by the UWC. Orme told the delegation that there was nobody to blame for the current situation other than the workers themselves. He then informed them that troops could be brought into the power stations. Paisley warned that 'such action would be disastrous; it would cause a blood bath . . . to use the Army would be a deliberate provocation'.[70] This comment illustrates the difficulty facing the government with regard to Army intervention. Not only was intervention likely to be ineffective, there was a credible threat that it would provoke further loyalist violence. A report by Frank Cooper of the NIO showed that the town of Larne was the 'most troublesome area' and that Craig was 'handling the "heavy" side of the operation' there: in other words, co-ordinating the action of the loyalist paramilitaries'.[71] The government, therefore, had good reason to take Craig's threats seriously. There is no evidence, however, that loyalist threats had a decisive influence on government policy. This was more likely to be influenced by constraining factors, such as the potential effectiveness of the Army at maintaining essential services in an emergency situation.

As the strike entered its second week, the credibility of the state was further damaged. An attempt to hold a 'back to work' march on 21 May, led by Len Murray, leader of Britain's Trades Union Congress (TUC), ended in a debacle. The public response was derisory. Scarcely 200 people turned up to support it, and its route, blocked by loyalist crowds, had to be defended from attack by the Army. The ugly mood of the march was captured by *The Sun* newspaper. Loyalist women, it reported, 'screamed, clawed, spat and kicked out at the marchers', whilst their male counterparts 'hurled lumps of metal and stones. They chanted "Communist bastards"'.[72]

Shortly after the failed back-to-work initiative, the Prime Minister met the Irish Ambassador, in London, to discuss the situation regarding the power stations. Wilson informed Dr Diarmuid O'Sullivan that a team of specialists had been flown to Northern Ireland for possible deployment at the power stations. He qualified this by saying that 'if troops were put into the power stations, the amount of power produced might, in fact, be less than at present, and such action might strengthen the UWC'.[73] The archival evidence suggests that there was conflicting information about whether or not electricity supplies could be maintained by the troops, since Rees had assured the executive that he had taken measures to ensure adequate supplies could be maintained. At the same time Wilson informed O'Sullivan that the troops might produce less power than the reduced amounts being generated by the UWC. Faulkner's memoirs, however, state that the executive was 'not told that the forces could not keep power supplies going'.[74]

The petrol and oil distribution plan went ahead on 27 May. This was approved by the British government at the request of the executive. Overall, the plan was unsuccessful, since its details appear to have been leaked by some Stormont civil servants, and loyalist paramilitaries remained in control of much of the distribution of fuel. As Seamus Mallon,[75] commented in the Northern Ireland Assembly: '[w]hen we have this type of situation [,] and when the massive force of our British Army, the R.U.C., the R.U.C. reserve and the U.D.R. are not in a position to take any action [,] I think we can safely say we have arrived at a state of anarchy'.[76] Further evidence that the UWC was considering more direct action against the executive was reported in the daily intelligence summary from Northern Ireland. The summary stated that the 'strike organisers [were] considering the takeover of Stormont with the help of Security men employed there', although there is no evidence that any such attempt was ever made. The summary also stated '[i]n three areas of Belfast the Officials and Provisionals are now collaborating and sealed arms dumps have been opened. They consider that the present situation is "their best chance since 1969"'.[77] The news that the IRA had taken over the distribution of food in West Belfast was seen as further evidence of the lack of authority of the executive, or the government, throughout Northern Ireland.[78] Soon afterwards, the Prime Minister delivered his notorious 'spongers' speech, which made matters even worse. It was broadcast the day after two Catholic publicans were shot dead by UDA and UVF elements in Ballymena, for refusing to close their business during the strike.[79] Wilson later admitted that his words were 'provocative and bitter'.[80] With support for the strike increasing daily, the executive attempted to counter this by issuing a statement on the phased implementation of the Sunningdale Agreement.

The phasing-in of Sunningdale caused serious difficulties within the SDLP, and, on 22 May, its Assembly party initially voted against the party leadership on this issue. Perhaps the most unusual aspect of this disagreement within the SDLP is that it did not occur earlier in the month – as the decision to implement Sunningdale in phases was actually taken some days previously. The records show that plans were made to arrange a meeting with ministers from the Republic at the end of May; the object of which was to agree on how the Council of Ireland provisions of Sunningdale could be implemented in phases. It was agreed that a council of ministers from the northern and southern jurisdictions would be established in the first instance, with the all-Ireland council to be developed on an agreed basis between the executive and the Irish government. The all-Ireland assembly, with thirty members from the two jurisdictions, would only be established when a test of opinion showed that implementation was undertaken 'with the whole-hearted consent of the people'.[81] At the next meeting of the executive, ministers 'again discussed the method by which progress could be made by phased implementation and further clarified their respective positions in relation to Council functions'.[82] On 20 May the following week, details of this agreement were confirmed when

Kenneth Bloomfield summarised the report of the executive sub-committee on Sunningdale for the executive members.[83]

It appears that the only debate within the executive, at this stage, was in relation to what the Council of Ireland would actually do once in existence. There is no record of any disagreement, at this time, over the issue of phased implementation which subsequently divided the SDLP later that month. Austin Currie claimed, in his memoirs, that the debate on phasing resulted in tensions within the executive. Archival evidence shows that the SDLP leader and his executive colleagues did not oppose the notion of phasing-in Sunningdale, but rather its timing, lest it appear as a concession to the UWC and lead to further demands from that organisation.[84] However, it appears as if there may have been disquiet within the SDLP Assembly party over the agreement reached on phasing, and that the backbenchers within the SDLP regarded this as an attempt by unionists to renege on their obligations on the Council of Ireland. The SDLP parliamentary party was relatively flexible on the issue of phasing, but the period of several years, as proposed by the executive, and accepted by the SDLP ministers, was regarded by some as a weakening of the agreement by unionists.[85] This division between the SDLP Assembly party and its executive members is further evident from examining the records of the meeting between the SDLP Assembly party and the Minister of State, Stanley Orme on 23 May, the day it was decided to issue the statement on the phasing of the Council of Ireland. Paul Dixon has argued that Orme used Labour's influence with the SDLP to press the Assembly party into accepting a 'compromise package to keep the power-sharing Executive alive'. He claims that Orme 'warned them that if they did not accept the new package they would lose the support of the British Labour Party, which because of bipartisanship, had been so important in giving the SDLP leverage over British Governments at Westminster'.[86] The minutes of the meeting make no mention of the British Labour Party or bipartisanship, but Orme did make a successful appeal to the SDLP warning that its rejection of the phasing plan would bring the executive down. He urged the party 'not to do something which would mean that Sunningdale would not be signed possibly for as long as 20 years'. While ultimately accepting the executive position, individual SDLP members took the opportunity to convey their dissatisfaction with the government to Orme. Aidan Larkin, Assembly member for Mid-Ulster, argued that the strike 'at last presented an opportunity for Fascist unionism to be confronted, but it was quite clear that the British Government was ducking away from the issue and was not dealing with the strike'.[87]

On 26 May, Merlyn Rees flew to Cornwall to seek Wilson's confirmation that the oil and petrol distribution plan should go ahead. He argued that if the government 'sat it out without taking decisive action, they would get the worst of all worlds'. Wilson stated that if pressure was yielded to one faction in Northern Ireland, the other would be offended, and there seemed little chance of compromise. He did agree to the dispatch of additional troops to Northern Ireland so that law and order could be enhanced. When questioned by Wilson about the unity of the loyalists, Rees replied that they were still relatively united, but that there had been rumours circulating that they were planning some form of Unilateral Declaration of Independence (UDI). The Prime Minister urged that a study of policy options open to the government in the event of a UDI be undertaken hastily. He discussed the issue of compensation to property that had been damaged during the strike due to paramilitary activity. He stated that it 'needed to be considered whether the community in Northern Ireland should not be required to tax themselves to pay their own compensation'. Wilson continued with the observation that if Britain 'decided to pull out in more or less peaceful circumstances some troops could be left behind and a diminished financial contribution could be continued. If, on the other hand, Britain were forced out, we would owe them nothing (except for such things as service pensions, etc)'. The conversation concluded that the executive was likely to fall whether or not firm action was taken by the British government. However, Wilson argued that the cabinet decision to implement the oil plan was the right thing to do 'in Great Britain terms'. He appears to have been particularly frustrated with the loyalists in Northern Ireland at this point. His remarks may be considered in the context of the 'spongers' speech made by him the previous night. It is apparent that the issue of a possible British withdrawal from Northern Ireland was discussed at the highest levels of government, even if withdrawal was never official government policy.[88]

Despite these discussions, little or no firm action was taken against the UWC. The oil plan, implemented on 27 May, was unsuccessful and, in any case, could not solve the problem of the control of the power stations by the UWC. On 27 May, Rees was informed by an NIES official (Mr Smith) that, even if troops were put into the power stations to generate a reduced level of electricity, at least fifty engineers would be required to distribute it although he stated that it might be possible 'that these could be provided by the Central Electricity Generating Board in Great Britain'. However, he advised Rees not to take any action until the following morning, to give the NIES time to assess how the 'men on the ground' would react to such army intervention.[89] In the end, the British engineers never materialised, as the executive collapsed the day after this meeting occurred. An eleventh hour offer to the British government from the President of the Republic of Uganda, Idi Amin Dada, to bring the Northern Ireland politicians to Africa, where he would act as a mediator in the dispute, was, politely, declined.[90] The 'Backbencher' column of the *Irish Times* was highly critical of Harold Wilson's handling of the strike. It lambasted the 'Huyton twit'[91] for calling a section of the Irish people spongers.

The UWC victory, it argued, had shown Wilson to be the real sponger, since he had 'soaked up the greatest piece of punishment ever handed out to a British Prime Minister'.[92]

Michael Kerr has argued that if Heath had been Prime Minister during the strike, he 'would certainly have acted' against the UWC.[93] He has also claimed that Heath and Whitelaw invested 'too much political capital in Northern Ireland to have allowed power-sharing to collapse in the face of such unconstitutional unionist opposition'.[94] Kerr's arguments are similar to those contained in Whitelaw's memoir. The latter claimed that Labour was not as committed to the new institutions in Northern Ireland as Heath's government had been.[95] However, there appears to be no archival evidence to support this contention, and what action the Conservatives may or may not have taken, had they been in power at this time, will never be known.

There were clear constraints on what the British government could do, both in terms of maintaining essential services, and keeping violence to a minimum. More forceful government intervention may even have worsened troublesome behaviour in the region. On the day the executive collapsed, there appear to have been some violent incidents in republican areas of Derry, possibly due to resentment at the behaviour of the security forces throughout the strike. The report of a senior British Army officer regarding these disturbances read: 'The *SCUM OF EUROPE* live west of the FOYLE.'[96] However, it has also been argued that the British government was considering more radical options concerning Northern Ireland, including withdrawal, in the event of an emergency situation. It is certainly true that Britain's future role in Northern Ireland was the subject of considerable discussion in Whitehall at the time, and this issue will now be discussed.

The aftermath of the strike and discussion of future Northern Ireland policy, May–June 1974

Documents written in the aftermath of the strike offer an insight into the government's policy motives during the UWC action. On 29 May 1974, the Liberal Party leader, Jeremy Thorpe, discussed the Northern Ireland situation with the Prime Minister. Harold Wilson informed Thorpe that the government was considering its policy on Northern Ireland, and that 'they would not go back to direct rule: the Secretary of State would be forming his own Executive'. The Prime Minister also confirmed that, in contrast to the government's stance in relation to the UWC, the Secretary of State would be in a position to negotiate 'with any other body which assumed powers and was not properly constituted'. A nominated executive could be put in place for four months and possibly extended under the provisions of the Northern Ireland Constitution Act (1973), which granted Rees considerable powers.

Some insight into the reasons why British policy towards the UWC was ineffective is provided by a further exchange between Thorpe and Wilson. The former asked the Prime Minister if, in the event of a resumption of the UWC strike, 'the best course might be to allow the economic life of the province to run down'. Wilson replied that 'this had been, in effect, the view of the Cabinet', that the government should 'sit it out' during the strike. The only exception made to that policy had been the decision to intervene over petrol supplies since the executive had made that an issue of confidence. Wilson agreed with Thorpe that, with the executive no longer in office, the government could afford to 'sit it out if the strike were resumed'. When questioned about the long-term role of Great Britain in Northern Ireland by Thorpe, Wilson appears to have ruled out withdrawal in the short term. Replying to his question about whether there would be some attraction in setting a timetable for withdrawal, the Prime Minister acknowledged that public support for such an idea was 'widespread'. Crucially, however, this 'was not reflected in Parliament – only a small number of Labour members such as Mr Dalyell and Mr Wellbeloved had supported withdrawal'. Also, withdrawal would mean 'giving in to the I.R.A.', and most likely result in the intensification of violence. Thorpe agreed that withdrawal would be 'disastrous'. This confirms the earlier suggestion that withdrawal was discussed by the government, but not that it became official government *policy*.[97]

At a meeting with Sir Alec Douglas-Home and Francis Pym, Wilson confirmed that the government proposed to attempt to continue power-sharing arrangements in Northern Ireland, although he believed that these had little chance of success. He expressed the hope that the SDLP would come to see that continued power-sharing was its best and indeed 'only hope'. Wilson argued that the possibility of a renewed strike was unlikely, but that the development of a coherent Protestant working class force was a 'new and . . . dangerous development'. The government, he stated, would not concede to the UWC demands for elections at this time, since it was vital, in his view, that time be allowed for 'moderate opinion to swing back again to the concept of power-sharing'. Rees, who was also at this meeting, expressed dissatisfaction with policing during the strike noting that 'the unreliability of the RUC had been regrettably demonstrated during this period'.[98]

Despite the hopes of the government, there was little appetite for power-sharing among loyalists in Northern Ireland. William Craig of the VUPP informed Merlyn Rees that he 'was against power sharing because it institutionalised conflict by ignoring the will of the people'. He stated that if elections were held, and there was a clear majority for power-sharing, then the loyalists would become the official opposition. However, if they were in the majority, they would reject the idea of power-sharing. When discussing the constitutional future of Northern Ireland, Craig stated that his preference was for devolution within the UK. However, he believed that the only 'realistic' possibility was that Northern Ireland should enjoy independence on a par with the Isle of Man.[99] When challenged by Rees that the adverse public opinion caused by any move towards such independence would make financial contributions from the UK to such a polity difficult, Craig retorted that 'in his youth they had been told that Eire would go under. It had not. Ulster started from a better position'. Given the huge subsidy received by Northern Ireland from the UK, it is likely that living standards in an independent Northern Ireland would have fallen well below those in the Republic. Craig also admitted that he had not thought through how the fears of the minority could be assuaged in an independent 'Ulster'.[100]

Ian Paisley (DUP) also opposed mandatory power-sharing, which he referred to as a 'dead duck', but stated his party was not against 'a freely entered into coalition'. He put forward more realistic proposals about Northern Ireland's future relationship with Great Britain than Craig. He argued that a new assembly might be elected to consider this question. He was 'interested in how Holland (and Belgium) had coped with different religious (or racial) groups'.[101] Harry West's unionists were even more opposed to power-sharing than the DUP; they were not even prepared to consider it. Former South Antrim Assembly member, Austin Ardill informed Rees that 'Unionists were not prepared to share power with Republicans even if they only had Irish unity as an aspiration'.[102] Only the former executive parties favoured power-sharing, and deemed it to be essential to any future settlement in Northern Ireland.[103] Gerry Fitt argued that power-sharing was the most important part of any settlement for his Belfast-based colleagues, but for those in border areas, the Council of Ireland was crucial.[104] Interestingly, Faulkner believed that there was a possibility that Paisley would accept the SDLP in government, with a Council of Ireland, if 'he could be on top'. Paisley's policies, he believed, were influenced by Glen Barr of the UDA, and were more realistic than those of Craig who, Faulkner argued, 'was off his nut'.[105]

Briefing the Prime Minister on these discussions, Rees concluded that British policy should be to hold an election within Northern Ireland. The purpose of this election would be to elect candidates who would sit in an assembly, wherein members would seek to agree on a form of government acceptable to the whole community. This was similar to the proposal made by Ian Paisley, although there is no direct evidence that he influenced Rees's thinking on the matter. Rees also informed Wilson that there was a growing feeling that the British could not solve 'the Irish problem and it would be better to let them have a shot at it themselves'. An assembly, along the lines proposed, would have provided an opportunity for a solution to emerge, although its chances of success must have appeared unlikely, even without the benefit of hindsight.[106] It is important to note that what Rees was proposing was an internal Northern Ireland solution with as little direct British involvement as possible, rather than advocating some kind of British withdrawal.[107]

Discussions concerning Northern Ireland's future within the UK began even before the fall of the executive. On 22 May, a report on its constitutional options came before the Prime Minister. The three options identified within this report were: (1) to retain the framework of the Constitution Act; (2) direct rule with greater responsibility for Northern Ireland (integration); or (3) withdrawal. None of these options were particularly attractive to British officials, particularly the issue of withdrawal, which was deemed problematic due to the amount of planning that would have to be undertaken before it could even be attempted. Other major arguments against option (3) included a potential increase in violence, the likelihood of the reintroduction 'of a force like the B-Specials' by the loyalists, damage to the UK's international reputation and the possibility of unfriendly governments such as the Soviet Union interfering in Ireland.[108]

Following the collapse of the executive, the question of British withdrawal from Northern Ireland was given more urgent consideration by the Prime Minister himself. He noted that, in the aftermath of the UWC strike, the government was in a position of 'responsibility without power', comparing its situation to that of a 'eunuch'.[109] Wilson suggested that the government would be at the mercy of the UWC if it pursued any policy unfavourable to that group. He rightly noted that the strike demonstrated that the British troops were powerless to maintain essential services in the face of mass civil disobedience, particularly highly specialised services such as electricity generation. Despite favourable post-strike press coverage for the government, he suspected that the Army 'and an increasing number of MPs' would be telling him that the Emperor had 'no clothes'. Crucially, he argued that power-sharing should still be the government's stated objective. However, he stated that preparations would have to be made regarding how best to manage a possible recurrence of the strike. 'In Doomsday terms', he added, 'which means withdrawal – I should like this scenario to be considered.' He noted that withdrawal was 'not the only' option, and was open to all the objections earlier raised by the officials. He then set out how he felt such a plan might operate in an emergency situation.

> At the moment we decided Doomsday was in sight we should proceed to prepare a plan for Dominion status for Northern Ireland. This would still mean that the Ulstermen were subjects of The Queen . . . Dominion status would not, of course, carry with it automatic entry into the Commonwealth. I should think this would be most unlikely, and so would membership of the United Nations.

He argued that Dominion status should not be granted to Northern Ireland without provision for the protection of minority rights, which amounted to a British veto on the change of the constitution for at least ten years. Wilson stated that there should be a 'tapering off over a period of three to five years' of revenue from the UK exchequer. 'After that they are out on their own, and have not got a prescriptive right to standards higher than those of the South.' In the event that the civil rights of the minority were violated, this financial support would stop immediately. The situation reminded the Prime Minister of Rhodesia's UDI in 1965, and the civil conflict which followed.[110] The issue of the armed forces was also crucial. Wilson believed that the British Army would have to retain control over what operations it would undertake in the hypothetical Dominion of Northern Ireland: 'we could hardly go in alongside the reconstituted B-Specials in an invasion of the Falls', he commented. He pessimistically concluded that although this was just one possible scenario, he felt that 'Parliamentary and other pressures' might drive the government to 'pretty early consideration of it, or of any appropriate alternative'.[111]

Robert Armstrong, Principal Private Secretary to the Prime Minister, informed Wilson that he had told the Cabinet Secretary, Sir John Hunt, that studies should be carried out of the ideas mentioned above, to which the latter agreed.[112] This suggests that the Prime Minister thought that a crisis similar to that previously envisaged in his 'Doomsday' document was likely to occur in the near future, and that withdrawal should be studied as one possibility of what to do in that event. The fact that withdrawal was considered at all reveals how serious a challenge to Westminster's authority in Northern Ireland the UWC strike had presented. On balance, however, withdrawal was at all times an unlikely option, given the serious problems which it would have created within Northern Ireland, and the damage to the international reputation of the UK. The 29 May diary entry of Bernard Donoughue, Wilson's senior policy advisor, claimed that Wilson favoured withdrawal from Northern Ireland. Importantly, Donoughue claimed that the 'machine [civil service] [was] preparing a counter-offensive', and did 'not want any moves towards a British withdrawal from Ulster'.[113] It is therefore likely that, even if Wilson had attempted to instigate withdrawal from Northern Ireland, he would have met with strong resistance from the civil service, and, from the cabinet also. Such resistance from the cabinet, upper echelons of the civil service, and the Army, made the prospect of withdrawal highly unlikely and potentially impracticable.

Conclusion

This chapter has illustrated how the divisions within unionist politics in Northern Ireland, following the collapse of Stormont, led to the conditions in which a successful loyalist political strike against British government policy in Northern Ireland occurred. Although divided on the future constitutional relationship between Northern Ireland and Great Britain, most unionists opposed the Council of Ireland provisions of Sunningdale. The strike had the expressed aim of securing fresh elections in Northern Ireland, but the UWC's own literature shows that there was also an explicitly sectarian character to its political agenda.

The response of the Northern Ireland Executive to the strike was ineffective. This was due to the fact that it had no control over security powers, either the police or the armed forces. It is also clear that the police did not act robustly against the strikers, prompting Merlyn Rees to remark that the RUC were unreliable in the face of the UWC action. Much of the wider Protestant community, to which most RUC officers belonged, sympathised with the overall aims of the strike. The executive itself remained relatively united throughout. The most significant disagreement was arguably the timing of the statement referring to the phased implementation of the Council of Ireland. However, as previously discussed, this issue was more problematic for the SDLP Assembly party than the executive. Despite the executive's relative unity, its standing among the unionist community, even those of a liberal or moderate persuasion, had been irrevocably damaged by the February general elections results.

It has been argued that the government had the power to 'tackle the strike', but failed to do so.[114] However, there were distinct limits to what the British government could do in the face of the strike. The UWC's control of the power-stations, coupled with the Army's inability to effectively generate and distribute power, without co-operation from senior management and technicians, gave the strikers a decisive advantage. Proposals to bring technicians from England to assist troops to run the stations, delayed on the advice of an NIES official, came too late in the day to attempt to save the executive. In any case, it will never be known whether such action might have succeeded, or whether, as Paisley suggested, a 'bloodbath' would have ensued. Wilson himself had inadvertently guaranteed the success of the strike following his infamous 'spongers' speech, which resulted in many moderate unionists siding with the UWC.

It has been argued that if Edward Heath had been Prime Minister, he would have acted against the strikers, but there appears to be no compelling evidence to support this view. The argument that British intervention would have defeated the strike tends to ignore the fact that, by the second week of the stoppage, a large number of the Protestant community was at least tacitly supportive of the strikers' aims. The government was not 'spineless' in avoiding a direct confrontation with the UWC: it simply recognised that the majority community was prepared to bring Northern Ireland to the brink in order to defeat Sunningdale and the executive. In this context, it would have been pointless for the government to attempt to save the unionists from themselves, as this may only have resulted in an increase in violent action. As Rees later commented, the UK was 'not Russia', and a popular uprising of this nature could not simply be put down by force.[115]

The strike led Harold Wilson to consider a plan for Dominion status for Northern Ireland, in the case of a complete breakdown of law and order. But too much significance should not be attributed to Wilson's 'Doomsday' document. There is no evidence that withdrawal from Northern Ireland was ever official government policy, or that it would have been countenanced by the government or higher civil service. The document, however, does offer a fascinating insight into aspects of the Prime Minister's thinking, and suggests, as Bew, Gibbon and Patterson have argued, that Wilson personally believed that 'no solution was possible except in the context of withdrawal'.[116] However, it was the long-term impact of the UWC strike on British government policy that was its most important legacy. The effects of the strike and the fall of the executive on British–Irish relations will be considered in the next chapter.

Notes

1 Kerr argues Wilson did not support power-sharing as it was arguably not the most realistic means of bringing about a united Ireland. See *Destructors*, p. 13; Kerr, *Imposing*, p. 68.

2 B. O'Leary, 'The Labour government and Northern Ireland' in J. McGarry and B. O'Leary, *The Northern Ireland Conflict: Consociational Engagements* (Oxford: Oxford University Press, 2004), p. 196.

3 J. Hume, *Personal Views: Politics, Peace and Reconciliation* (Dublin: TownHouse, 1996), p. 38.

4 Jackson, *Home Rule*, p. 280; F. Wright, *Northern Ireland: A Comparative Analysis* (Dublin: Gill and Macmillan, 1987), p. 238; Anderson, *14 May Days*, p. 103.

5 P. Bew, P. Gibbon and H. Patterson, *Northern Ireland 1921–1996: Political Forces and Social Classes* (London: Serif, 1996).

6 Craig, *Crisis*, pp. 180; 194.

7 Lee, *Ireland*, p. 445.

8 Wood, *Crimes*, pp. 3; 16.

9 Walker, *Unionist Party*, pp. 193–4. See chapter 1.

10 Wood, *Crimes*, p. 33.

11 This is not to suggest 'unionism' was a monolithic entity prior to this event, but the divisions certainly were more serious afterwards.

12 *Irish Times*, 6 May 1974.

13 Faulkner, *Memoirs*, p. 259.

14 Ibid., pp. 256–9.

15 For more on these unionist divisions, S. McDaid, 'Divided loyalties: Faulkner unionists and the Ulster Workers Council, 1974' in O. Coquelin, P. Galliou and T. Robin (eds), *Political Ideology in Ireland: From the Enlightenment to the Present* (Newcastle: Cambridge Scholars Press, 2009), pp. 258–74.

16 *Irish Times*, 23 April 1974.

17 Anderson, *14 May Days*, p. 148.

18 *Newsletter*, 17 May 1974.

19 Faulkner, *Memoirs*, p. 261.

20 Anderson, *14 May Days*, p. 97.

21 S. Wichert, *Northern Ireland since 1945* (London: Longman, 1991), p. 167.

22 Lee, *Ireland*, p. 445; Faulkner, *Memoirs*, pp. 262–3.

23 *Ulster General Strike: Strike Bulletins of the Workers' Association* (Belfast: Workers' Association, 1974), p. 70.

24 TNA, FCO 87/312, Thom to Harding, 31 July 1974.

25 J. Bennett (NILP) *Fourteen Days of Fascist Terror: The Truth about the Lock-out That Toppled the Assembly Government* (London: Connolly Publications, 1974), p. 5.

26 Bloomfield, *Tragedy*, p. 48.

27 Lee, *Ireland*, p. 445.

28 PRONI, D/4211/4/1/23, Roy Bradford Papers [papers relating to UWC strike].

29 Fisk, *The Point of No Return*, p. 46. S. Nelson, *Ulster's Uncertain Defenders: Protestant Political, Paramilitary and Community Groups and the Northern Ireland Conflict* (Belfast: Appletree, 1984), p. 155.

30 *UWC News Sheet*, no. 15, May 1974. Linen Hall Library Fiche (LLF) 2014.

31 Ibid., no. 19, May 1974.

32 PRONI OE/2/22, executive minutes, 14 May 1974.

33 Anderson, *14 May Days*, p. 4. See also Walker, *Unionist Party*, p. 216.

34 PRONI, OE/2/23, executive minutes, 17 May 1974.

35 PRONI OE/2/24, situation report by Maurice Hayes, [DHSS], executive minutes, 20 May 1974.

36 Ibid., executive minutes, 20 May 1974. It is not clear who made the above comment.

37 PRONI, OE/2/25, executive minutes, 21 May 1974. Bradford is not named in the records, but he had issued a public statement previously calling for negotiations with the UWC. See Faulkner, *Memoirs*, p. 270.

38 PRONI, OE/2/26, executive minutes, 22 May 1974. The meeting between Orme and the SDLP is discussed below. Thus, the executive never officially decided this matter by majority vote.

39 PRONI, OE/2/27, executive minutes, 22 May 1974.

40 Bruce, *Paisley*, pp. 106–7. David Trimble is also reported to have been sympathetic towards the UWC in the early days. Wood, *Crimes*, p. 46. Craig, however, is reported to have believed the strike would fail. Anderson, *14 May Days*, ch. 3.

41 PRONI, OE/2/27, executive minutes, 22 May 1974.

42 PRONI, OE/2/28, executive minutes, 23 May 1974.

43 PRONI, Central Secretariat files (CENT)/1/3/34, meeting at Chequers between the Prime Minister, the Secretary of State for Northern Ireland, the Secretary of State for Defence and the Attorney General with Mr Brian Faulkner, Mr Gerry Fitt and Mr Oliver Napier [Chequers meeting], 24 May 1974.

44 Fisk, p. 102.

45 PRONI, CENT/1/3/34, Chequers meeting, 24 May 1974.

46 PRONI, OE/2/30 executive minutes, 24 May 1974.

47 PRONI, OE/2/31, executive minutes, 27 May 1974.

48 Jackson, *Home Rule*, p. 279.

49 J. Bardon, *A History of Ulster* (Belfast: Blackstaff, 2001), p. 710.

50 Lee, *Ireland*, p. 444.

51 PRONI, OE/2/32, executive minutes, 28 May 1974.

52 PRONI, OE/1/24, meeting between Northern Ireland administration and the Secretary of State, 17 May 1974.

53 Ibid. Maurice Hayes also used the Weimar analogy when discussing the emergence of middle-class Protestant support for the strike. See *Minority*, p. 198.

54 PRONI, OE/2/32, executive minutes, 28 May 1974.

55 *UWC News Sheet*, no. 19, 29 May 1974.

56 TNA, CJ4/838, HQNI policy towards UDA and CESA, 6 November 1972. See also Fisk, p. 94

57 TNA, CJ4/491, the strike in Northern Ireland. Entry for 17 May 1974 notes 'Men in combat jackets and carrying sticks and cudgels stood beside the barricades and turned back many people trying to get to work.'

58 Currie, *All Hell*, p. 266.

59 TNA, PREM 16/146, note by Lord Bridges of a telephone conversation between the Prime Minister and the Secretary of State for Northern Ireland, 16 May 1974.

60 Kerr, *Destructors*, p. 171.

61 TNA, PREM 16/146, note by Lord Bridges of a telephone conversation between the Prime Minister and the Secretary of State for Northern Ireland, 16 May 1974.

62 Ibid., record of a conversation between Prime Minister and the Secretary of State, 17 May 1974.

63 Ibid., Nicholls to Butler, 17 May 1974.

64 TNA, CJ4/504, meeting between the Secretary of State, the GOC, Chief of Staff, Chief Constable and Officials, 17 May 1974.

65 PRONI, OE/1/24, meeting between the Northern Ireland Administration and the Secretary of State, 17 May 1974.

66 TNA, CJ4/504, confidential note on fuel reserves, 22 May 1974.

67 M. Dewar, *The British Army in Northern Ireland* (London: Arms and Armour, 1985), p. 100.

68 Wood, *Crimes* p. 45; Anderson, *14 May Days*, p. 68.

69 TNA, CJ4/504, meeting between the Secretary of State, the GOC, Chief of Staff, Chief Constable and Officials, 17 May 1974; ibid., meeting between the Prime Minister and the Chief Executive, 24 May 1974; TNA, CJ4/502, meeting between the Secretary of State and representatives of the Confederation of British Industry (CBI), 26 June 1974.

70 TNA, CJ4/504, meeting between the Minister of State and a delegation led by Dr Paisley, 15 May 1974.

71 Ibid., Cooper to Secretary of State, 16 May 1974.

72 *The Sun*, 22 May 1974.

73 TNA, CJ4/504, note for the record of a conversation between the Prime Minister and Dr O'Sullivan, 23 May 1974.

74 Faulkner, *Memoirs*, p. 274.
75 SDLP Assembly member for Armagh, later Deputy First Minister of Northern Ireland (1999–2001).
76 *Northern Ireland Assembly: Official Report*, vol. 3, col. 1220, 23 May 1974.
77 TNA, PREM 16/147, daily intelligence summary, 23 May 1974.
78 PRONI, OE/2/30, executive minutes, 24 May 1974.
79 D. McKittrick, B. Feeney, S. Kelters and C. Thornton, *Lost Lives: The Stories of the Men, Women and Children Who Died as a Result of the Northern Ireland Troubles* (Edinburgh: Mainstream, 2nd edn, 2007), pp. 454–5. One of the gang was sentenced to life imprisonment for murder, Wood, *Crimes*, p. 45.
80 Wilson, *Final Term*, p. 76.
81 PRONI, OE/2/21, executive minutes, 13 May 1974.
82 PRONI, OE/2/22, executive minutes, 14 May 1974.
83 PRONI, OE/2/24, executive minutes. 20 May 1974.
84 See Currie, *All Hell*, p. 264; PRONI, OE/2/26, executive minutes, 23 May 1974.
85 Currie, *All Hell*, p. 270.
86 P. Dixon, '"A house divided cannot stand": Britain, bipartisanship and Northern Ireland', *Contemporary Record*, ix: 1 (1995), pp. 147–87, p. 169.
87 TNA, CJ4/501, Note for the Record, 23 May 1974.
88 TNA, CJ4/1147, record of a conversation between the Prime Minister and the Secretary of State for Northern Ireland at RNAS Caldrose, Penzance, 26 May 1974.
89 Ibid., meeting between the Secretary of State and senior commerce officials, 27 May 1974.
90 TNA, PREM 16/148, Kampala to FCO, 28 May 1974.
91 Wilson was MP for the Huyton Constituency (located in the Liverpool region) from 1950 to 1983.
92 *Irish Times*, 1 June 1974.
93 Kerr, *Imposing*, p. 68.
94 Kerr, *Destructors*, p. 13.
95 Whitelaw, *Memoirs*, p. 156.
96 TNA, CJ4/501, summary of main incidents for Chief of Staff by Major W. E. Rous, 29 May 1974.
97 TNA, CJ4/491, note for the record, 29 May, 1974. Dalyell was an outspoken critic of devolution within Great Britain, and author of *Devolution: The End of Britain* (London: Jonathan Cape, 1977). Wellbeloved was Labour MP for Erith and Crayford, but defected to the Social Democratic Party in 1981.
98 TNA, CJ4/491, note for the record, 29 May 1974 (Meeting between Wilson, Rees, Sir Alec Douglas-Home and Francis Pym). For the RUC during the strike, see K. Sheehy, *More Questions Than Answers: Reflecting on a Life in the RUC* (Dublin: Gill and Macmillan, 2008), pp. 23–4. Sheehy argues that he received orders to ignore loyalist barricades from his superiors in Bangor during the UWC strike. For histories of the RUC, G. Ellison and J. Smyth, *The Crowned Harp: Policing Northern Ireland* (London: Pluto Press, 2000); C. Ryder, *The RUC: A Force under Fire* (London: Methuen, 1989).

99 The Isle of Man is a British Crown dependency, which is responsible for its domestic affairs. Its foreign relations and defence are the responsibility of the UK government, but it is neither a part of the UK nor a member of the European Union.

100 TNA, CJ4/491, meeting between Secretary of State and William Craig, 30 May 1974.

101 Ibid., meeting between Secretary of State and Dr Paisley, 30 May 1974.

102 Ibid., meeting between Secretary of State and Harry West, 30 May 1974.

103 Ibid., meeting between Secretary of State and Oliver Napier, 30 May 1974; meeting between Secretary of State and Gerry Fitt, 30 May 1974.

104 Ibid., meeting between Secretary of State and Gerry Fitt, 30 May 1974.

105 Ibid., meeting between Secretary of State and Brian Faulkner, 30 May 1974.

106 Ibid., Rees to Wilson, 31 May, 1974.

107 The following year, elections to the Northern Ireland Convention took place. This is discussed in the final chapter.

108 TNA, PREM 16/147, constitutional options in Northern Ireland, report by group of officials, 22 May 1974.

109 TNA, PREM 16/148, Wilson to Robert Armstrong, 30 May 1974 [Principal Private Secretary to the PM]. A similar phrase is used in Joe Haines' memoirs (Wilson's Press Secretary). 'In the Province, we have responsibility without power, the prerogative of the eunuch throughout the ages'. J. Haines, *The Politics of Power* (London: Jonathan Cape, 1977), p. 121.

110 TNA PREM 16/148, Wilson to Robert Armstrong, 30 May 1974. Wilson was affected by the Rhodesian negotiations. Unlike Rhodesia. [Northern Ireland's] 'landed frontier would not be with a country (such as Salazar's Mozambique) through whom no help or comfort could come'.

111 Ibid., Wilson to Armstrong, 30 May 1974.

112 Ibid., Armstrong to Wilson, 31 May 1974. Wilson's official biographer has suggested that withdrawal was only discussed with a few senior officials. P. Zeigler, *The Authorised Life of Lord Wilson of Rievaulx* (London: Weidenfeld and Nicolson, 1993), p. 466. As the following chapter demonstrates, discussions concerning withdrawal took place within the cabinet later in 1974.

113 B. Donoughue, *Downing Street Diary: With Harold Wilson in No. 10* (London: Jonathan Cape, 2004), p. 130.

114 Kerr, *Imposing*, p. 69.

115 P. Taylor, *Brits: The War Against the IRA* (London: Bloomsbury, 2001), p. 162

116 Bew, Gibbon and Patterson, *Northern Ireland*, p. 191.

6

Government policy after the UWC strike and British–Irish relations, 1974–75

In the aftermath of the UWC strike, the British government reconsidered its policy in relation to Northern Ireland. A number of options were examined by officials and politicians, including repartition, withdrawal and total integration. However, these were all reckoned too problematic. The Labour government refused to abandon the principles of policy established by the previous Conservative administration. The only solution acceptable to it was one based on power-sharing with an Irish dimension. In the absence of politicians in Northern Ireland agreeing to such a solution, direct rule would continue indefinitely.

Following the executive's collapse, the British–Irish relationship came under considerable strain. The Irish government feared that the British were considering disengagement from Northern Ireland. These fears were compounded by the British government's decision to engage in secret discussions with paramilitary groups, in a tentative attempt to steer them away from political violence. High level negotiations took place between government representatives and the PIRA, aimed at establishing an enduring ceasefire. These talks caused much anxiety among Dublin politicians. However, the Irish government's fears were misplaced. Engaging with paramilitaries was not a prelude to British withdrawal. It was merely part of a wider attempt to reduce violence, since the persistence of paramilitary attacks diminished the prospects of any future political initiative. Notwithstanding these tensions, cross-border security co-operation appeared to improve steadily throughout 1974 and 1975. It was logical for the Irish government to take steps to improve security co-operation, since it recognised that maintaining a British presence in Northern Ireland was essential to the stability of the southern state.

The immediate aftermath of the strike: relations with the Republic and British Northern Ireland policy

To understand the motivations behind the Republic's Northern Ireland policy, it is necessary to return to one of the key events during the UWC strike. On

17 May 1974, a series of loyalist bombs were detonated in Dublin and Monaghan. Thirty-three civilians were killed, the highest loss-of-life in a single day during the Northern Ireland conflict.[1] The attacks demonstrated the Republic's vulnerability to violence spreading over the border. To strengthen the Republic's frontier defences, 300 Irish troops, on peace-keeping duty in the Middle East, were recalled for deployment to the Northern Ireland border.[2]

Although these bombings were the work of loyalists, Arthur Galsworthy, the British Ambassador to Ireland, reported an outpouring of anti-IRA sentiment in the aftermath. This was because many people in the Republic blamed the IRA for initiating the violence. This anti-IRA sentiment, he claimed, augured well for more overt security co-operation. However, he advised caution regarding Irish public opinion, which had 'long been content to watch violence in the North'. It was only when the Republic itself experienced violence that it reacted in the way that the North had 'sought for so long'. However, Galsworthy warned that 'it would be a mistake . . . to rub this point in.'[3]

Some tensions between Dublin and London arose during the UWC strike. The Irish government privately criticised the Westminster government for its handling of the stoppage. It was particularly disappointed with the response of the British security forces. On 24 May, the Taoiseach, Liam Cosgrave, conveyed these views to Harold Wilson. He condemned the RUC and Army for their 'frequent consultation and negotiation with the armed gangs involved'. Such inaction, he argued, might lead the minority to 'swing over to the I.R.A.'.[4] Despite these criticisms, the two governments maintained frequent contact, both during, and immediately after the strike.

Following the collapse of the executive, the Irish government's public response was one of 'profound and muted regret'. Arthur Galsworthy reported that the Dublin coalition's statements about its collapse were 'free from recrimination' against the British government.[5] Indeed, the Irish coalition had 'no disagreement with the broad strategy' of British Northern Ireland policy following the strike, as Garret FitzGerald confirmed to the British Ambassador.[6] Throughout June 1974, Galsworthy noted that the Irish government's statements, concerning Northern Ireland, attempted to reassure the unionist community of its friendly intentions. The Taoiseach spoke publicly about the need to create a spirit of friendship between the northern and southern states.[7] Furthermore, the Minister for Posts and Telegraphs, Conor Cruise O'Brien, stated that there was no hope of securing unionist consent for Irish unity for many years. While welcoming these remarks, Galsworthy was concerned that Fianna Fáil might attempt to portray the coalition as being opposed to a united Ireland.[8] As 1974 progressed, however, the Irish government became increasingly pessimistic about the prospects for stability. Some disagreements emerged between Dublin and London over the latter's Northern Ireland policy. In June of that year, the Northern Ireland Secretary, Merlyn Rees, believed that any political settlement in Northern Ireland should originate with the region's own politicians. A solution imposed by Westminster would, in his opinion, not succeed.

Rees favoured the establishment of an elected Constitutional Convention. It would act as a forum for political debate, and produce a report outlining its preferred future form of government. However, he confirmed that a 'number of principles' would have to be adhered to if the Convention report was to be accepted. The form of government acceptable to both communities, should involve 'some form of power-sharing', and also recognise the need for co-operation 'between North and South'.[9] The Prime Minister, at a meeting with the SDLP leadership, confirmed that power-sharing remained central to government policy. According to Wilson, Northern Ireland could either 'stay in the United Kingdom with power-sharing', or have 'an independent status'. However, this amounted to no choice at all, since the only form of independence the government would concede, was one with guaranteed 'power-sharing' for the minority community.[10] Later, in a letter to Jack Lynch, leader of the Fianna Fáil party, the Prime Minister again emphasised that his government, and the Conservative and Liberal parties, believed that 'power-sharing must be the basis and the essence of any future solution'.[11] Michael Kerr has claimed that Heath and Wilson had 'contrasting approaches' to power-sharing, and that Wilson did not support the idea, since it was not the 'most realistic means of bringing about a united Ireland.'[12] However, the evidence demonstrates that Wilson's government refused to countenance any settlement which did *not* involve power-sharing. Thus, without power-sharing, there would be no devolution and no independence: direct rule would continue instead.

This commitment to power-sharing was confirmed on 4 July 1974, when a White Paper, *The Northern Ireland Constitution*, was published. Consistent with Rees's thinking, the document stated that an elected Convention should meet to consider the future government of Northern Ireland. However, the White Paper re-emphasised what had been decided in 1973: that '[t]here is an Irish dimension', and that any recommendation made by the Constitutional Convention must command 'widespread support from its members'. In practice, this meant that it must be acceptable to unionists *and* nationalists. Importantly, it explicitly stated that 'there must be some form of power-sharing and partnership' in any new political arrangement. Only if these conditions were met, would the government give 'serious consideration' to the Convention's proposals.[13] Shortly thereafter, the Northern Ireland Act (1974) was passed, which reintroduced direct rule, and also legislated for the holding of the proposed Convention elections at a later date.[14]

The Irish government reacted negatively to the proposed Constitutional Convention. Cosgrave asked Wilson to consult with Dublin before taking any new initiative, since it might also have implications for the political stability of the Republic. Particularly, he requested to be informed before any revision of the Sunningdale agreement was contemplated, such as the devolution of extra powers to any new Northern Ireland Assembly.[15] However, no such plan actually existed. The aim of British policy was, in the short term, to proceed with the Convention in the hope that a 'Northern Ireland' solution might emerge. The Dublin government, however, became increasingly fearful that withdrawal from Northern Ireland was being seriously considered in Whitehall.

On 25 July, Maurice Hayes, a prominent Catholic civil servant in Northern Ireland, wrote a memorandum entitled 'Political Developments in the Irish Republic'. This memorandum mentioned Dublin's concerns about the direction of British policy. According to Hayes, the Irish government was 'living in fear of a British withdrawal' from Northern Ireland. He reported that most people in the Republic wished the North would 'go away – preferably not in their direction'. Because Dublin would be powerless in the event of a British withdrawal, Hayes concluded that the coalition would accept 'virtually any [Northern Ireland] settlement which . . . [would give] some degree of equity to the Catholic in the North, while preserving the stability of society'.[16] The memorandum was intended for Kenneth Bloomfield, former Secretary to the Executive, but it also reached Frank Cooper, Permanent Under-Secretary (PUS) of the NIO and the British Ambassador in Dublin.[17] Garret FitzGerald retrospectively confirmed that, following the collapse of the executive, the Irish cabinet feared that British withdrawal was an imminent possibility.[18]

That same month, Merlyn Rees announced plans which he claimed were designed to assist former detainees upon their release. He informed the House of Commons that a group known as the Resettlement Agency of Northern Ireland (RANI) would receive a grant of £20,000 from the Treasury.[19] RANI was ostensibly independent of government, and designed to help ex-detainees reintegrate into their communities. However, the group was also designed to encourage contact between various paramilitary groups, and to engage them in political dialogue. Whilst the government's policy of dialogue with paramilitary groups continued, its relationship with the SDLP, the representatives of constitutional nationalism, became more fraught.

One source of tension was the SDLP's involvement in the European Court of Human Rights (ECHR) case between Ireland and the UK. The case, originally taken by the Irish government, alleged that the British Army was guilty of torturing detainees in Northern Ireland. Former SDLP executive ministers Gerry Fitt and Paddy Devlin gave evidence in the case, criticising Army behaviour. Both the British and Irish delegates had difficulty understanding Devlin's evidence, on account his strong Northern Ireland accent, which also caused problems for the Strasbourg translators. Following his evidence, one interpreter reportedly asked the Irish delegation 'please, what is a f*** the Pope band?'.[20]

By far a more serious cause of friction between the two sides was the proposed Constitutional Convention. On 9 August, *The Guardian* published a statement by John Hume claiming that the London government intended to use the Convention to 'prepare the ground' for withdrawal from Northern Ireland.[21] Merlyn Rees, however, dismissed the SDLP's concerns in a letter to the Prime Minister. The party's distrust of the government was 'quite indefensible in view of [the SDLP's] "connexion" with the Labour Party'.[22] Rees's assumption, that the SDLP did not trust the Labour government, was confirmed at a meeting with the SDLP leadership on 29 August. The party was bitterly disappointed with the government's performance during the UWC strike. Gerry Fitt accused it of 'total and abject surrender' to the loyalists, and claimed that the strike could have been dealt with had the government taken 'early action'. He further alleged that the Conservative government had honoured its Sunningdale pledges, 'but the Labour government had not kept their word'. The behaviour of the British Army in nationalist areas was also harshly criticised. Seamus Mallon complained that 'virtually every young Catholic in Armagh had been detained at one time or another, sometimes repeatedly'. The SDLP also suggested that the 'British government was harassing the Catholics because it was powerless to cope with the Protestants', and also indicated that it was seriously considering boycotting the proposed Convention, which it described as a 'farce'. Fitt also complained that the government's commitments in the White Paper regarding power-sharing were 'inadequate'. He then mentioned the possibility of Irish military intervention in the event of an attempted loyalist takeover: 'in a Doomsday situation it had to be remembered that Ireland was an island and that the Army of the South might march North to defend their Catholic brothers'.[23] However, this was never the policy of the Irish government, which was primarily concerned with preventing violence from spreading to the southern state. Relations were not only tense between the SDLP and the British government; the party's dealings with the Irish government were often stressed and difficult also.

The SDLP's abrasive political style was not appreciated by the Irish government, which attempted to keep the party at 'arm's length'. British documents record that the SDLP was dissatisfied with the level of support it received from the government in the Republic. This was referred to in an August meeting between Merlyn Rees and Diarmuid O'Sullivan, the Irish Ambassador to the UK. O'Sullivan claimed that the SDLP had been 'stirring things up' in the media, with reports that Dublin was unhappy with the frequency of contact between itself and London.[24] The documentary evidence clearly demonstrates that the prevalent presumption, that Dublin and the SDLP shared the same aims and policies, greatly oversimplifies the historical reality of the period.

The SDLP's political isolation was recognised by London officials. Adrian Carter (NIO), in a 9 September letter to Lord Bridges (Wilson's Private Secretary) stated that relations between the Dublin government and the SDLP were 'somewhat strained'. Carter claimed that recent (separate) statements by both the Taoiseach and Conor Cruise O'Brien, which downplayed the possibility of a united Ireland, came as an 'unwelcome shock' to the SDLP. Consequently, he argued, the party was fearful of losing Catholic support and being 'outflanked' by the IRA. Thus, the SDLP began highlighting issues such as the unduly aggressive behaviour of the British Army in nationalist areas. The letter concluded with the observation that the SDLP needed the government's help, because of its difficult relations with Dublin and the 'constant Protestant scrutiny' which it found itself under.[25]

The following day, members of the SDLP met the Prime Minister in London. Gerry Fitt outlined the feelings of despair and isolation in the Catholic community, and the particular concern about the proposed Constitutional Convention. This, he argued, was an 'open cheque' to the Protestants, who were 'now looking for total ascendancy'. Wilson, however, reassured Fitt that any recommendations which the proposed Convention might make would have to be approved by the government, ratified by Parliament, and based 'on a power-sharing plan'. When pressed by John Hume, as to whether this meant 'power-sharing in Government', Wilson confirmed that 'this was his meaning'. The only alternative for the loyalists was a Unilateral Declaration of Independence (UDI). Hume then asked how the government would react to this. Wilson replied that it would be both unacceptable and impractical. Northern Ireland 'would not last three weeks without British support'.[26] Nevertheless, the SDLP remained apprehensive about the future stability of Northern Ireland, and the government's intentions towards the region.

Later that month, secret talks between opposing factions of paramilitary groups took place. It was reported that leaders from both the OIRA and PIRA were in contact with loyalists. These talks were initiated by the UDA leader, Andy Tyrie, a central figure in the UWC strike committee, and were attended by over sixty people. The British government reported that there were indications that some of the 'politically minded provisional leaders (particularly the Belfast ones) . . . wished to find an opportunity of halting their terrorist campaign'. The various paramilitaries displayed 'a certain amount of camaraderie' towards one another, and further meetings were planned. Rees reported that the talks were being kept strictly secret, but that the government was providing modest 'unattributable [sic] support'. Of all the paramilitary groups, the OIRA was reportedly most in favour of political dialogue. The PIRA was apparently less enthusiastic, and the UDA 'merely willing to experiment'. The

UVF did not participate in the inter-paramilitary talks due to the 'extreme attitude of the majority of its members'. Discreet funding was also provided for a series of university seminars to promote contacts between the competing paramilitary groups. If these talks proved fruitful, the government expected to organise further meetings between the opposing sides. These initiatives, whilst potentially embarrassing for the government, were deemed politically worthwhile.[27] The existing literature concerning this period tends only to emphasise the government's contact with the PIRA, but archival evidence shows that secret exchanges with loyalist paramilitaries were also ongoing and extensive.[28]

As 1974 progressed, new policy initiatives were considered by the British government. However, whilst several options were examined, there was little deviation from the principle that any restoration of devolution would include power-sharing. Failing that, direct rule would remain the fallback option for the government.

British policy proposals: the difficulties of radical options

The United Kingdom general election was held on 10 October 1974. Labour returned to power with a majority of just three seats.[29] Coincidentally, the weeks following the election witnessed an upsurge in sectarian violence in Northern Ireland. The intensity of this violence prompted media speculation about potential British withdrawal, and what the Irish Army might do in that event. An *Irish Times* report claimed that plans had been made which envisaged the Irish Army crossing the border in the event of having to fill a 'political vacuum'.[30] However, the actual plan was only one of contingency, and, as Paul Bew correctly suggested, merely reaffirmed the inability of the Irish Army to defend the Republic in the event of island-wide civil war.[31] It is clear that the media's reporting of the Irish contingency plan stirred up unionist feeling. The United Ulster Unionist Coalition (UUUC) leaders complained to Merlyn Rees about it. However, he reassured them it was merely a *contingency plan*, of the kind made by most governments, and affirmed that there would be no withdrawal on the basis of 'letting the people of Ulster "get on with it"'.[32]

On 23 October, Harold Wilson wrote to Merlyn Rees outlining his thoughts regarding possible future Northern Ireland policy. He believed there was a strong case for reviving one of the ideas contained in his 1971 'fifteen point plan': an all-party conference on the future of Northern Ireland. This would include all the Northern Ireland parties and the three major parties from Great Britain. However, Wilson argued that no statement referring to this proposed conference should be issued until after the Convention elections.[33] In the absence of any viable alternative, the government decided that the Convention, as outlined in the July 1974 White Paper, should proceed (although the Convention election itself did not take place until the following year).

That same day, the Cabinet Secretary, John Hunt, wrote a memo concerning the Convention elections. He believed the elections should proceed, despite the Convention itself being 'likely to fail.' He also highlighted the need to reassure the SDLP regarding power-sharing, lest it boycott the Convention election and return to its 'traditional practice of abstention'. The memo also noted the need to downplay the Irish dimension. Hunt did not think that the Irish dimension should be abandoned. Indeed, he argued for closer co-operation with the Republic especially on security matters. However, owing to loyalist sentiment, he thought the government should abandon the 'political trimmings' of the Irish dimension in the form of institutionalised co-operation.[34]

Wilson's Private Secretary, Lord Bridges, discussed power-sharing in a letter to the Prime Minister, Robert Armstrong and Robin Butler, dated 23 October.[35] Bridges believed that power-sharing was the only 'just solution', but that it was unattainable in present circumstances. Neither was it within the government's power to impose it. He suggested there were two options: either withdrawal or re-partition – the latter involving the cession of parts of Northern Ireland to the Republic. The former was deemed to be too problematic to attempt, given the bloodshed and international humiliation which it would precipitate. Re-partition was also considered to be distasteful, problematic, and expensive and carried the risk of violent enforced population transfers.[36] Bridges's letter demonstrated the extreme difficulty of undertaking any radical political initiative. It reinforced the idea that direct rule was the only acceptable interim solution, if Northern Ireland's politicians could not agree on a power-sharing settlement.

Merlyn Rees believed that if the proposed Convention broke down, or failed to produce a report acceptable to the Westminster parties, the government should be prepared to develop a new 'political policy'. However, he was clear on two points: there was no chance of a united Ireland, and the complete integration of Northern Ireland with the rest of the UK was out of the question. He added that, politically, Great Britain 'must, in the end, move away from our present relationship with the North', although it would be incumbent on the British government to 'reassure the South and others that we will not leave a Congo situation there'.[37] Viewed in isolation, this document might be considered as evidence that the government was contemplating a managed disengagement from Northern Ireland. However, read in the context of other documentation produced at this time, what Rees was referring to was not disengagement in the sense of withdrawal, but having the government take a less prominent role in any future discussions. It should attempt to allow an 'internal settlement', to be worked out by Northern Ireland politicians themselves, with direct rule continuing while the search for a solution was ongoing. The importance of the Irish government to any future settlement was also referred to in Whitehall at this time. It was clear that a formal Council of Ireland was impossible.

In an October memorandum, it was noted that 'formal *institutionalised* co-operation between North and South [was] now dead. *We need to develop practical contacts in its stead*.'[38] It stated that the goal of British policy should leave 'room for closer and more regular contact with the Irish Government leading to a firmer basis for relations between the two countries'. It was also asserted that the Irish government's main concern was a 'guaranteed share in government' for the minority community, and that Dublin would be content with 'much less formal' cross-border co-operation. However, for the British government, the problem was 'to get the Northern Protestants to believe this, and accept that "good neighbourliness" should imply a degree of fraternisation, as distinct from a negative and stand-offish concept of non-interference'. Privately, the British government resolved to keep the Irish informed, and provide a greater consultative role for Dublin regarding Northern Ireland policy. This co-operation involved more than going 'through the motions' of simply informing Dublin about policy proposals. It also meant providing the Irish government with 'an opportunity to contribute to ideas' which would be taken into account 'in the formulation of [British] policy'. This approach carried some security risks, given the 'Irish government's propensity to leaks in the press'. Nonetheless, the memo argued that Dublin's views 'on the future Constitutional pattern for Northern Ireland' should be sought.[39] In Dublin, however, uncertainty continued to characterise the coalition's attitude to Northern Ireland, as the Irish contingency plans from the period reveal.

Irish contingency planning: fears of a British withdrawal

Senior Irish politicians and officials were deeply concerned by the proposed Constitutional Convention. They feared that loyalist paramilitaries, with the tacit or active support of unionist politicians, would attempt a Unilateral Declaration of Independence. On 23 October, Conor Cruise O'Brien, MEP Justin Keating and Dermot Nally from the Department of the Taoiseach met the British Ambassador, Arthur Galsworthy. They expressed fears about the outcome of the planned Convention. A loyalist majority would, they argued, be unwilling to support power-sharing, or anything 'smacking of an Irish dimension'. They put it to Galsworthy that, should this occur, HMG would not face up to the 'runaway horse', and would effectively acquiesce in a 'new version of Protestant supremacy'. Replying, Galsworthy argued that the outcome might be worse if the government refused to hold the Convention elections. Loyalist violence might increase due to frustration at a perceived inability to have a say in how Northern Ireland should be governed. He concluded that, although O'Brien, Keating and Nally were not speaking in an official capacity, a loyalist takeover of Northern Ireland was considered possible by the Irish government.[40] Evidence emerged the following month which confirmed Galsworthy's suspicions.

On 13 November 1974, the Irish Embassy wrote to the Foreign and Commonwealth Office (FCO) to request the following specific and unusual information.

1. What ex-colonial grant-in-aid, if any, was paid by the United Kingdom to former British colonies such as Cyprus, Aden, Kenya, on their gaining of independence?
2. On what criteria, if any, was the amount of aid determined in each case
3. How long did the aid continue?[41]

Further enquiries were made to the Home Office. These concerned the financial arrangements between the UK, the Isle of Man and the Channel Islands. An FCO official had no doubt why these requests were made. It did 'not require a great leap of the imagination to see the answers to these questions being incorporated in Irish thinking about the viability of an independent Northern Ireland'. The official speculated, correctly, that the reason for this thinking was that the Irish could not accept the repeated British assurances that no withdrawal of troops would take place as long as the security situation required their presence.[42] However, given that the Irish government had supposedly heard rumours of Wilson's May 1974 'Doomsday' document, its apprehension was understandable.[43]

A note by Walter Kirwan from the Department of the Taoiseach, commenting on a memorandum by Garret FitzGerald, demonstrates how concerned the Irish government was about potential British withdrawal. This minute shows that the government considered seeking an arrangement with the British to put Northern Ireland under a UN trusteeship. Kirwan recognised that the likelihood of UN involvement was minimal and, in any case, might not reduce violence. He foresaw three possible outcomes if the Convention failed: (1) the concession of devolved government to the loyalists by the British; (2) Unilateral Declaration of Independence by the loyalists; or (3), an autonomous Northern Ireland associated with the UK, 'in the same way as the Isle of Man or the Channel Islands'. He concluded that the most likely options were either a return to indefinite direct rule or 'negotiated independence over the full six county area or smaller area'. He confirmed that an Interdepartmental Unit on Northern Ireland (IDU) was studying the possible implications of the latter.[44]

The Irish government's other main concern was the sovereignty of the southern state. Dublin was particularly troubled by the threat republican and loyalist subversives posed to that sovereignty, in the event of a British with-drawal. A government memorandum referred to what might happen in such a '"doomsday" situation', were loyalists to forcibly take over Northern Ireland. Bloody civil war was considered the likely outcome, which could 'spill over' into the Republic. On a slightly more positive note, the Gardaí considered that no faction of the IRA would be able to 'take over' areas of either the northern or southern state for any considerable period of time. Loyalist paramilitaries were considered potentially more dangerous. It was also thought that, in the absence of the British Army, the RUC would 'side with the loyalists', with the latter embarking on a concerted campaign against the northern Catholic community.[45]

The further evolution of Irish government thinking on Northern Ireland is evident in a DFA memorandum of November 1974. The memo was con-cerned with what initiatives the British government might take in Northern Ireland in advance of the Convention elections. One of the possibilities con-sidered was that the British government might attempt an initiative to end IRA violence, in the hope of creating 'a new climate of opinion for discussion'. It was reported that the SDLP, acting on information from a source within the Northern Ireland Office, informed the Department of Foreign Affairs (DFA) that the British government was considering withdrawing the Army to barracks 'and the ending of internment'. The DFA thought this might be pos-sible in the context of Merlyn Rees's statement issued on 12 November. Here, Rees stated that if violence was ended, there was a potential to bring about a new situation in Northern Ireland.[46] However, a new initiative was thought too difficult in light of the hard-line statements made by the PIRA's Dáithí Ó Conaill in an Independent Television Network interview on 17 November. Here, Ó Conaill stated that the PIRA planned to escalate its bombing cam-paign in Great Britain.[47] Further dangers mentioned in the memorandum included the possibility of 'a de facto IRA takeover of areas evacuated by the army' and the perception that the British were 'looking to the IRA rather than to the SDLP as the representatives of the minority'. The potential hostility of the northern majority was also mentioned. Nevertheless, it was thought that an initiative, of the kind mentioned by Rees, might lead to an ending of PIRA violence, creating conditions from which a solution might emerge. However, the chances of such an initiative were considered '*possible*, but improbable'. The memorandum outlined three possible outcomes in the present situation. These were: developments leading to a peaceful solution within the UK; developments leading to 'large-scale civil war'; and developments leading to a peaceful solution outside the UK. In the event of an outbreak of civil war, the Irish government could do little to prevent the spread of violence, or to protect the lives of Irish citizens in Northern Ireland. Indeed, it was thought that the government had insufficient capacity to 'prevent the emergence of a *de facto* independent Protestant state in East Ulster or a *de facto* independent state controlled by the Provisional IRA in West Ulster'. In the unlikely event that an international peace-keeping force was deployed, such a force was unlikely to be able to do 'more than patrol the border or borders between any new de facto states . . . or between the Republic . . . and a new de facto Protestant state in East Ulster'. The other possible solutions envisaged in the memo were a peacefully achieved independent Northern Ireland, or a Northern Ireland placed under UN trusteeship.

A peaceful solution within the UK was considered unlikely. Indefinite direct rule was thought objectionable to most loyalists, although integration was believed to be potentially more favourable to that community. It was thought that, on the minority side, integration would 'perhaps command more acceptance than might be expected a priori'. However, the percentage of nationalists opposed to such a solution was thought sufficient to sustain the PIRA's armed campaign. For the Irish government, total integration was 'the least easy to accept', since it would appear as a reversal of movement 'towards an ultimate political relationship between North and South'.[48]

The DFA memorandum stated that Dublin should consider accepting an independent Northern Ireland in very specific circumstances, including guarantees for the minority, or some UN involvement.[49] However, independence should only be considered acceptable if it was 'based on power-sharing in government, guarantees for the minority and a built-in possibility of maximum co-operation' between the Dublin and Belfast administrations. This was a slightly modified version of the Sunningdale formula. The memorandum supported the continued presence of British troops in Northern Ireland, since any withdrawal endangered the minority, 'especially in East Ulster'.[50] An outbreak of civil war in Northern Ireland was thought likely to discredit both the SDLP and the Irish government in the eyes of the minority, particularly if 'the IRA could claim credit for achieving the departure of Britain and its army despite the opposition of the Irish government and the SDLP to such an outcome'. A solution to these potential problems was not forthcoming, but the memorandum concluded by urging the Irish government to examine policies that might avert the 'very grave' danger of civil war in Northern Ireland.

A further DFA memorandum asserted that discussions with the SDLP should begin regarding the policy options open to it in the event of the predicted loyalist rejection of power-sharing with an Irish dimension at the Convention.[51] However, further evidence of the distance between the policies of the SDLP, and those of the Dublin government, emerged that same month. The memorandum also stated that the SDLP should not be 'encouraged to think in terms of military intervention' from the Republic in Northern Ireland. As mentioned, the SDLP informed the British government that this might occur if loyalists attacked the minority community. However, such intervention by the Republic would have required up to 60,000 troops, and cost an estimated £220 million per annum to sustain. The Irish Army had a potential strength of 14,231 professional soldiers, and 16,219 members of the army reserve. It is therefore apparent that it had neither the human or financial resources to become involved in an operation in Northern Ireland. Even with 60,000 troops (the memorandum stated), intervention would be futile and essential services could not be guaranteed.[52] The Irish government was clearly more concerned with the interests of the Republic, than in lending support to the Northern Ireland minority, and it is evident that the Irish government had differing priorities to those of the SDLP.

The potential of a loyalist takeover was not the only issue of concern for the government of the Republic during this period. As 1974 progressed, the British policy of engaging in speculative dialogue with paramilitaries caused much anxiety in Dublin. There was considerable discussion between British officials and the PIRA, as the latter began making tentative moves towards a ceasefire at the end of 1974. However, despite Dublin's fears, the British government's engagement with the PIRA was not a prequel to British withdrawal from Northern Ireland.

Power-sharing and PIRA ceasefires

On 1 November 1974, the Taoiseach met with Harold Wilson in London to discuss Dublin's concerns regarding the future of Northern Ireland. Liam Cosgrave was anxious about what action the British government might take in the event of a deadlock situation in the Convention. He asked what Wilson would do if unionists refused to countenance a power-sharing solution. The Prime Minister assured him that the newly elected British parliament 'would refuse to consider any scheme for the Province which was not based on power-sharing'. Any form of a revived Stormont would not be acceptable, and his government was doing all it could to convince public opinion that 'the only future still lay in a power-sharing scheme'.[53] Later that morning, a further meeting took place between British and Irish ministers and officials. The Prime Minister repeated that neither his government, nor the Westminster parliament, would accept any solution not based on the principle of power-sharing. However, Irish ministers were concerned that the Protestant community might stage another strike if its preferred solution, a return to the old Stormont, was not granted. Replying, Wilson suggested that the UWC strike had succeeded due to Protestant fears of the Irish dimension. He did not believe that 'power-sharing by itself' was likely to provoke a similar reaction. Indeed, he stressed that the target of the UWC had been the executive. It would be a quite different matter for unionists to try to force the British parliament, united in its opposition, to agree to 'the resurrection of a new type of Stormont'.[54] Irish ministers asked Wilson and Rees, who was also in attendance, what steps would be taken to protect Catholic areas in the event of loyalist attacks and intimidation. The British suggested that the Army could be deployed, and that economic sanctions against the Protestant community would also be considered. Wilson stated that, if the loyalists attempted a coup, 'it would be relatively easy to prevent the shipment of heavy goods which the Protestant community would need'. Some differences arose between the two sides concerning the Army's behaviour in Catholic areas. Garret FitzGerald (Minister for Foreign Affairs) argued that the Army should be confined to a policing role, and its presence reduced in these districts. Rees and Wilson, on the other hand, claimed that this would effectively mean handing the areas 'over to the IRA', with the risk of increased violence and many more deaths. This meeting concluded with Irish ministers being told that the discussion could be continued with Merlyn Rees, as the Prime Minister's time was limited due to other engagements.

Meanwhile, the British government, through interlocutors, was involved in secret discussion with the IRA during this period. On 13 November, Lord Bridges wrote about the clandestine discussions between NIO officials and the PIRA. The Prime Minister was reportedly 'content that officials should continue these very secret contacts on a non-attributable basis'. However, he was not prepared to offer any 'easement on internment', since he did not believe that senior members of the Belfast PIRA leadership, could 'deliver' a ceasefire.[55] Nevertheless, contacts between government representatives and the PIRA continued as the year drew to a close. Politically, the proposed Constitutional Convention remained the focus of attention.

It is clear that there was likely to be only one realistic option available if the planned Convention could not agree on power-sharing: an indefinite period of direct rule. A memo by John Hunt for the Prime Minister, dated 22 November, confirmed that this was the case. Unilateral British withdrawal was deemed particularly objectionable, although it was not entirely without its advocates in cabinet. The Home Secretary, Roy Jenkins, believed that if the Convention failed, the government 'would probably have to withdraw'. Likewise, negotiated independence was also ruled out, failing 'some miracle' where the two communities 'both came down in favour of it'. Given these difficulties, officials concluded that the only 'practical option' available to the government was 'to persevere with some form of direct rule', albeit with 'some differences'. The emphasis would shift from a British search for a solution to allowing Northern Ireland politicians to 'see what they could make of the problem'. Meanwhile, the UK government would concentrate on 'administering the Province' in a 'low key' fashion. Importantly, it was noted that, whether the Convention succeeded or failed, the government had a 'further considerable period of direct rule' ahead of it. The remaining options, independence or withdrawal, were simply not viable.[56] Meanwhile, there were signs that the PIRA was considering stepping-up its political involvement, and was willing to offer a ceasefire to allow discussions with government representatives to take place.

On 10 December, senior republicans, including Ruairí Ó Brádaigh, Dáithí Ó Conaill and Máire Drumm, held secret discussions with a number of prominent Protestant clergymen at Smyth's Village Hotel in Feakle, Co. Clare.[57] The meeting ended abruptly when the Garda Special Branch arrived to arrest them, a move which was blamed on the intervention of their arch-nemesis, Conor Cruise O'Brien.[58] These discussions were not officially facilitated by Westminster. Shortly after the Feakle talks, however, the British government proposed entering talks with the PIRA with the aim of establishing an enduring ceasefire. Reducing republican violence was a top priority for the government. PIRA attacks in Great Britain increased significantly during this time. The most notorious were the Guildford and Birmingham public house bombings in October and November 1974 respectively. A total of twenty-six people were killed in these two attacks. A number of innocent Irish people living in Britain were wrongfully convicted of the Guildford and Birmingham bombings, many receiving life sentences.[59] For several weeks after the Birmingham atrocities, members of the Irish community in England were subjected to assaults and abuse.[60] The Prime Minister himself called for an end to these attacks.[61] In retrospect, the bombings provide an insight into the context in which the government stepped-up its attempts to secure a PIRA ceasefire.

A secret document by John Hunt, dated 16 December 1974, and entitled 'New Initiatives in Northern Ireland' demonstrates that Merlyn Rees brought forward a new proposal which he deemed 'radical in nature'. Rees planned to 'offer a phased release of detainees and an increasingly low profile by the Army, in return for an enduring [PIRA] cease-fire'. It was thought that if a bargain could be struck with the PIRA, this could radically transform the situation in Northern Ireland. Also, if the PIRA refused to accept any offer, it might become more marginalised in Catholic communities. If a ceasefire was brokered and held, detention could be brought to an end by '1975 or mid-1976'. For security reasons, the Army advised a three-month delay before any releases were contemplated. However, Hunt posed the question of whether it would be 'politically advisable' to delay releases for more than one month, if the ceasefire was 'seen to be working'. He argued that any releases, although risky, might 'bring considerable benefits'. However, there were potential risks to this strategy, including possible violence by dissidents attempting to derail the ceasefire. The document noted that the government should remain resolute if there was any challenge from 'extremists, on either side, or splinter-groups'. Hunt recommended consulting with the opposition before making any public pronouncements about talks with the PIRA, to minimise the risk of a negative reaction.[62] However, some of the most serious opposition to engaging with the PIRA came not from the Westminster parties, but from the Irish government.

On 19 December 1974, Garret FitzGerald met Merlyn Rees and his Minister of State Stanley Orme to discuss political developments. Officials from both sides were also present. The issue of the recent Feakle talks was raised. Rees denied that the British government had anything to do with these talks. One of the British officials present claimed that the Feakle meeting was merely a propaganda move by the PIRA, designed to regain some of its lost support following the Birmingham bombings. The Irish delegation was unconvinced by these denials. (Indeed, the minutes of the meeting record some doubt 'that the British were not directly involved' in the negotiations). FitzGerald then asked where the British stood regarding power-sharing and the Irish dimension. He expressed concern that London was attempting to 'down-play the significance of the Irish dimension'. Rees dismissed his concerns. The fact that the British government had not emphasised it did not mean that its 'attitude [towards] it was changing'. It was simply thought unhelpful to emphasise it in the aftermath of the UWC strike, given the hostility of loyalist opinion.[63]

Despite Rees's assurances about the continued importance of the Irish dimension to government policy, Stanley Orme had earlier informed the Irish Minister for Justice, Paddy Cooney, that any institutionalised Irish dimension must be regarded as 'out', and that Dublin should assist in conveying this point to the SDLP. Orme 'in quite forcible terms' stated that it would be 'wrong to assume' that a prolonged period of direct rule would follow if the Convention failed to produce an acceptable solution. He noted the 'growing feeling among the major parties at Westminster that the sooner direct rule [could] be brought to an end the better', and claimed that pressure within the House of Commons to end it would soon follow.[64] While Orme did not explicitly mention withdrawal, his remarks could have been interpreted as such by the Dublin government, already pessimistic about future developments in Northern Ireland. It can be seen from Orme's remarks, during this meeting, why the Irish government was suspicious about Britain's future intentions towards Northern Ireland.

Conor Cruise O'Brien, in a memorandum on Northern Ireland, written for Garret FitzGerald, argued that there was no chance that unionists would accept a multi-national UN peace-keeping force. He also stated that it was not in the Irish government's interest to publicly suggest that such a force would be desirable, since this might actually encourage British disengagement. O'Brien's memorandum stated:

There is no doubt the British Government – and Harold Wilson in particular – would dearly like to get rid of Northern Ireland if they could do so without international obloquy that would be drawn on them by the process of simple withdrawal. If however an Irish Government were even to hint at the possibility of UN trusteeship, this would offer the British Government exactly what we must assume they want: the possibility of honourable withdrawal.

He argued that there were 'no attractive solutions' to the Northern Ireland conflict. The choice faced was a stark one: 'either the British stay or they go'. He was firmly in favour of the British remaining, since, in his view, the worst that could occur was a prolongation of the conflict at roughly the present levels of violence. Alternatively, British withdrawal would lead to civil war which neither the Irish Army nor a UN force could control. He advocated that the government 'make it as difficult as possible for the British to extricate themselves from their present responsibilities', since it was in the 'best interests of the over-whelming majority of the people in this island to keep them'.[65] It is clear that O'Brien's line of thinking was accepted by the Irish government at the time, but its fears about British disengagement remained.[66]

On 22 December 1974, the PIRA called an eleven-day ceasefire over the Christmas and New Year period. It was extended on 2 January 1975 for a further two weeks, ending on 16 January.[67] During this time, secret contacts between British officials and PIRA representatives took place, in the hope of securing a more long-term ceasefire, in return for a reduction of the Army's presence in republican areas. The British government's policy was bitterly opposed by the Dublin government, and raised fears about British withdrawal. Cosgrave informed Sir Arthur Galsworthy of the 'traumatic effect it would have throughout Ireland if the impression gained ground that [the British] were prepared to negotiate in any way with the Provisionals, in any of their manifestations'.[68]

Despite a major reduction of the security force presence, and significantly fewer weapons searches in republican strongholds, the PIRA claimed that the Army had failed to observe the truce, and it resumed armed struggle.[69] However, the government hoped that the levels of PIRA violence would be less intense in the medium-term future. Rees informed the cabinet that it might face a period of several months where 'there was no formal and complete ceasefire but a measure of restraint' from the PIRA.[70] Rees's optimism was proven correct, when, on 9 February, following discussions between NIO officials and the PIRA leadership, the PIRA announced an indefinite, but erratic, ceasefire.[71]

During this 'ceasefire', which was marred by outbreaks of violence (and intra-republican feuding), talks between government representatives and the PIRA Army Council took place.[72] The PIRA delegation was primarily represented by Ruairí Ó Brádaigh, Billy McKee, and another republican, whose name is not publicly known.[73] Secret Intelligence Service (SIS) officer Michael Oatley, and James Allan from the NIO, were among those who represented the British side. The British representatives mentioned a number of radical possibilities to the PIRA leadership, including possible disengagement from Northern Ireland.[74]

During this renewed truce, the British government established 'incident centres' in republican areas throughout the region.[75] These centres, staffed twenty-four hours a day by civil servants, were put in place to monitor the capricious ceasefire. If any threats to the truce arose, the centres would serve as a point of contact between Provisional Sinn Féin (PSF) and the NIO. Following this, the former then set up its own incident centres, manned by its local representatives, to increase its profile in republican areas.[76] Extreme loyalists complained forcefully about the PSF centres at a meeting with NIO officials. A UDA delegation, including Andy Tyrie and Glen Barr, complained that PSF was using the incident centres as bases for unofficial republican policing activities. The UDA demanded that action be taken, otherwise it would declare 'no go' areas in loyalist parts of Belfast in response. The loyalists argued that the government had been 'duped' and that PSF would try to obtain government sanction for its 'policing' networks, once these had been established and 'accepted' in republican communities. Frank Cooper (of the NIO), assured the delegation that there would be no acceptance of any police force other than the RUC. He denied that 'anything sinister' was going on. However, he mentioned the difficulty of policing republican areas, due to the absence of widespread nationalist acceptance of the RUC. The UDA leaders were clearly unsatisfied with Cooper's reassurances, and further criticised the government's policy. They claimed it had no chance of changing 'the Provisionals into a political organisation'. The meeting ended without significant accord, although Cooper agreed with the loyalists, that the incident centres were a 'nuisance', and had been cleverly exploited for propaganda purposes by PSF.[77] Whilst the PIRA was engaging in dialogue in Northern Ireland, the Dublin government came under increasing pressure from the republican movement in the southern state.

In early February 1975, several PIRA prisoners in Portlaoise went on hunger strike to protest against the conditions in the prison.[78] The IRA prisoners had '17 or 18 demands, particularly in relation to food parcels, the exclusion of "ordinary" criminals from the prison, searching, visiting arrangements, procedures and handicrafts'.[79] One of their number, Patrick Ward, was determined to stay on hunger strike until the demands were met. The strike was discussed at a meeting of the ILP's parliamentary party. The Tánaiste Brendan Corish stated that he had 'always believed the Provisional IRA would eventually turn on the Irish government and state [,] and this had now happened'. Corish was concerned that yielding to the prisoners would lead to increasing demands from them.[80] Three (un-named) leading members of the PIRA were apparently allowed into Portlaoise prison in an attempt to end the strike. The Irish government refused direct negotiations, despite threats received 'through highly placed clerics that two members of the government would be assassinated for each hunger striker who died'.[81] The Portlaoise strike was discussed at a meeting between British and Irish officials in February 1975. However, Sean Donlon of the DFA discounted any threat to Irish ministers, since 'Rule 6 of the IRA precluded them from actions against the Government in the South'. However, he admitted that the IRA had 'an endearing habit of changing the rules after making them!'[82] The strike ended on 17 February 1975, when republicans claimed their dispute with prison authorities was resolved 'satisfactorily'.[83]

Meanwhile, discussions between the PIRA and British continued. Despite the protracted negotiations between British officials and the PIRA, both the talks and the ceasefire faltered. The ceasefire officially ended in January 1976, although statistics of PIRA attacks during the course of the truce suggest that, as the *Irish Independent* later commented, 'it never really started'.[84] PIRA violence escalated in late 1975. The ever-increasing number of sectarian attacks by loyalist groups, and vicious intra-republican feuding, did little to help the security situation.[85] The PIRA leadership concluded that nothing significant would arise from the British discussions. The necessarily slow speed which the government attempted to phase out detention without trial, following Lord Gardiner's recommendation that it should not remain in force in the long-term, was arguably a major reason why the PIRA returned to violence.[86]

Niall Ó Dochartaigh has recently argued that, for the British and the PIRA, the ceasefire initially represented 'a genuine attempt to negotiate a settlement while both sides simultaneously manoeuvred for advantage in the event of failure'. He further posits that the PIRA's call for a British declaration of intent to withdraw from Northern Ireland was 'an issue for negotiation' rather than an absolute for the PIRA.[87] However, despite cryptic references to creating 'structures of disengagement' referred to by the British interlocutors, there were no signs the British government would accede to the PIRA's key demand: the withdrawal of British forces from Ireland.[88] In the absence of withdrawal, it is unclear what else the British could have offered the PIRA by way of a compromise, given that the latter opposed power-sharing on the Sunningdale model. Equally, given the levels of violence throughout this period, the extent to which it can be referred to as a genuine ceasefire is debatable.

Following the breakdown of the discussions, the government's incident centres were closed down, but PSF's own centres remained open.[89] These centres were an important feature in the political development of PSF, giving it an enhanced standing and a physical presence in nationalist areas.[90] Whilst many people found the discussions with the PIRA objectionable, they were designed to lead to the diminution of its military capacity, for as long a period as possible, without making substantial concessions to the republicans.[91] These discussions should be seen in the context of the government's need to take any possible measures to reduce violence. The government's other strategy, attempting to cajole Northern Ireland politicians to devise an acceptable solution, was attempted in May 1975, when elections to the Constitutional Convention took place.

Before the elections, reference to the Irish dimension was more muted in government literature. However, its commitment to power-sharing remained. A government publication stated that any solution must involve the 'sharing of power and responsibility'.[92] As predicted, loyalists triumphed at the polls: the UUUC candidates won 46 of the 78 seats. Most of the unionists remained committed to the return of a majority rule, Stormont-type system. Sensing the unionist mood, Ian Paisley performed a trademark *volte face* and came out in favour of restoring the Stormont system, having previously argued in favour of total integration with the rest of the UK.[93] The SDLP's rhetoric was relatively moderate during the Convention. Its pre-election manifesto stated that any solution to the conflict must recognise both the Irish and the British dimensions in Northern Ireland.[94] Even John Hume, one of the party's more stridently nationalist members, called for an end to direct rule, replacing it with 'direct rule by the people of Northern Ireland through their own administration'.[95] In August 1975, representatives of the UUUC met the SDLP to discuss the possibility of forming a voluntary coalition.[96] The UUUC proposals, however, did not amount to power-sharing 'as of right' which was a *sine qua non* for the British government and the SDLP. The UUUC plan, based on ideas proposed William Craig, was designed for an emergency situation, and was, as such, only temporary. This, combined with the rejection of the proposals by Harry West and Ian Paisley, meant the idea came to nothing.[97] Following protracted debates, the majority report of the Convention was published in November 1975 and discussed in parliament in January 1976.[98] Predictably, it called for a return to Stormont-style devolution with majority rule. However the government refused to deviate from the principle that any restoration of devolution must involve power-sharing and recognise the Irish dimension. Thus the Convention report, out of step with government policy, was shelved.[99]

Increasing alienation? Developments in British–Irish relations

Despite the tensions caused by the British decision to proceed with the Convention elections, and its negotiations with the PIRA, the British and Irish governments continued *prima facie* to enjoy cordial relations. At a meeting between governmental officials in February 1975, the Dublin delegation stated that it wanted the Irish dimension to remain a part of any future Northern Ireland settlement, but claimed to be 'much more sensitive to Protestant opinion' than previously. Dublin officials also stated that the Irish government 'would not make an issue of [the Irish dimension]' in public. The Irish officials stressed their desire for departmental contacts between Northern Ireland and the Republic to be increased to the level that pertained during 'the Lemass/O'Neill period in the late 1960s'. Sean Donlon stated that the most important issue concerning inter-governmental co-operation was security. It was a 'first priority' for the Irish government, although it was restricted from saying this due to potentially hostile public opinion. Douglas Janes of the NIO expressed satisfaction at the progress made at meetings between Merlyn Rees and Paddy Cooney to discuss security co-operation, although he admitted that progress was not as rapid as he wished.[100]

Throughout 1975, therefore, British–Irish security co-operation in Northern Ireland became closer and more overt, as is evidenced both by contemporary media reports and official documents. For example, a British memorandum from September 1975 recorded that, following a meeting in Dublin the previous year, cross-border security co-operation made significant improvements. Four 'technical panels' had been established comprising members of the security forces on both sides of the border. The panels were concerned with such matters as the exchange of information regarding paramilitary activity and the detection of arms and explosives. Importantly, the memo noted the 'co-operative attitude of the Irish government' and the British government's gratitude 'for the co-operation being given on security matters'. The previously mentioned ECHR case was also referred to in this note. However, it appears that the FCO, while aggrieved, and indeed frustrated, by the case, regarded it as more of a nuisance than a serious threat to the stability of British–Irish relations. The document stated that the 'Irish action in this case has always been difficult to reconcile with the constructive role which the Irish Government have played in other matters'.[101] This was particularly true of security co-operation. A briefing note prepared for the Prime Minister's meeting with Ulster Unionist politician Enoch Powell the following month confirmed that the government was generally 'satisfied with the co-operation received' from the Irish security forces.[102] In December 1975, both the RUC and the Gardaí publicly stated that co-operation was at a 'highly satisfactory' level. It was reported that the two police forces were operating an unpublicised two-way radio link, with meetings between superintendents in border regions held twice a year to discuss joint problems. It was further claimed that a 'free air' corridor was in place above the frontier which allowed British Army helicopters to conduct surveillance on the Irish side of the border, with permission from the DFA.[103]

The British policy of close co-operation and exchange of information with Dublin continued into early 1976. On 6 January that year, Wilson informed Cosgrave of his plan to dispatch units of the Special Air Service (SAS) to South Armagh, in a bid to weaken the PIRA in that area. While the letter highlighted the need to further improve border co-operation, Wilson expressed his government's gratitude for 'all the help that has been given to us in the past months and for the excellent results that the Garda have achieved' in the fight against paramilitary violence.[104]

It is unsurprising that the Irish government wished to strengthen its co-operation with the British security forces, given that elements within it believed some kind of British disengagement from Northern Ireland was likely. British officials and politicians were generally satisfied with the levels of co-operation received from the Irish. However, the British Army felt that co-operation could have been better if the Irish Army was allowed to communicate directly with British forces in Northern Ireland. This, though, would have breached the Republic's Constitution, which only permits the Defence Forces to act in support of the Gardaí. Despite the difficulties and disputes, such as Dublin's opposition to the Convention elections, its suspicions about potential British withdrawal, and the ongoing ECHR case, diplomatic relations throughout 1974–75 were generally solid, and showed no signs of imminent collapse. Anthony Craig has suggested that, post-collapse of the executive, the two governments had become 'alienated from each other'.[105] But archival evidence suggests that this is not an entirely accurate characterisation of the British–Irish relationship at this time. Indeed, this material demonstrates that both sides recognised that there should be closer co-operation and discussion regarding the future of Northern Ireland.

Conclusion

In the aftermath of the UWC strike, direct rule was restored under the terms of the Northern Ireland Act (1974). A number of radical options, including withdrawal, repartition and total integration were discussed, but all were deemed too problematic to attempt. The only viable alternative was continued direct rule, 'with some differences'. The British government recognised that no solution could be imposed, and that plans for a settlement were best left to those within the region. It pressed ahead with elections to the Constitutional Convention. This gave Northern Ireland's politicians a chance to express a preference for what form of government the region should have. However, the British government realised that there was little chance that the unionist dominated Convention would produce any suggestions which would be acceptable, since power-sharing was the only acceptable formula for political progress.

The Convention report predictably called for a return to the old Stormont system. This was unacceptable both to the government and the SDLP, since both demanded power-sharing as a *sine qua non* for the restoration of devolved political institutions. The SDLP also rejected William Craig's 'emergency' power-sharing proposals since, to have accepted power-sharing as temporary, would have been a major setback. Concerns remained within the Labour government that the loyalists might attempt some form of UDI, as is evident from contemporary British documents. However, whilst disengagement was discussed as a contingency plan, there is no evidence that it was ever official government policy.

Throughout this period, British–Irish relations remained solid, and co-operation continued at both political and official level. Undeniably, there were tensions between the sides, some serious. The Irish government was firmly opposed to the Constitutional Convention. Like some on the British side, it believed that the loyalists could use the opportunity to declare a UDI. The recent horror of the Dublin and Monaghan bombings also caused deep concern in Dublin that the violence would spread across the border. The Irish government was also suspicious about British engagement with the PIRA. Senior Irish officials and politicians were concerned that Britain wished to withdraw, or at least disengage, from Northern Ireland. This concern is evident from the contingency planning undertaken in Dublin throughout 1974. Difficulties also remained between Britain and Ireland over the ECHR case concerning the treatment of detainees by the British Army, but the two governments remained in close contact throughout.

During this period, the British government engaged in discussions with the PIRA about a possible prolonged ceasefire, in exchange for the reduction of Army activity in republican areas. This process culminated in the PIRA 1975–76 ceasefire which 'petered out' by September 1975, and was officially declared over early the following year.[106] During the ceasefire, which was 'more honoured in the breach than in the observance',[107] public monies were used to fund 'truce incident centres' manned by NIO officials. Public funds were also used to help set-up the RANI. The latter was ostensibly a service to assist former detainees. In reality, it was used to foster contacts between the various loyalist and republican paramilitary groups, in order to involve them in the political process. This was a rational step, since the British government recognised that there was little hope of improving the security situation, unless paramilitaries exchanged violence for politics.

In the Republic, the IRA caused a number of problems for the Irish government. These included the Portlaoise hunger strikes, and assassination threats to government ministers. The Irish government feared that both republicans and loyalists posed a significant threat to the security of the state, if civil war erupted in Northern Ireland. However, despite occasional differences over

Northern Ireland policy, the Dublin government continued to favour close co-operation with the British. It was in the interests of *both* governments to maintain good diplomatic relations. The Irish needed the British to remain in Northern Ireland, whilst the British needed Dublin's co-operation on security. The London government also required Dublin's support for its preferred policy of a settlement based on the recognition that Northern Ireland's constitutional status could only be altered with the consent of the majority, power-sharing and an Irish dimension: the formula for political progress established as part of the Sunningdale package.

Notes

1 The bombings were the work of elements within the Lurgan/Portadown UVF. Houses of the Oireachtas Joint Committee on Justice, Equality, Defence and Women's Rights, *Final Report on the Report of the Independent Commission of Inquiry into the Dublin and Monaghan Bombings, March 2004* (Dublin: Stationery Office, 2004), p. 57. See also D. Mullan, *The Dublin and Monaghan Bombings* (Dublin: Wolfhound Press, 2003). A further independent report concluded that the idea that rogue elements in British intelligence colluded with the bombers was 'neither fanciful nor absurd'. Houses of the Oireachtas, *Interim Report of the Independent Commission of Inquiry into the Dublin and Monaghan Bombings, December 2003* [Barron Report] (Dublin, Stationery Office, 2003), p. 286.
2 TNA, PREM 16/146, Galsworthy to NIO Belfast, 20 May 1974.
3 Ibid.
4 TNA, FCO 87/311, Cosgrave to Wilson, 24 May 1974.
5 TNA, CJ4/491, Galsworthy to NIO Belfast (Tel. No. 277), 29 May 1974.
6 TNA, FCO87/311, Galsworthy to NIO Belfast, 6 June 1974.
7 Ibid., Galsworthy to NIO Belfast, 6 June 1974.
8 Ibid., 17 June 1974.
9 TNA, CAB 128/54/19, Cabinet, confidential annex (Northern Ireland), 13 June 1974.
10 TNA, PREM 16/148, note for the record, 5 June 1974.
11 TNA, PREM 16/149, Wilson to Lynch, 10 June 1974.
12 Kerr, *Destructors*, pp. xviii; p. 13.
13 CAIN website. *The Northern Ireland Constitution* (HMSO, 1974). Available: http://cain.ulst.ac.uk/hmso/cmd5675.htm.
14 CAIN website. *The Northern Ireland Act* (HMSO, 1974). Available: http://cain.ulst.ac.uk/hmso/nia1974.htm.
15 TNA, FCO 87/311, Cosgrave to Wilson, 3 July 1974.
16 Ibid, Hayes to Bloomfield, 25 June 1974.
17 Ibid., covering note from Harding to Galsworthy.
18 G. FitzGerald, 'The 1974–75 Threat of a British Withdrawal from Northern Ireland', *Irish Studies in International Affairs*, xvii (2006), pp. 141–50.
19 HC Debates, vol. 876, 9 July 1974, col. 1268.
20 TNA, FCO 87/312, Thom to Harding, 29 July 1974.

21 *The Guardian*, 9 August, 1974.
22 TNA, PREM 16/150, Rees to Wilson, 9 August, 1974.
23 Ibid., record of a meeting between the Secretary of State and leaders of the SDLP, 29 August, 1974.
24 TNA, FCO 87/312, James Callaghan to Galsworthy, 19 August 1974.
25 TNA, PREM 16/151, Carter to Bridges, 9 September 1974.
26 Ibid., meeting between the Prime Minister and the SDLP, 10 September 1974.
27 Ibid., Rees to Wilson, 26 September 1974. In June 1974, Rees had publicly stated that he would welcome paramilitary groups becoming more involved in politics. His remarks followed a conference between loyalist groups (UWC, UVF, UDA). He further stated such discussions should be extended on a 'more widespread basis throughout the community.' See *Irish Times*, 17 June; 25 June 1974.
28 Bew, Frampton and Gurruchaga, *Talking to Terrorists*, p. 51.
29 D. Childs, *Britain since 1945: A Political History* (London: Routledge, 6th edn, 2006), p. 157.
30 *Irish Times*, 14 October 1974.
31 Bew, *Ireland*, p. 517.
32 TNA, PREM 16/151, meeting between the Secretary of State and UUUC leaders, 22 October 1974.
33 Ibid., Wilson to Rees, 22 October 1974.
34 Ibid., Northern Ireland: future trends of policy (IRN (74) 22). John Hunt to Wilson, 23 October 1974.
35 Armstrong was Principal Private Secretary to the Prime Minister; Butler Private Secretary to the Prime Minister. Both men later held the posts of Cabinet Secretary and Head of the Home Civil Service.
36 The extreme violence which occurred during the large-scale population transfers during the partition of India in 1947 would no doubt have been remembered by many senior officials, and was thus unlikely to be considered.
37 TNA, PREM 16/151, Rees to Wilson, 28 October 1974.
38 TNA, FCO 87/351, Brief – Cabinet, ministerial committee on Northern Ireland, 24 October 1974, emphasis added.
39 Ibid.
40 TNA, FCO 87/350, Galsworthy to FCO, 23 October 1974.
41 TNA, FCO 87/312, Embassy of Ireland to FCO, 13 November 1974.
42 Ibid., J.B. Donnelly to B.A. Major, British Embassy, Dublin, 29 November 1974.
43 Bew, *Ireland*, p. 514; FitzGerald, 'Threat of a British withdrawal', pp. 141–50. See also chapter 5.
44 NAI, DT 2005/7/663, minute by Walter Kirwan, 20 November 1974. The Channel Islands and the Isle of Man – neither of which is part of the UK – both opted not to join the EEC upon the UK's accession in 1973.
45 Ibid., assessment of capacity of IRA to take over areas North and South of the border in the event of a 'doomsday' situation in the North [Memo undated, cover letter to W. Kirwin, 19 November 1974].
46 *Irish Times*, 12 November 1974.
47 Ibid., 18 November 1974.

48 NAI, DT 2005/7/663, Department of Foreign Affairs, memorandum for the government, Northern Ireland Situation, 19 November 1974.

49 Ibid. It was thought unlikely that the British would '"return" Northern Ireland to the Irish state, from which it opted out in 1922'.

50 Ibid., Department of Foreign Affairs, memorandum for the government, Northern Ireland Situation, 19 November 1974.

51 Ibid.

52 NAI, DT 2005/7/640, Department of Foreign Affairs., memorandum for the government, Northern Ireland situation, November 1974.

53 TNA, PREM 16/152, record of conversation between the Prime Minister and the Taoiseach, 10 am, 1 November 1974.

54 Ibid., record of discussion between the Prime Minister and the Taoiseach, 11 am, 1 November 1974.

55 Ibid., Bridges to K. J. Jordan, 13 November 1974.

56 Ibid., Northern Ireland: future trends of policy, 22 November 1974. Industry minister Tony Benn also appears to have supported withdrawal in November 1974. His diary entry for 25 November states that there is 'no doubt in my mind that we shall have to get out [of Northern Ireland]'. Almost a year later he wrote 'My God, we shall have to get out of Ireland . . . because the English cannot solve the Irish problem'. T. Benn, *The Benn Diaries* (London: Hutchinson, 1995), pp. 305, 335. Benn, however, was not involved in the formulation of Northern Ireland policy.

57 Bew, Frampton and Gurruchaga, pp. 53–4; English, *Armed Struggle*, p. 178. Ó Brádaigh was PSF President and former IRA Chief-of-Staff. Ó Conaill and Drumm were the then Vice-Presidents of PSF.

58 *Irish Times*, 16 December 1974.

59 Taylor, *Provos*, pp. 173–4.

60 A. Beckett, *When The Lights Went Out: What Really Happened to Britain in the Seventies* (London: Faber and Faber, 2009), p. 124.

61 *The Times*, 23 November 1974.

62 TNA, PREM 16/152, new initiatives in Northern Ireland (IRN (74) 26), 16 December 1974.

63 NAI, DT 2005/7/664, Secret: meeting between Garret FitzGerald and Merlyn Rees and Stanley Orme, 19 December 1974.

64 Ibid., Northern Ireland situation, note by Diarmuid O'Sullivan, 16 December 1974. British officials made similar comments at a meeting with their Irish counterparts on 12 December 1974. Ibid., Meeting of Officials at Department of Foreign Affairs 12 December 1974.

65 Ibid., Northern Ireland Situation – Comments by the Minister for Posts and Telegraphs on the Memorandum from the Minister for Foreign Affairs. [December 1974].

66 FitzGerald 'The 1974–75 threat of a British withdrawal', pp. 141–50.

67 English, *Armed Struggle*, p. 179.

68 TNA, PREM 16/515, Galsworthy to FCO and NIO, 10 January 1975.

69 *Irish Times*, 18 January 1975.

70 TNA, CAB 128/56/5, Cabinet conclusions, 23 January 1975. See *Irish Times*, 23 January 1975 for details of NIO–PIRA discussions.
71 English, *Armed Struggle*, p. 179; *The Times*, 10 February 1975.
72 Taylor, *Provos*, pp. 177–82.
73 R. W. White, 'The 1975 British–IRA truce in perspective', *Éire-Ireland*, xlv: 3 and 4 (2010), p. 216.
74 R. W. White, *Ruairí Ó Brádaigh: The Life and Politics of an Irish Revolutionary* (Bloomington: Indiana University Press, 2006), p. 227.
75 Centres were located in Belfast (2); Derry; Dungannon; Armagh; Newry and Enniskillen. *Irish Times*, 13 February 1975.
76 Ibid., 12 February 1975.
77 TNA, CJ4/838, note of a meeting between NIO Officials and UDA delegation, 27 February 1975.
78 A republican riot occurred at the same prison in December 1974. Troops were used to restore order. *Irish Times*, 30 December 1974.
79 Labour Party Archives, Dublin (LPA) Parliamentary Labour Party (PLP) Minutes, 5 February 1975. The Fine Gael Minister for Justice, Paddy Cooney, was allowed to address this meeting to update the PLP on the IRA hunger strikes.
80 LPA, PLP Minutes, 5 February 1975. For more on Ward's hunger strike, see *Irish Times*, 22 February 1975.
81 LPA, PLP Minutes, 24 January 1975.
82 TNA, CJ4/806, note by G. W. Watson, NIO, 12 February 1975.
83 *Irish Times*, 17 February 1975.
84 *Irish Independent*, 10 February 1976. The PIRA was responsible for approximately 90 deaths during the course of its supposed ceasefire (9 February 1975 to 23 January 1976). M. Sutton, *Bear In Mind These Dead . . . An Index of Deaths from the Conflict in Ireland, 1969–1993* (Belfast: Beyond the Pale, 1994), pp. 70–86.
85 Taylor, *Provos*, pp. 194–7. For the republican feuds, see Rekawek, *Terrorism*, pp. 24–9. In December 1974, a split in the OIRA resulted in the formation of the Irish National Liberation Army (INLA), a small, but deadly, Marxist–Leninist republican paramilitary organisation. See J. Holland and H. McDonald, *INLA: Deadly Divisions. The Story of One of Ireland's Most Ruthless Terrorist Organisations* (Dublin: Poolbeg, 1994).
86 English, *Armed Struggle*, p. 179. Gardiner wished to recommend the end of detention outright, but, due to the security situation, was unable to suggest a precise time when this should occur. *Report of a Committee to Consider, in the Context of Human Rights, Measures to Deal with Terrorism in Northern Ireland* (HMSO, 1975).
87 Ó Dochartaigh, '"Everyone Trying"', p. 59.
88 Taylor, *Provos*, pp. 181–2.
89 Ibid., p. 196. *Irish Times*, 13 November 1975.
90 According to former PSF strategist, Tom Hartley. Taylor, *Provos*, p. 186.
91 S. Aveyard, 'No solution: British government policy in Northern Ireland under Labour, 1974–79' (PhD dissertation, Queen's University Belfast, 2012), p. 81.
92 Northern Ireland Discussion Paper 3. *Government of Northern Ireland: A Society Divided* (HMSO: 1975).

93 *Northern Ireland Constitutional Convention: Report of Debates (Convention Report)*, 17 June 1975, p. 240.
94 *SDLP: Speak with Strength. Constitutional Convention Election Manifesto May 1975* (Belfast, 1975).
95 *Convention Report*, 19 June 1975, p. 287.
96 Jackson, *Home Rule*, p. 329.
97 Ibid., pp. 329–30 for discussion of these proposals, and the potential involvement of David Trimble in their formulation. See also, Lee, *Ireland*, p. 450. Many VUPP members left the party in protest following Craig's coalition proposals. See J. Greer, 'Paisley and his Heartland: A Case Study of Political Change' in C. NicDháibhéid and C. Reid (eds), *From Parnell to Paisley: Constitutional and Revolutionary Politics in Ireland* (Dublin: Irish Academic Press, 2010), p. 245.
98 Northern Ireland Constitutional Convention Report. CAIN website. Available: www.cain.ulst.ac.uk/events/convention/nicc75report.htm.
99 Bourke, *Peace*, p. 230.
100 TNA, CJ4/806, note of a meeting with Irish Officials, 11 February 1975.
101 TNA, PREM 16/520, North–South security co-operation, minute by ROI department, 10 September 1975 (European political co-operation: Ministerial meeting, Venice 11–12 September 1975. Additional brief: Northern Ireland).
102 TNA, PREM 16/531, brief for Prime Minister's meeting with Enoch Powell, 30 October 1975. Official sources also expressed satisfaction with the Republic's co-operation the following month. *Irish Times*, 27 November 1975.
103 *Irish Times*, 6 December 1975.
104 NAI, DT 2006/133/691, Wilson to Cosgrave, 6 January 1976.
105 Craig, *Crisis*, p. 3.
106 Bourke, *Peace*, p. 163.
107 Hanley and Millar, *Lost Revolution*, p. 297.

Conclusion

The period from 1972 to 1975 was witness to a number of significant political initiatives, aimed at bringing stability to Northern Ireland. Arguably the most 'radical and far-sighted' of these was the attempt to establish a power-sharing executive, comprised of moderate nationalists and unionists, and the cross-community Alliance Party.[1] Power-sharing was perhaps the single most important transformation in the political culture of Northern Ireland, and was integral to future attempts to secure a political settlement in the region.

As Alvin Jackson argued, the central interpretive problem of the Sunningdale 'débâcle' was 'the issue of causation and blame: why did the power sharing executive fall, and who carried the responsibility?'[2] The executive failed because it did not have the necessary support from the majority community.[3] The outrage expressed by that majority community following the introduction of direct rule demonstrated the importance of the Stormont parliament to unionist political culture.[4] Without it, unionists feared British withdrawal and potential Irish unification, since many of them did not trust the government of the nation they professed to be a part of. Many unionists also lost trust in the UUP leader, Brian Faulkner.

Faulkner's decision to work within the parameters of the British White Paper resulted in a split within his party. This undermined both his personal credibility and the legitimacy of the new institutions for many unionists. More importantly, the proposed Sunningdale Council of Ireland was perceived by many unionists as a step towards future Irish unity. The SDLP's portrayal of the proposed Council as a staging-post to Irish unity, and the readiness of unionists to believe these assertions, ensured that only a minority of unionists supported the new arrangements. However, both nationalist and hard-line unionist depictions of what the Council *could* become were inaccurate, since the Irish government was not prepared to vest it with any significant powers.

Only the Irish Department of Foreign Affairs (DFA) favoured a strong Council of Ireland with major evolutionary potential. Nonetheless, most other Irish departments refused to countenance any transfer of their responsibilities to the proposed Council, despite prompting from DFA officials, and their minister, Garret FitzGerald. The Republic's attitude towards the Council was similar to that of the Northern Ireland officials and unionist politicians, who viewed it as a necessary nonsense,[5] to ensure continued SDLP participation in power-sharing arrangements. The SDLP applied significant pressure on the Dublin government to create a strong Council, but its requests largely fell on deaf ears. As the evidence herein has shown, the party's influence on the policies of the Dublin coalition has been overstated by both party members, and academic commentators. The Irish government would not accede to any demand that compromised its national interest, including a costly and potentially unwieldy all-Ireland Council.

The ongoing security crisis was also a major obstacle to the executive's chances of success, with high levels of both republican and loyalist violence marring its tenure. Executive members themselves recognised that violence seriously hindered its ability to garner support in the community. Unlike the old Stormont, the executive had no security powers, and could thus have appeared ineffective to some voters, who may have been unaware of the constraints in which it operated.

The increase in PIRA cross-border attacks also caused consternation among the unionist community. This increase was due to the enhanced effectiveness of the security forces in urban areas following Operation Motorman. The fact that the perpetrators of such attacks could escape over the border, occasionally evading capture, convinced some unionists that the Republic of Ireland was a haven for militant republicans. This was an inaccurate perception. Indeed, the Republic's draconian security legislation was purposefully designed to deal with republican subversion.[6] Although, there is evidence to suggest that cross-border security co-operation was not as effective as it could have been, especially during the premiership of Jack Lynch. Yet, this improved significantly with the election of the Fine Gael–ILP coalition in February 1973. Under the coalition, better co-ordination and intelligence-sharing existed between the Garda and the RUC. The coalition was regarded as much more effective in tackling cross-border violence than its Fianna Fáil predecessor. Nevertheless, its election was not a panacea for the security crisis. Its slender parliamentary majority, and vulnerability to Fianna Fáil criticism, meant that most cross-border co-operation was kept secret. Consequently, many unionists were unaware of the impact that the change of government had on security matters. PIRA attacks also remained frequent during this time, despite this improved co-operation. Yet, the tendency of unionists and British Army personnel to blame the Republic for the persistence of these attacks, disguised an unpalatable reality: British forces were not in total control of security within Northern Ireland, and enhanced co-operation alone could not eliminate this violence.

Domestic political pressure also meant that the Republic's government was unable to change the parts of its Constitution (Articles 2 and 3), which claimed Northern Ireland as part of the national territory. These articles were particularly offensive to unionists. The Irish government's declaration accepting Northern Ireland's constitutional status, announced at Sunningdale, was devalued by Kevin Boland's legal challenge. The government's defence, that the declaration was merely a statement of policy, increased unionist suspicions that the Dublin government was not acting in good faith. Some believed the declaration to be merely cosmetic, and held that the government was actually committed to Irish reunification. Like its predecessors, however, the Fine Gael–ILP government was more concerned with the stability of the southern state than a united Ireland.[7] An excerpt from Roy Bradford's quasi-autobiographical novel, *The Last Ditch*, wherein the protagonist, Desmond Carson, discusses the Republic's attitude to Irish unity, aptly captures the coalition's approach to this subject between 1972 and 1975:

> [Irish politicians] instead of 'Pray God we'll be together again' are blessing themselves gratefully and saying 'thank God a united Ireland is still just a national aspiration and thank God we don't have to cope with the problem of assimilating a million Prods from Ulster into our nice little, tight little, Catholic Republic.[8]

With events such as Bloody Sunday still fresh in the electorate's minds, the emotive nature of Irish public opinion meant that changing the Constitution to reflect this political reality would have been difficult, if not impossible. Nevertheless, this was another reason why some unionists could not, or would not, support the Sunningdale settlement.

Political and security crises were not the beleaguered executive's only problems. The administration came into office during a period of economic uncertainty for both the UK and the wider world, as evidenced by the collapse of the Bretton Woods system, and the economic shock following the Oil Crisis. Despite the differing political backgrounds of its members, the executive was relatively united in its approach to socio-economic policy. It was not constrained by ideological dogma, and its policies were generally progressive. Its priorities were the creation of jobs, with state intervention if necessary. It also sought to improve the region's comparatively poor housing stock, and made speculative attempts to tackle sectarian division. The far-sighted, if necessarily limited attempts, to introduce integrated education, suggests that the power-sharing administration was earnest about improving community relations. Whether or not its plans would have come to fruition, had it survived, is an open question, given the fiscal constraints facing the UK at that time. Paramilitary violence also threatened economic recovery; this included the PIRA's insidious targeting of foreign industrialists.[9]

However, the executive's expansive socio-economic programme was not enough to ensure widespread public support, particularly from the unionist community. This lack of unionist support was publicly manifest during the paramilitary-backed Ulster Workers' Council (UWC) strike of May 1974. The UWC's control of key industries, especially the main electricity generating stations, severely limited the executive's capacity to break the strike (such as it was). The British government's freedom to act against the UWC was also limited, lest it angered both loyalist *and* republican groups. The constraints within which the government operated cannot be ignored when assessing its response to the strike. The General Officer Commanding informed Merlyn Rees that the British Army could not guarantee essential services, particularly the generation and distribution of electricity.[10] This would require the support of engineers and middle-management in the power stations. Rees was informed that engineers from Great Britain might be able to come to Northern Ireland and distribute power, but the plan was delayed following the advice of a Northern Ireland Electricity Service official. However, this speculative plan came to naught, as, the following day, the executive collapsed. Support for the strike had, in any case, been galvanised by Wilson's churlish 'spongers' speech. It has been suggested that, had the Conservative government been in power, it would have acted decisively against the UWC.[11] This argument is speculative, lacking a compelling evidential basis. Anthony Craig contended that Wilson sought 'to give the UWC what *they* wanted' and 'turn to full withdrawal'.[12] However, the British government's response to the strike was not part of a wider plot to extricate itself from Northern Ireland. While the 'Doomsday' document may indicate what Paul Bew has described as Wilson's 'subjective support'[13] for withdrawal, it was never government policy, and Wilson could not have imposed it on his reluctant cabinet or senior officials. Those who argue that the government abandoned the power-sharing executive fail to address the question of unionists' resistance, and the lengths to which they were prepared to go to defeat Sunningdale.

Following the UWC strike, British officials considered the implications of withdrawal from Northern Ireland as a policy option. Other alternatives, such as re-partition and integration, were also examined by officials. Cillian McGrattan has argued that there was 'an overabundance of options and a cacophonous polyphony of ideas and voices within the governmental decision making process'.[14] However, archival evidence demonstrates that only one option was viable: the continuation of direct rule until Northern Ireland's politicians would accept a power-sharing settlement. The government's policy on power-sharing remained consistent, as was confirmed in the wake of the Constitutional Convention report. This report, calling for a return to Stormont-style, majority-rule devolution, was immediately shelved, because it did not meet the 'Sunningdale principles'. The government was also consistent in recognising the need for a meaningful Irish dimension as part of any future settlement.

There were a number of policy differences between the British and Irish governments during this period, for example the ongoing ECHR case. The Dublin government also feared that British withdrawal from Northern Ireland was being considered, as is evidenced by its contingency plans of late 1974. It also opposed the Constitutional Convention and the British discussions with representatives of the PIRA during its 1975–76 'ceasefire'. Despite these tensions, concerted efforts were made to ensure British–Irish relations remained on a cordial footing, and there is evidence that these efforts were successful, particularly in the enhanced security and intelligence co-operation achieved throughout 1974 and 1975. Whilst not ignoring the differences between the two states, the overall picture of the British–Irish relations is one of improvement rather than estrangement. An intergovernmental approach was crucial in the later attempts to make peace in the 1990s.[15]

The policies established during the 1972 to 1975 period, that Northern Ireland should remain in the UK for as long as the majority so wished (the principle of consent), power-sharing, and an Irish dimension, were central to the Belfast (Good Friday) Agreement of 1998. All other matters were negotiable, but these core principles were not. As Lord Bew noted, 'all the parties [to the Belfast Agreement] were told in political terms, "You can have whatever settlement you want as long as you accept the principle of consent, power sharing plus an Irish dimension". It was Henry Fordism in politics; that is what they were all told'.[16] However, Seamus Mallon's description of the Belfast Agreement as 'Sunningdale for slow learners' is inaccurate, since it implies that a settlement could have been reached much earlier. The basic principles of both accords were indeed similar, but the political contexts in which they were agreed were entirely different. Most significantly, paramilitaries and extreme parties were excluded from political negotiations during the 1970s, but played a key role in the peace talks of the 1990s. The contention that the Sunningdale settlement was a 'lost peace process' is therefore erroneous.[17] The years between 1972 and 1975 were the most violent of the conflict. By contrast, after the republican and loyalist ceasefires of 1994, the number of violent deaths decreased significantly from pre-ceasefire levels.[18] This 'peace dividend' suggested that real change was possible, whereas in the 1970s, no end to the violence was in sight.

However, Sunningdale did not fail simply because extremists were excluded. It failed because of opposition from unionists, who were prepared to support a paramilitary-backed strike in order to wreck it. Much anti-Sunningdale sentiment was motivated by inflated fears concerning the threat of a united Ireland. However, whilst in 1974, changes to the Irish Constitution were impossible, this was not the case following the 1998 accord. Following the Belfast Agreement, over 94 percent of the Irish electorate endorsed the removal of the Republic's territorial claim on Northern Ireland, and substantive changes to Articles 2 and 3 of its Constitution.[19] The structures of inter-governmental co-operation agreed in 1998 were also more 'unionist friendly', comprising not just a North–South Ministerial Council, but also a British–Irish Council, with devolved administrations in the UK, the Channel Islands and Isle of Man all represented.[20] This was a more acceptable settlement for unionists than either Sunningdale or the 1985 Anglo-Irish Agreement, the latter having given the Republic a consultative role in Northern Ireland's affairs, without unionist consent.[21]

The Belfast Agreement also included aspects which republicans insisted on, which were not part of the Sunningdale package. These included wholesale reform of policing and the enactment of strict equality legislation. During the 1970s, the importance of police reform was recognised, but no systematic attempts were made to change the RUC in order to make it more acceptable to the nationalist community. By contrast, the Independent Commission on Policing for Northern Ireland established in 1998, and chaired by Chris Patten, recommended radical reform of the RUC. This included re-naming the force, and the equal recruitment of Catholics and Protestants.[22] The Good Friday Agreement also included commitments to an 'equality agenda', frequently highlighted by Sinn Féin during the 1990s negotiations.[23] This commitment to equality is reflected in Section 75 of the Northern Ireland Act 1998, which prevents discrimination on grounds of age, race, sex, religion and political opinion. By contrast, the Northern Ireland Constitution Act of 1973 expressly prohibited discrimination only on grounds of religion and political opinion.[24]

Another important reason why the Belfast Agreement cannot accurately be described as Sunningdale for slow learners is because it has itself evolved since it was first enacted. The St Andrews Agreement of 2006, a revised and updated version of the Belfast Agreement, but still based on the same three core principles of consent, power-sharing and an Irish dimension, superseded the 1998 accord via the introduction of a number of fundamental changes to the way that the Northern Ireland Assembly functioned. This included the requirement that Ministers endorse the Police Service of Northern Ireland (PSNI).[25]

One could question why the current settlement has thus far proven more successful than the Sunningdale package. Sunningdale was perceived as disproportionately favourable to republicans and nationalists. The loss of Stormont, coupled with the proposed Council of Ireland, led many unionists to believe that they had conceded too much, with no improvement in security to show for it. By comparison, both sides could legitimately claim to have made gains from the Belfast Agreement, particularly once both communities became accustomed to a relatively peaceful political dispensation, thus increasing the Belfast Agreement's chances of success. In the immediate aftermath of the collapse of the first executive in May 1974, the *Newsletter* perceptively observed that, in any new formula for a settlement, there could be:

> [N]o repetition of a situation where one side or the other is asked to sign merely in the hope that, somehow, everything will turn out alright. If a pact is needed, both must be able to sign in full confidence that they are enshrining the prospect of a happy, prosperous, power-sharing united Ulster.[26]

While it would be asking a lot of any settlement to meet all of these criteria, the Belfast and St Andrews Agreements have at least established an acceptable institutional framework within which the region's politicians can work to ensure a return to the bloodshed and misery of the 1970s is avoided.[27] These institutions, based on the 'Sunningdale principles', have provided the template for one of the most enduring periods of peace in Northern Ireland's turbulent history.[28]

Notes

1 The Sunningdale settlement as described in P. Wilkinson, *Terrorism and the Liberal State* (Basingstoke: Palgrave Macmillan, 2nd edn, 1986), p. 161.

2 Jackson, *Home Rule*, pp. 368–9.

3 For a contrary view see, Kerr, *Destructors*, p. 5–6.

4 For more on this, J. Todd, 'Two traditions in Unionist political culture', *Irish Political Studies*, ii: 1 (1987), pp. 1–26.

5 Faulkner, *Memoirs*, p. 229.

6 Fanning, *Independent Ireland*, p. 134.

7 Lee, *Ireland*, p. 301.

8 R. Bradford, *The Last Ditch* (Dundonald: Blackstaff, 1981), p. 116.

9 High profile cases of this kind also occurred in the Republic, such as the kidnapping of Dutch industrialist Tiede Herrema on 3 October 1975. *Irish Times*, 4 October 1975.

10 D. Hammill, *Pig in the Middle: The Army in Northern Ireland 1969–1984* (London: Methuen, 1985), p. 152. See also Dewar, p. 100, which states that Sir Frank King, GOC Northern Ireland, informed the Chief of the General Staff, Sir Peter Hunt, that the Army could not cope with a power failure.

11 Kerr, *Imposing*, p. 68; *Destructors*, p. 13; Whitelaw, *Memoirs*, p. 156.

12 Craig, *Crisis*, p. 182.

13 Bew, *Enmity*, p. 517.

14 McGrattan, 'Learning from the past of laundering history? Consociational narratives and state intervention in Northern Ireland', *British Politics*, v: 1 (2010), p. 93.

15 These foundations were further cemented by the Anglo-Irish Agreement of 1985.

16 *House of Lords Debates*, 22 January 2008, c209. Available: www.publications. parliament.uk/pa/ld200708/ldhansrd/text/80122–0014.htm.

17 Kerr, *Destructors.*
18 See Sutton Index of Deaths, CAIN website. Available: http://cain.ulst.ac.uk/sutton/tables/Year.html.
19 *Irish Times,* 25 May 1998.
20 McLoughlin, *John Hume,* p. 177.
21 J. Tonge, *The New Northern Irish Politics?* (Basingstoke: Palgrave Macmillan, 2005), pp. 26–8.
22 Ibid., p. 223.
23 See for example, G. Adams, *Hope and History: Making Peace in Ireland* (Dingle: Brandon, 2003), pp. 310–13.
24 Section 75, Office of First and Deputy-First Minister Website. Available: www.ofmdfmni.gov.uk/section_75; *Northern Ireland Constitution Act* (HMSO, 1973).
25 E. O'Kane, *Britain, Ireland and Northern Ireland since 1980: The Totality of Relationships* (London: Routledge, 2007), p. 178. The post-1998 attempts at devolution were largely unsuccessful, until the decommissioning of PIRA weapons in 2005 made the chances of a new deal more likely. See Bew, *Ireland,* pp. 552–5 and G. K. Peatling, *The Failure of the Northern Ireland Peace Process* (Dublin: Irish Academic Press, 2004), pp. 68–89.
26 *Newsletter,* 30 May 1974.
27 Recent outbreaks of dissident republican violence appear to have galvanised, rather than destabilised, the political institutions.
28 This is not to ignore the tragic fact that deaths did occur since 1998, but that, relatively speaking, Northern Ireland was much more peaceful than had previously been the case. Between 1998 and 2011, there were 141 deaths attributable to the conflict, of which 42 were paramilitaries. By contrast, between 1972 and 1975 alone, there were almost 1,300 deaths. Source: *The Guardian* Datablog. Available: www.guardian.co.uk/news/datablog/2010/jun/10/deaths-in-northern-ireland-conflict-data#data.

Select bibliography

State papers

National Archives of Ireland, Dublin
Attorney General's Office (AG) files
Department of Finance (FIN) files
Department of Foreign Affairs (DFA) files
Department of Justice (JUS) files
Department of the Taoiseach (DT) files

The National Archives, Kew
Cabinet Office (CAB) files
Foreign and Commonwealth Office (FCO) files
Ministry of Defence (DEFE) files
Northern Ireland Office (CJ4) files
Prime Minister's Office (PREM) files

Public Record Office of Northern Ireland, Belfast
Basil McIvor Papers (D/2962)
Brian Faulkner Papers (D/3591)
Central Secretariat (CENT) files
Office of the Executive (OE) files
Roy Bradford papers (D/4211)
Secretary of State's Executive Committee (SOSEC) files

Political party archives

Fianna Fáil Party, University College Dublin
Parliamentary Party Minutes, 1957–1970

Irish Labour Party, Head Office, Ely Place, Dublin
Parliamentary Party Minutes, 1973–1980

Printed primary sources

House of Commons: Official Report of Debates (HMSO, 1974)
House of Lords: Official Report of Debates (HMSO, 1972)
Northern Ireland Act (HMSO, 1974)
Northern Ireland Assembly Official Report of Debates, vols i–iii (HMSO, 1973–74).
Northern Ireland Assembly Papers, 1–8, 1973–74 (HMSO, 1974)
Northern Ireland Constitutional Proposals (HMSO, 1973)
Northern Ireland, Discussion Paper: Finance and the Economy (HMSO, 1974)
Northern Ireland: Finance and the Economy, paper 1 (HMSO, 1974)
Report of Debates: Northern Ireland Constitutional Convention, vols i–ii (HMSO, 1975–76)
Report of the Bloody Sunday Inquiry, x vols (HMSO, 2010)
The Future of Northern Ireland: A Paper for Discussion, NIO, 1972.
The Sunningdale Communiqué (HMSO, 1973)

Irish government publications

Dáil Éireann: Official Report, various vols (Dublin, Stationery Office)
Final Report on the Report of the Independent Commission of Inquiry into the Dublin and Monaghan Bombings, March 2004 (Dublin, Stationery Office)
Interim Report of the Independent Commission of Inquiry into the Dublin and Monaghan Bombings, December 2003 [Barron Report] (Dublin, Stationery Office)

London School of Economics archives

Merlyn Rees Diaries, Transcripts of tapes, MERLYN-REES/1/1

Newspapers and periodicals

Anglo-Celt
Belfast News Letter
Belfast Telegraph
Combat
Connacht Tribune
Die Zeit [Germany]
Fortnight
Irish Independent
Irish Times
Leitrim Observer
National Post [Canada]
Sunday Independent
The Guardian
The Sun
The Times
Time Magazine
UWC News Sheet

Political pamphlets: Linen Hall Library

1973 Assembly Manifesto, Belfast: Ulster Democratic Unionist Party, 1973

A Statement of Policy: Power for the People: Power for Our Land, Belfast: Ulster Vanguard, 1973

Another Step Forward with the SDLP: Manifesto 1974, Belfast: SDLP, 1974

Assembly Election Manifesto, Belfast: Alliance Party, 1973

Assembly Election Manifesto: SDLP Manifesto. Assembly Elections: A New North, a New Ireland, Belfast: SDLP, 1973

Community of the British Isles, Belfast: Ulster Vanguard, 1973

Consistent or Inconsistent, Newtonards: Ulster Democratic Unionist Party, 1972

Co-operative Ideas: Dáil Ceantair Sinn Féin, Beal Feirsde, Belfast: Provisional Sinn Féin, n.d.

District Council Election Manifesto, Belfast: SDLP, 1973

Dominion of Ulster, Belfast: Ulster Vanguard, 1972

Éire Nua, Provisional Sinn Féin, Dublin: Provisional Sinn Féin, 1974

Government without Right, Belfast: Ulster Vanguard, 1973

Manifesto:October 1974 Election, Belfast: Volunteer Political Party, 1974

NILP: The Way Ahead. Second Manifesto: Assembly Election, June 1973, Belfast: Northern Ireland Labour Party, 1973

Peace Order and Good Government, Belfast: Ulster Unionist Party, 1973

Policies for Reconstruction, Belfast: Alliance Party, 1973

Pro-Assembly Unionists: Imperial General Election Campaign, February 1974, Belfast: Unionist Party of Northern Ireland, 1974

Red Hand Commandos: Within the Context of Northern Ireland, Belfast: Red Hand Commandos, 1974

SDLP: Second Annual Conference, Belfast: SDLP, 1972

Sinn Féin (Official) *Ard Fhéis*, Dublin: Official Sinn Féin, 1973

Speak With Strength. Constitutional Convention Election Manifesto May 1975, Belfast: SDLP, 1975.

Spelling It Out: A Brief Statement of Basic Principles, Ulster Vanguard: Belfast, 1972

Statement of Alliance Party's Position for Constitutional Conference, Belfast: Alliance Party, 1972

The Labour Party: Annual Reports, 1969–77, Dublin: Labour Party, 1969–77

The Northern Ireland Constitutional Proposals: A Constructive Approach, Belfast: Ulster Unionist Party, 1973

The Policies of Alliance, Belfast: Alliance Party, 1972

The Unionist Party: Fundamental Principles, Belfast: Ulster Unionist Party, 1973

Towards a New Ireland, Belfast: SDLP, 1972

Towards the Future: A Unionist Blueprint, Belfast: Ulster Unionist Party, 1972

Ulster: A Nation. Belfast: Ulster Vanguard, 1972

Ulster General Strike: Strike Bulletins of the Workers Association, Belfast: The Association, 19–31 May 1974

Union with Great Britain, extract from speech by Ian Paisley, Belfast: DUP, 1972

Unionist Local Government Manifesto, Belfast: Ulster Unionist Party, 1973

Secondary sources

Akenson, D. H., *Conor: A Biography of Conor Cruise O'Brien* (New York: Cornell University Press, 1994)

Alonso, R., *The IRA and Armed Struggle* (London: Routledge, 2007)

Amuzegar, J., *Managing the Oil Wealth: OPEC's Windfalls and Pitfalls* (London: I. B. Tauris, 2001)

Anderson, D., *14 May Days: The Inside Story of the Loyalist Strike of 1974* (Dublin: Gill and Macmillan, 1994)

Arnold, B., *Jack Lynch: Hero in Crisis* (Dublin: Merlin, 2001)

Arthur, P., *Government and Politics of Northern Ireland* (London: Prentice Hall, 1984)

Arthur, P., *Special Relationships: Britain, Ireland and the Northern Ireland Problem* (Belfast: Blackstaff, 2000)

Arthur, P. and K. Jeffrey, *Northern Ireland since 1968* (Oxford: Wiley-Blackwell, 2nd edn, 1996)

Aughey, A., *Under Siege: Ulster Unionism and the Anglo-Irish Agreement* (London: Hurst, 1989)

Aveyard, S., 'No solution: British government policy in Northern Ireland under Labour, 1974–79' (PhD dissertation, Queen's University Belfast, 2012)

Balabkins, N., *West German Reparations to Israel* (New Brunswick: Rutgers University Press, 1971)

Bardon, J., *A History of Ulster* (Belfast: Blackstaff, 2001)

Bean, K., *The New Politics of Sinn Féin* (Liverpool: Liverpool University Press, 2007)

Beckett, A., *When the Lights Went Out: Britain in the Seventies* (London: Faber and Faber, 2009)

Benn, T., *The Benn Diaries* (London: Arrow, 1995)

Bennett, J., *Fourteen Days of Fascist Terror: The Truth about the Lock-out That Toppled the Assembly Government* (London: Connolly Publications, 1974)

Bew, P., *Ireland: The Politics of Enmity, 1789–2006* (Oxford: Oxford University Press, 2007)

Bew. P. and H. Patterson, *The British State and the Ulster Crisis: From Wilson to Thatcher* (London: Verso, 1985)

Bew, P., P. Gibbon and H. Patterson, *Northern Ireland 1921–1996: Political Forces and Social Classes* (London: Serif, 1996)

Bew, P., P. Gibbon and H. Patterson, *Northern Ireland 1921/2001: Political Forces and Social Classes* (London: Serif, 2002)

Bew, J., M. Frampton and I. Gurruchaga, *Talking to Terrorists: Making Peace in Northern Ireland and the Basque Country* (London: Hurst, 2009)

Birrell D. and A. Murie, *Policy and Government in Northern Ireland: Lessons of Devolution* (Dublin: Gill and Macmillan, 1980)

Bleakley, D., *Faulkner: Conflict and Consent in Irish Politics* (London: Mowbrays, 1974)

Bloomfield, K., *Stormont in Crisis: A Memoir* (Belfast: Blackstaff, 1994)

Bloomfield, K., *A Tragedy of Errors: The Government and Misgovernment of Northern Ireland* (Liverpool: Liverpool University Press, 2007)

Bogdanor, V., *Devolution in the United Kingdom* (Oxford: Oxford University Press, 2nd edn, 2001)

Boland, K, *Up Dev!* (Dublin: Kevin Boland, 1976)

Boland, K, *Fine Gael: British or Irish?* (Dublin: Mercer, 1984)

Bourke, R., *Peace in Ireland: The War of Ideas* (London: Pimlico, 2003)

Bowyer Bell, J., *The Secret Army: The IRA 1916–1979* (Dublin: Academy Press, 1979)

Boyce, D. G., *The Irish Question in British Politics, 1868–1986* (Basingstoke: Macmillan, 1988)

Bradford, R., *The Last Ditch* (Dundonald: Blackstaff, 1981)

Bruce, S., *The Red Hand: Protestant Paramilitaries in Northern Ireland* (Oxford: Oxford University Press, 1992)

Bruce, S., *Paisley: Religion and Politics in Northern Ireland* (Oxford: Oxford University Press, 2007)

Buckland, P., *James Craig: Lord Craigavon* (Dublin: Gill and Macmillan, 1980)

Buckland, P., *A History of Northern Ireland* (Dublin: Gill and Macmillan, 1981)

Buxton, T., P. Chapman and P. Temple, *Britain's Economic Performance* (London: Routledge, 2nd edn, 1998)

Callaghan, J., *A House Divided: The Dilemma of Northern Ireland* (London: Collins, 1973)

Clarke, P., *Hope and Glory: Britain 1900–2000* (London: Penguin, 2nd edn, 2004)

Clancy, M. A. C., *Peace without Consensus: Power-sharing Politics in Northern Ireland* (Farnham: Ashgate, 2010)

Collins, S., *The Cosgrave Legacy* (Dublin: Blackwater, 1996)

Coogan, T. P., *Ireland in the Twentieth Century* (London: Hutchinson, 2003)

Craig, A., *Crisis of Confidence: Anglo-Irish Relations in the Early Troubles, 1966–1974* (Dublin: Irish Academic Press, 2010)

Cunningham, M., *British Government Policy in Northern Ireland, 1969–2000* (Manchester: Manchester University Press, 2001)

Currie, A., *All Hell Will Break Loose* (Dublin: O'Brien, 2004)

Devlin, P., *The Fall of the N.I. executive* (Belfast: Paddy Devlin, 1975)

Devlin, P., *Straight Left: An Autobiography* (Belfast: Blackstaff, 1993)

Dewar, M., *The British Army in Northern Ireland* (London: Arms and Armour, 1985)

Dillon, M. and D. Lehane, *Political Murder in Northern Ireland* (London: Penguin, 1973)

Dillon, M., *The Dirty War* (London: Arrow, 2nd edn, 1991)

Dixon, P., '"A house divided cannot stand": Britain, bipartisanship and Northern Ireland', *Contemporary Record*, ix: 1 (1995)

Dixon, P., 'Consociationalism and the Northern Ireland peace process: the glass half full or half empty?', *Nationalism and Ethnic Politics*, iii: 3 (1997)

Dixon, P., 'Paths to peace in Northern Ireland (I): civil society and consociational approaches', *Democratization*, iv: 2 (1997)

Dixon, P., 'Paths to peace in Northern Ireland (II): the peace processes 1973–74 and 1994–96', *Democratization*, iv: 3 (1997)

Dixon, P., 'Why the Good Friday Agreement in Northern Ireland is not consociational', *Political Quarterly*, lxxvi: 3 (2005)

Dixon, P., *Northern Ireland: The Politics of War and Peace* (Basingstoke: Palgrave Macmillan, 2nd edn, 2008)

Donoughue, B., *Downing Street Diary: With Harold Wilson in No. 10* (London: Jonathan Cape, 2004)

Doody, J., 'Exclusion orders under the Prevention of Terrorism Acts 1974–1989: a social harm analysis' (PhD dissertation, University of Ulster, 2010)

Dow, C., *Major Recessions in Britain and the World, 1920–1995* (Oxford: Oxford University Press, 1998)

Dwyer, T. Ryle, *Nice Fellow: A Biography of Jack Lynch* (Cork: Mercier Press, 2001)

Edwards, A., *A History of the Northern Ireland Labour Party: Democratic Socialism and Sectarianism* (Manchester: Manchester University Press, 2009)

Ellison, J. and J. Smyth, *The Crowned Harp: Policing Northern Ireland* (London: Pluto Press, 2000)

English, R., *Armed Struggle: The History of the IRA* (London: Macmillan, 2003)

English, R., *Irish Freedom: A History of Nationalism in Ireland* (London: Macmillan, 2007)

Fanning, R., *Independent Ireland* (Dublin: Helicon, 1983)

Fanning, R., '"The great enchantment": uses and abuses of modern Irish history' in Ciaran Brady (ed.), *Interpreting Irish History: The Debate on Historical Revisionism 1938–1994* (Dublin: Irish Academic Press, 1994)

Fanning, R., 'Playing it cool: the response of the British and Irish governments to the crisis in Northern Ireland, 1968–69', *Irish Studies in International Affairs*, xii (2001)

Farrell, M., *Northern Ireland: The Orange State* (London: Pluto Press, 1976)

Farrell, M., *Arming the Protestants: The Formation of the Ulster Special Constabulary and the Royal Ulster Constabulary, 1920–27* (London: Pluto Press, 1983)

Farrington, C., 'Reconciliation or irredentism: the Irish government and the Sunningdale Communiqué 1973', *Contemporary European History*, xvi: 1 (2007)

Faulkner, B., *Memoirs of a Statesman* (London: Weidenfeld and Nicolson, 1978)

Ferriter, D., *The Transformation of Ireland, 1900–2000* (London: Profile, 2004)

Fisk, R., *The Point of No Return: The Strike Which Broke the British in Ulster* (London: Deutsch, 1975)

FitzGerald, G., *All in a Life: An Autobiography* (Dublin: Gill and Macmillan, 1991)

FitzGerald, G., 'The 1974–75 threat of a British withdrawal from Northern Ireland', *Irish Studies in International Affairs*, xvii (2006)

Follis, B. A., *A State under Siege: The Establishment of Northern Ireland, 1920–25* (Oxford: Clarendon Press, 1995)

Foster, R. F., *Modern Ireland 1600–1972* (London: Allen Lane, 1988)

Foster, R. F., *Luck and the Irish: A Brief History of Change, 1970–2000* (London: Allen Lane, 2007)

Frampton, M., *The Long March: The Political Strategy of Sinn Féin, 1981–2007* (Basingstoke: Palgrave Macmillan, 2009)

Gallagher, M., *The Irish Labour Party in Transition, 1957–82* (Manchester: Manchester University Press, 1982)

Gillespie, G., 'The Sunningdale Agreement: lost opportunity or an agreement too far?', *Irish Political Studies*, xiii (1998)

Gillespie, G., *Years of Darkness: The Troubles Remembered* (Dublin: Gill and Macmillan, 2008)

Gillespie, S. G., 'Loyalist politics and the Ulster Workers' Council strike of 1974' (PhD dissertation, Queen's University Belfast, 1994)

Godson, D., *Himself Alone: David Trimble and the Ordeal of Unionism* (London: Harper Collins, 2004)

Greer, J., 'The Paisleyites: from protest movement to electoral breakthrough', *The Sixties*, ii: 2 (2009)

Greer, J., 'Paisley and his heartland: a case study of political change' in C. NicDháibhéid and C. Reid (eds), *From Parnell to Paisley: Constitutional and Revolutionary Politics in Ireland* (Dublin: Irish Academic Press, 2010)

Greer, J., 'Losing the province: a localised study of Ulster unionism, 1968–1974' (PhD dissertation, Queen's University Belfast, 2011)

Haines, J., *The Politics of Power* (London: Jonathan Cape, 1977)

Hall, P. A., 'Policy paradigms, social learning and the state: the case of economic policymaking in Britain', *Comparative Politics*, xxv: 3 (1995)

Hamill, D., *Pig in the Middle: The Army in Northern Ireland, 1968–1984* (London: Methuen, 1985)

Hanley, B. and S. Millar, *The Lost Revolution. The Story of the Official IRA and the Workers' Party* (Dublin: Penguin Ireland, 2009)

Harkness, D., *Northern Ireland since 1920* (Dublin: Helicon, 1983)

Harris, J. A., 'The Conservative government and the Sunningdale Agreement, 1972–74' (PhD dissertation, Queen's University Belfast, 2008)

Harte, P., *Young Tigers and Mongrel Foxes: A Life in Politics* (Dublin: O'Brien, 2005)

Hayes, M., *Minority Verdict: Experiences of a Catholic Public Servant* (Belfast: Blackstaff, 1995)

Healey, D., *The Time of My Life* (London: M. Joseph, 1989)

Heath, E., *The Course of My Life: An Autobiography* (London: Coronet, 1999)

Hennessey, T., *A History of Northern Ireland, 1920–1996* (Dublin: Gill and Macmillan, 1997)

Hennessey, T., *Northern Ireland: The Origins of the Troubles* (Dublin: Gill and Macmillan, 2005)

Hennessey, T., *The Evolution of the Troubles, 1970–72* (Dublin: Irish Academic Press, 2007)

Hine, D., 'Factionalism in Western European parties: a framework for analysis', *West European Politics*, v (1982)

Holland, J. and H. McDonald, *INLA: Deadly Divisions* (Dublin: Torc, 1994)

Hume, J., *Personal Views: Politics, Peace and Reconciliation in Ireland* (Dublin: Town-House, 1996)

Isaacs, J. and T. Downing, *Cold War* (London: Abacus, 2nd edn, 2008)

Jackson, A., 'Unionist Myths, 1912–1985', *Past and Present*, cxxxvi (1992)

Jackson, A., *Ireland 1798–1998: Politics and War* (Oxford: Blackwell, 1999)

Jackson, A., *Home Rule: An Irish History, 1800–2000* (London: Weidenfeld and Nicolson, 2003)

Jackson, A., '"Tame Tory hacks"? The Ulster Party at Westminster, 1922–1972', *Historical Journal*, liv: 2 (2011)

Jackson, A., *The Two Unions: Ireland, Scotland and the Survival of the United Kingdom, 1707–2007* (Oxford: Oxford University Press, 2011)

Jeffery, K. and P. Hennessy, *States of Emergency: British Governments and Strikebreaking since 1919* (London: Routledge, 1983)

Jenkins, R., *A Life at the Centre* (London: Macmillan, 1991)

Kaufmann, E. P., *The Orange Order: A Contemporary Northern Irish History* (Oxford: Oxford University Press, 2007)

Kennedy, D., *The Widening Gulf: Northern Attitudes to the Independent Irish state, 1919–49* (Belfast: Blackstaff, 1988)

Kennedy, M., *Division and Consensus: The Politics of Cross-border Relations, 1925–1969* (Dublin: Institute of Public Administration, 2000)

Keogh, D., *Jack Lynch: A Biography* (Dublin: Gill and Macmillan, 2008)

Kerr, M., *Imposing Power-sharing: Conflict and Co-existence in Northern Ireland and Lebanon* (Dublin: Irish Academic Press, 2005)

Kerr, M., *The Destructors: The Story of Northern Ireland's Lost Peace Process* (Dublin: Irish Academic Press, 2011)

Kitson, F., *Low Intensity Operations: Subversion, Insurgency, Peace-keeping* (London: Faber and Faber, 1971)

Lee, J. J., *Ireland 1912–1985: Politics and Society* (Cambridge: Cambridge University Press, 1989)

Lijphart, A., 'Consociational democracy', *World Politics*, xxi: 2 (1969)

Lijphart, A., 'Comparative politics and the comparative method', *American Political Science Review*, lxv: 3 (1971)

Lijphart, A., 'The Northern Ireland problem: cases, theories and solutions', *British Journal of Political Science*, v: 1 (1975)

Lijphart, A., *Democracy in Plural Societies* (New Haven: Yale University Press, 1977)

Lijphart, A., 'Consociation: the model and its applications in divided societies' in D. Rea (ed.), *Political Co-operation in Divided Societies* (Dublin: Gill and Macmillan, 1982)

Mair, P., *The Changing Irish Party System: Organisation, Ideology and Electoral Competition* (London: Pinter, 1987)

Major, J., *John Major: The Autobiography* (London: HarperCollins, 2000)

MacGréil, M., *Prejudice and Tolerance in Ireland: Based on a Survey of Intergroup Attitudes of Dublin Adults and Other Sources* (Dublin: College of Industrial Relations, 1977)

McAllister, I., 'The legitimacy of opposition: the collapse of the 1974 Northern Ireland executive', *Éire-Ireland*, xii: 4 (1977)

McAllister, I. *The Northern Ireland Social Democratic and Labour Party: Political Opposition in a Divided Society* (London: Macmillan, 1977)

McDaid, S., 'Divided loyalties: Faulkner unionists and the Ulster Workers Council, 1974' in O. Coquelin, P. Gaillou and T. Robin (eds), *Political Ideology in Ireland: From the Enlightenment to the Present* (Newcastle: Cambridge Scholars Publishing, 2009)

McDaid, S., 'The David Thornley affair: republicanism and the Labour party' in C. NicDháibhéid and C. Reid (eds), *From Parnell to Paisley: Constitutional and Revolutionary Politics in Ireland* (Dublin: Irish Academic Press, 2010)

McDaid, S. and K. Rekawek, 'From mainstream to minor and back: the Irish Labour Party, 1987–1992', *Irish Political Studies*, xxv: 4 (2010)

McDonald, H., *David Trimble* (London: Bloomsbury, 2000)

McDonald, H., *Gunsmoke and Mirrors: How Sinn Féin Dressed Up Defeat as Victory* (Dublin: Gill and Macmillan, 2008)

McDonald, H. and J. Cusack, *The UDA: Inside the Heart of Loyalist Terror* (Dublin: Penguin Ireland, 2004)

McGarry, J. (ed.), *Northern Ireland and the Divided World: Post Agreement Northern Ireland in Comparative Perspective* (Oxford: Oxford University Press, 2001)

McGarry. J. and B. O'Leary (eds), *Explaining Northern Ireland: Broken Images* (Oxford: Blackwell, 1995)

McGarry, J. and B. O'Leary, *The Future of Northern Ireland* (Oxford: Clarendon Press, 2nd edn, 2004)

McGarry, J. and B. O'Leary, *The Northern Ireland Conflict: Consociational Engagements* (Oxford: Oxford University Press, 2004)

McGrattan, C. 'Dublin, the SDLP and the Sunningdale Agreement: maximalist nationalism and path dependency', *Contemporary British History*, xxiii: 1 (2009)

McGrattan, C., 'Learning from the past or laundering history? Consociational narratives and state intervention in Northern Ireland' in *British Politics*, v: 1 (2010)

McGrattan, C., *Northern Ireland 1968–2008: The Politics of Entrenchment* (Basingstoke: Palgrave Macmillan, 2010)

McIvor, B., *Hope Deferred: Experiences of an Irish Unionist* (Belfast: Blackstaff, 1998)

McKibben, J. A., 'Ulster Vanguard: a sociological profile' (M.Soc.Sci. dissertation, Queen's University Belfast, 1991)

McKittrick, D. and D. McVea, *Making Sense of the Troubles* (London: Penguin, 2001)

McKittrick, D., B. Feeney, S. Kelters, C. Thornton, *Lost Lives: The Stories of the Men, Women and Children Who Died as a Result of the Northern Ireland Troubles* (Edinburgh: Mainstream, 2nd edn, 2007)

McLean, I. and A. McMillan, *State of the Union: Unionism and the Alternatives in the United Kingdom since 1707* (Oxford: Oxford University Press, 2005)

McLoughlin, P. J., '"Dublin is just a Sunningdale away?" The SDLP and the failure of Northern Ireland's Sunningdale Experiment', *Twentieth Century British History*, xx: 1 (2009)

McLoughlin, P. J., *John Hume and the Revision of Irish Nationalism* (Manchester: Manchester University Press, 2010)

Maudling, R., *Memoirs* (London: Sidgwick and Jackson, 1978)

Miller, D. W., *Queen's Rebels: Ulster Loyalism in Historical Perspective* (Dublin: UCD Press, 2nd edn, 2007)

Mitchell, J., 'Undignified and inefficient: financial relations between London and Stormont', *Contemporary British History*, xx: 1 (2006)

Moloney, E., *A Secret History of the IRA* (London: Allen Lane, 2002)

Moloney. E., *Paisley: From Demagogue to Democrat* (Dublin: Poolbeg, 2008)

Moloney, E., *Voices from the Grave: Two Men's War in Ireland* (London: Faber and Faber, 2010)

Moloney, E. and A. Pollak, *Paisley* (Dublin: Poolbeg, 1986)

Mulcahy, A., *Policing Northern Ireland: Conflict, Legitimacy and Reform* (Collumpton: Willan, 2006)

Mulholland, M., 'Assimilation versus segregation: Unionist strategy in the 1960s', *Twentieth Century British History*, xi: 3 (2000)

Mulholland, M., *Northern Ireland at the Crossroads: Ulster Unionism in the O'Neill Years, 1960–9* (Basingstoke: Palgrave Macmillan, 2000)

Mullan, D., *The Dublin and Monaghan Bombings* (Dublin: Wolfhound Press, 2003)

Mulvenna, G., 'The Protestant working class in Northern Ireland: political allegiance and social and cultural challenges since the 1960s' (PhD Dissertation, Queen's University Belfast, 2009)

Mumford, A., 'Covert peacemaking: clandestine negotiations and backchannels with the Provisional IRA during the early "Troubles", 1972–76', *Journal of Imperial and Commonwealth History*, xxxix: 4 (2011)

Murphy, M. A., *Gerry Fitt: A Political Chameleon* (Cork: Mercier Press, 2007)

Murray, G., *John Hume and the SDLP: Impact and Survival in Northern Ireland* (Dublin: Irish Academic Press, 1998)

Murray, G. and J. Tonge, *Sinn Féin and the SDLP: From Alienation to Participation* (Dublin: O'Brien, 2005)

NicAoláin, F., *The Politics of Force: Conflict Management and State Violence in Northern Ireland* (Belfast: Blackstaff, 2000)

NicDháibhéid, C. and C. Reid (eds), *From Parnell to Paisley: Constitutional and Revolutionary Politics in Ireland* (Dublin: Irish Academic Press, 2010)

Ó Broin, E., *Sinn Féin and the Politics of Left Republicanism* (London: Pluto Press, 2009)

Ó Dochartaigh, N., *From Civil Rights to Armalites: Derry and the Birth of the Irish Troubles* (Basingstoke: Palgrave Macmillan, 2nd edn, 2004)

Ó Dochartaigh, N., 'Bloody Sunday: error or design?', *Contemporary British History*, xxiv: 1 (2010)

Ó Dochartaigh, N., '"Everyone trying", the IRA ceasefire, 1975: a missed opportunity for peace?', *Field Day Review*, vii (2011)

Ó Dochartaigh, N., 'Together in the middle: back-channel negotiation in the Irish peace process', *Journal of Peace Research*, xlvii: 6 (2011)

O'Brien, C. C., *States of Ireland* (London: Hutchinson, 1972)

O'Brien, C. C., *Memoir: My Life and Themes* (London: Profile, 1998)

O'Brien, J., *The Arms Trial* (Dublin: Gill and Macmillan, 2000)

O'Duffy, B., *British–Irish relations and Northern Ireland: From Violent Politics to Conflict Regulation* (Dublin: Irish Academic Press, 2007)

O'Halloran, C., *Partition and the Limits of Irish Nationalism: An Ideology under Stress* (Dublin: Gill and Macmillan, 1987)

O'Kane, E., *Britain, Ireland and Northern Ireland since 1980: The Totality of Relationships* (London: Routledge, 2007)

O'Kane, E., 'Learning from Northern Ireland? Uses and abuses of the Irish "model"', *British Journal of Politics and International Relations*, xii: 2 (2010)

O'Malley, P., *The Uncivil Wars: Ireland Today* (Belfast: Blackstaff, 1983)

Oppenheimer, A. R., *IRA: The Bombs and the Bullets. A History of Deadly Ingenuity* (Dublin: Irish Academic Press, 2008)

Parkinson, A. F., *Ulster loyalism and the British Media* (Dublin: Four Courts, 1998)

Patterson, H., *The Politics of Illusion: A Political History of the IRA* (London: Serif, 2nd edn, 1997)

Patterson, H., *Ireland since 1939: The Persistence of Conflict* (Oxford: Oxford University Press, 2002)

Patterson, H., 'The British state and the rise of the IRA, 1969–71: the view from the Conway Hotel', *Irish Political Studies*, xxiii: 4 (2008)

Patterson, H., 'Sectarianism revisited: the Provisional IRA campaign in a border region of Northern Ireland', *Terrorism and Political Violence*, xxii: 3 (2010)

Patterson, H. and E. P. Kaufmann, *Unionism and Orangeism in Northern Ireland since 1945: the Decline of the Loyal Family* (Manchester: Manchester University Press, 2007)

Peatling, G. K., *The Failure of the Northern Ireland Peace Process* (Dublin: Irish Academic Press, 2004)

Peck, J., *Dublin from Downing Street* (Dublin: Gill and Macmillan, 1978)

Pimlott, B., *Harold Wilson* (London: HarperCollins, 1992)

Powell, J., *Great Hatred, Little Room: Making Peace in Northern Ireland* (London: Bodley Head, 2008)

Prince, S., *Northern Ireland's '68: Civil Rights, Global Revolt and the Origins of the Troubles* (Dublin: Irish Academic Press, 2007)

Prince, S. and G. Warner, *Belfast and Derry in Revolt: A New History of the Start of the Troubles* (Dublin: Irish Academic Press, 2011)

Probert, B., *Beyond Orange and Green: The Political Economy of the Northern Ireland Crisis* (London: Zed Press, 1978)

Puirséil, N., *The Irish Labour Party, 1922–73* (Dublin: UCD Press, 2007)

Ramsay, R., *Ringside Seats: An Insider's View of the Crisis in Northern Ireland* (Dublin: Irish Academic Press, 2009)

Rees, M., *Northern Ireland: A Personal Perspective* (London: Methuen, 1985)

Rekawek, K., 'How terrorism does not end: the case of the Official Irish Republican Army', *Critical Studies on Terrorism*, i: 3 (2008)

Rekawek, K., *Irish Republican Terrorism and Politics: A Comparative Study of the Official and the Provisional IRA* (London: Routledge, 2011)

Robbins, K., *The World Since 1945: A Concise History* (Oxford: Oxford University Press, 1998)

Rose, R., *Governing without Consensus: An Irish Perspective* (London: Faber and Faber, 1971)

Routledge, P., *John Hume: A Biography* (London: HarperCollins, 1997)

Rowthorn, B. and N. Wayne, *Northern Ireland.: The Political Economy of Conflict* (Cambridge: Polity Press, 1988)

Ruane, J. and J. Todd (eds) *The Dynamics of Conflict in Northern Ireland: Power, Conflict and Emancipation* (Cambridge: Cambridge University Press, 1997)

Ryder, C., *The RUC: A Force under Fire* (London: Methuen, 1989)

Ryder, C., *The Ulster Defence Regiment: An Instrument of Peace?* (London: Methuen, 1991)

Ryder, C., *Fighting Fitt: The Gerry Fitt Story* (Belfast: Brehon, 2006)

Sandbrook, D., *State of Emergency: The Way We Were: Britain 1970–1974* (London: Penguin, 2011)

Schneckener, U., 'Making power-sharing work: lessons from successes and failures in ethnic conflict regulation', *Journal of Peace Research*, xxxix: 2 (2002)

Sela, A., 'The 1973 Arab war coalition: aims, coherence and gain distribution' in P. R. Kumarswamy (ed.), *Revisiting the Yom Kippur War* (London: Frank Cass, 2000)

Sheehy, K., *More Questions Than Answers: Reflecting on a Life in the RUC* (Dublin: Gill and Macmillan, 2008)

Smith, M. L. R. and P. Neumann, 'Motorman's long journey: changing the strategic setting in Northern Ireland', *Contemporary British History*, xix: 4 (2005)

Smyth, C., *Ian Paisley: Voice of Protestant Ulster* (Edinburgh: Scottish Academic Press, 1987)

Subacchi, P., 'From Bretton Woods onwards: the birth and rebirth of the world's hegemon', *Cambridge Review of International Affairs*, xxi: 3 (2008)

Sutton, M., *Bear In Mind These Dead . . . An Index of Deaths from the Conflict in Ireland, 1969–1993* (Belfast: Beyond the Pale, 1994)

Swan, S., *Official Irish Republicanism 1962 to 1972* (Lulu.com, 2007)

Taylor, P., *Provos: The IRA and Sinn Féin* (London: Bloomsbury, 1997)

Taylor, P., *Loyalists* (London: Bloomsbury, 2000)

Taylor, P., *Brits: The War Against the IRA* (London: Bloomsbury, 2001)

Taylor, R. (ed.), *Consociational Theory: McGarry and O'Leary and the Northern Ireland Conflict* (London: Routledge, 2009)

Todd, J., 'Two traditions in Unionist political culture', *Irish Political Studies*, ii: 1 (1987)

Tomlinson, J., 'Tale of a death exaggerated: how Keynesian policies survived the 1970s', *Contemporary British History*, xx: 4 (2007)

Tonge, J., 'From Sunningdale to the Good Friday Agreement: creating devolved government in Northern Ireland', *Contemporary British History*, xiv: 3 (2000)

Tonge, J., *Northern Ireland: Conflict and Change* (Harlow: Pearson Education, 2nd edn, 2002)

Tonge, J., *The New Northern Ireland Politics?* (Basingstoke: Palgrave Macmillan, 2005)

Townshend. C., *Ireland: The 20th Century* (London: Hodder, 1999)

Turner, A. W., *Crisis? What Crisis?: Britain in the 1970s* (London: Aurum, 2008)

Utley, T. E., *Lessons of Ulster* (London: Dent, 1975)

Walker, G., *A History of the Ulster Unionist Party: Protest, Pragmatism and Pessimism* (Manchester: Manchester University Press, 2004)

Walker, G., 'The Protestant working class and the fragmentation of Ulster Unionism' in M. Busteed, F. Neal and J. Tonge (eds), *Irish Protestant Identities* (Manchester: Manchester University Press, 2008)

Wallace, M., *British Government in Northern Ireland. From Devolution to Direct Rule* (Newton Abbot: David and Charles, 1982)

Warner, G., 'Putting pressure on O'Neill: the Wilson government and Northern Ireland, 1964–69', *Irish Studies Review*, xiii: 1 (2005)

Wass, D., *Decline to Fall: The Making of British Macroeconomic Policy and the 1976 IMF Crisis* (Oxford: Oxford University Press, 2008)

Wharton, K., *Bloody Belfast: An Oral History of the British Army's War against the IRA* (Stroud: History Press, 2010)

White, B., *John Hume: Statesman of the Troubles* (Belfast: Blackstaff, 1984)

White, R. W., *Ruairi Ó Brádaigh: The Life and Politics of an Irish Revolutionary* (Bloomington: Indiana University Press, 2006)

White, R. W., 'The 1975 British–IRA truce in perspective', *Éire-Ireland*, xlv: 3 and 4 (2010)

Whitelaw, W., *The Whitelaw Memoirs* (London: Aurum, 1989)

Whyte, J., *Interpreting Northern Ireland* (Oxford: Clarendon Press, 1990)

Wichert, S., *Northern Ireland since 1945* (London: Longman, 2nd edn, 1999)

Wilford, R., *Aspects of the Belfast Agreement* (Oxford: Oxford University Press, 2001)

Wilkinson, P., *Terrorism and the Liberal State* (Basingstoke: Palgrave Macmillan, 2nd edn, 1986)

Wilson, H., *Final Term: Labour Government 1974–76* (London: Weidenfeld and Nicolson, 1979)

Wilson, R., *The Northern Ireland Experience of Conflict and Agreement: A Model for Export?* (Manchester: Manchester University Press, 2010)

Wood, I. S., *Crimes of Loyalty: A History of the UDA* (Edinburgh: Edinburgh University Press, 2006)

Wright, F., *Northern Ireland: A Comparative Analysis* (Dublin: Gill and Macmillan, 1987)

Ziegler, P., *The Authorised Life of Lord Wilson of Rievaulx* (London: Weidenfeld and Nicolson, 1993)

Ziegler, P., *Edward Heath: The Authorised Biography* (London: Harper Press, 2010)

Internet sources

ARK Election Results. Available: www.ark.ac.uk

Conflict Archive on the Internet. Available: www.cain.ulst.ac.uk

Die Zeit. Available: www.zeit.de

House of Lords Debates Online. Available: www.publications.parliament.uk

Privy Council Office Website. Available: www.pco.gov.uk/

The Guardian Datablog. Available: www.guardian.co.uk/news/datablog

Index

Note: 'n.' after a page reference indicates the number of a note on that page

Lightning Source UK Ltd.
Milton Keynes UK
UKOW06f0905210216

268774UK00004B/77/P